M000306392

Narratives of the
French and Indian War: 4

Narratives of the French and Indian War: 4

Captain Orme's Journal

George Croghan's Statement

Royal Navy Officer's Journal

French and Indian Cruelty

Recollections of an Old Soldier the Life of Captain David Perry

Luke Gridley's Diary of 1757

LEONAUR

Narratives of the French and Indian War: 4
Captain Orme's Journal
Royal Navy Officer's Journal
George Croghan's Statement
French and Indian Cruelty
Recollections of an Old Soldier the Life of Captain David Perry
Luke Gridley's Diary of 1757

FIRST EDITION

Leonaur is an imprint of Oakpast Ltd

Copyright in this form © 2019 Oakpast Ltd

ISBN: 978-1-78282-810-5 (hardcover)
ISBN: 978-1-78282-811-2 (softcover)

http://www.leonaur.com

Publisher's Notes

The views expressed in this book are not necessarily
those of the publisher.

Contents

Captain Orme's Journal   7

Royal Navy Officer's Journal   67

George Croghan's Statement   91

French and Indian Cruelty   93

Recollections of an Old Soldier the Life of Captain
David Perry   169

Luke Gridley's Diary of 1757   197

Captain Orme's Journal

Sir:

I am ordered to send this packet to you to be delivered to his Royal Highness. I am sorry the plans are not finished, but I am to have them tomorrow night.

Sir

    Your most humble and obedient servant,

Robert Orme.

Thursday morning.

(This letter was doubtless addressed to Col. Napier, the Duke of Cumberland's *aide-de-camp*.)

The general arrived at Hampton in Virginia, the 20th of February, 1755, and set out immediately for Williamsburgh, where Commodore Keppel agreed to meet him, to settle the properest place for the disembarkment of the troops. Orders were left on board the *Centurion* to be delivered to each transport as she arrived, directing the commanding officer to send the sick on shore to the hospitals provided for them by Sir John St. Clair; and orders were given to Mr. Hunter, the Agent at Hampton, to supply the sick and well with fresh provisions at the fullest allowance.

★★★★★★

Robert Orme, the author of this *Journal*, entered the army as an ensign in the 35th Foot. On 16th Sept. 1745, he exchanged into the Coldstreams, of which he became a lieutenant, April 24, 1751. He was never raised to a captaincy, though always spoken of as such. (II. MacKinnon.) He probably obtained leave of absence to accompany General Braddock, with whom he was a great favourite. He was an honest and capable man, says Shirley (VI. *Col. Rec.*), and it was fortunate that the general was so much under his influence. He brought letters of introduction from Thomas Penn to Gov. Morris (II. *Penn. Arch.*) and seems to have made a most favourable impression on all whom he encountered. Two months after the battle we find him a guest of Morris's, and nearly recovered of his wound.

"Captain Orme is going to England," writes he to General Shirley on Sept. 5th, 1755 (II. *P. A.*), "and will put the affair of the western campaign in a true light, and greatly different from what it has been represented to be; and you know his situation and abilities gave him great opportunities of knowing everything that passed in the army or in the colony, relative to military matters, and I am sure he will be of great use to the Ministry in the measures that may be concerted for the future safety and defence of these provinces. . . . .

"The opportunities which Mr. Orme will have with the duke, and all the king's ministers, upon his return, of explaining American affairs, makes it quite necessary that you should agree in general in your representations, that both may have the greater weight; and my friendship for you obliges me to hint this matter for your consideration, that you may in your letters to the Ministry refer to him, and give him an opportunity of enforcing what you may write; the substance of which you will, I believe, think it necessary to communicate to him."

Orme went from Philadelphia to New York, whence, or from Boston, he embarked for England. In Oct. 1756, he resigned his commission in the Guards (probably on occasion of his marriage) and retired into a private life. It seems that Orme was as bold in the *boudoir* as on the battlefield, and had already before going to America, "made some noise in London by an affair of gallantry." On his return, a mutual attachment sprung up between himself and the Hon. Audrey Townshend, only daughter of Charles, 3rd Viscount and the celebrated Audrey (Harrison), Lady Townshend. The lady had no little motive of interest in one who had gone through an American campaign; for of her brothers, one, Lieut.-Col. Roger Townshend, was slain in this very war at Ticonderoga (July 25, 1759); and another, George (the first Marquess), succeeded to Wolfe's command at the capture of Quebec.

However, much to the displeasure of her family, who had destined her for Lord George Lenox, she was married to Capt.

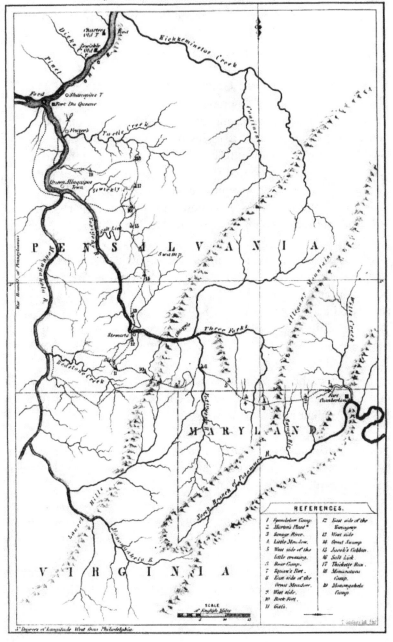

A MAP OF THE COUNTRY BETWEEN WILLS CREEK & MONONGAHELA RIVER,
shewing the route and Encampments of the English Army in 1755.

Pl. I.

REFERENCES.

1. Spendelow Camp.
2. Martin's Plant.
3. Savage River.
4. Little Meadow.
5. West side of the little crossing.
6. Bear Camp.
7. Squaw's Fort.
8. East side of the Great Meadow.
9. West side.
10. Rock Fort.
11. Guets.
12. East side of the Youghyar.
13. West side.
14. Great Swamp.
15. Jacob's Cabbin.
16. Salt Lick.
17. Thickette Run.
18. Monacatuca Camp.
19. Monongahela Camp.

SCALE of English Miles.

5 Degrees of Longitude West from Philadelphia.

Orme, and went to reside at Hartford, Eng. Nothing further can be traced of Captain Orme, save that he died in Feb, 1781. It is more than likely, however, that he belonged to the family of that Robert Orme whose name seems through continued generations to be identified with that of the East India Company. (III. Walpole *Corr.*; II. Collins' *Peerage*.)

★★★★★★

The general acquainted Governor Dinwiddie with His Majesty's pleasure, that the several assemblies should raise a sum of money to be employed towards defraying the expenses of the expedition and desired he would propose it to his Assembly; and that His Majesty also expected the provinces to furnish the troops with provisions and carriages. The general desired the governor would use all imaginable dispatch in raising and convening the levies to augment the two battalions to 700 each. He also proposed to the governor to make an establishment for some provincials, amongst which he recommended a troop of light horse.

The governor told the general his Assembly had voted twenty thousand pounds, which sum was to be employed in the purchasing provisions, and the payment of their own troops. That many men were already raised, and that Sir John St. Clair had promised him to select the best for the two regiments, and that the others should be formed into companies; accordingly, two of hatchet men or carpenters, six of Rangers, and one troop of light horse were raised, and their pay fixed at the same, in the currency of that country, as our officers of the same rank in sterling. Alexandria was named as the headquarters, as the most convenient place for forming and cloathing them.

Sir John St. Clair came to Williamsburgh and informed the general of his having draughted the best men of the Virginia levies for the two battalions; and that about three hundred which were not of proper size remained for the provincial companies.

★★★★★★

St. Clair remained for a long time in service in America. On the 20th March, 1756, he was made a Lieut.-Col. of the 60th; in Jan. 1758, the local rank of colonel in America was bestowed on him; and on Feb. 19th, 1762, he was made a full colonel. He is said to have dwelt near Tarbet, in Argyleshire. At the defeat he "was shot through the body, under the right pap," (Sharpe's *MS. Corr.*), but soon recovered.

★★★★★★

Sir John St. Clair laid before the general a roll of the independent companies, upon which were several men from sixty to seventy years of age, lame and everyway disabled; many were enlisted, only for a term of one, two, or three years; some were without discipline and very ill-appointed; in short, they were invalids with the ignorance of militia. These were all to be recruited with men who would otherwise have served in the regiments or Virginia Companies.

Sir John St. Clair gave General Braddock a plan for cantoning the two regiments; one, with part of the artillery, was to disembark at Alexandria, where five companies were to remain; two and a half were to canton at Frederick in Maryland, half a one at Conegogee, one at Marlborough and one at Bladensburgh. The other regiment and the rest of the artillery were to disembark about twenty miles from Fredericksburg upon the Potomack, at which place and Falmouth five companies were to be cantoned, and the other five at Winchester.

As these cantonments, of only a thousand men, took in a circuit of more than three hundred miles, the general thought it advisable to encamp them on their arrival; especially as the severity of the weather was then over. He knew that much confusion must arise in disembarking at different places: That it would be impossible to cloath, arm and discipline the levies when so much dispersed, and that soldiers are sooner and better formed in camps than in quarters. He therefore, in conjunction with Mr. Keppel, fixed upon Alexandria to disembark and encamp at; and the levies for the two regiments were ordered to that place.

The general desired Governor Dinwiddie would inform him of the present disposition of the Indians towards the English; what nations and number he might expect, and what steps were already taken to obtain them.

The governor said he had sent a proper person, (Mr. Gist, son of Washington's guide in 1753), to bring with him the Cherokee and Catawber nations, the latter being about one hundred and twenty fighting-men, and much the bravest of all the Indians: He added a peace was to be concluded at Winchester in April, between the Catawbers and the Six Nations through the mediation of his Government: That he had intended to be present at the Congress; but that he should be prevented by the meeting of his Assembly. However, he would take care, at the Ratification of the Peace, that they should take up the hatchet, and act under the general.

★★★★★★

11

The Six Nations, who were not on friendly terms with these Southern Indians, alleged that their refusal to assist Braddock was based on their reluctance to be brought in contact with the Catawbas and Cherokees. II. *Doc. Hist. N.Y.*

★★★★★★

Mr. Dinwiddie laid before the general contracts made for eleven hundred head of cattle, eight hundred of which were to be delivered in June and July, and three hundred in August; he said that he had also written to Governor Shirley, for a large quantity of salt fish, that a great deal of flour was already at Fort Cumberland, and that the assembly of Pensylvania had promised to deliver flour, to the amount of five thousand pounds of their currency, at the mouth of Conegogee, in April, which was to be carried up the Potomack to Fort Cumberland: He had also ordered a great quantity of bacon to be made at the fort. There were on board the transports one thousand barrels of beef, for which the general applied to Mr. Keppel and they were landed at Alexandria. Upon making a calculation on these estimates, there was found to be six months provisions for four thousand men.

General Braddock apprehended the greatest difficulty in procuring waggons and horses, sufficient to attend him upon his march, as the assembly had not passed an Act for the supplying them, but Sir John St. Clair assured the general that inconveniency would be easily removed, for, in going to Fort Cumberland, he had been informed of a great number of Dutch settlers, at the foot of a mountain called the Blue Ridge, who would undertake to carry by the hundred the provisions and stores, and that he believed he could provide otherwise two hundred waggons and fifteen hundred carrying horses to be at Fort Cumberland by the first of May.

The general desired him to secure the former of these, upon his return to the fort. At Williamsburgh the general wrote circular letters to all the governors upon the Continent, informing them of his commission, and recommending to them the constituting of a common fund, and desiring them to assist and forward as much as possible the general service, that it might answer the end, for which His Majesty had sent troops to their assistance. And, in the letters to Governors Shirley, Delancey, Morris and Sharpe, he desired they would meet him at Annapolis the beginning of April, that he might confer with them on some matters of the greatest importance to the Colonies and settle with them a general plan of operation for the approaching campaign.

★★★★★★

Robert-Hunter, second son of Governor Lewis Morris of Morrisania, after twenty years of public service in the council and as Chief Justice of New Jersey, was appointed Deputy Governor of Pennsylvania: a post he filled during two stormy years. I do not learn that he left any descendants; but the line was continued through those of his elder brother, Lewis; one of whom married the celebrated Duchess Dowager of Gordon; and others established some of the more distinguished families in America.

A character of Mr. Delancy is given in the *Review of Military Operations in North America*; and of Shirley, in I. Entick, *General History of the Late War*.

★★★★★★

Two transports being arrived at Hampton, the general and commodore went thither immediately, and orders were given to the commanding officer of each ship to sail as soon as they had received their fresh provisions, and to disembark their men at Alexandria. The soldiers were to take their beds ashore, and Lieutenant Colonel Burton was ordered to quarter the troops in the town till the arrival of more ships, in case the weather should prove severe. The general waited here three days, but no more ships arriving, he, and the commodore, returned to Williamsburgh.

The general applied to Mr. Keppel for some blocks, cordage, and other stores, and also for thirty seamen, who he thought would be very serviceable on the march, if it should be found necessary to pass the rivers in floats or in boats. He also desired a carpenter to direct the construction of them; with which the commodore complied very readily, constantly expressing an ardent desire to forward the success of the expedition, and never, I believe, two men placed at the head of different commands co-operated with more spirit, integrity and harmony for the publick service.

In about ten days, all the transports being arrived, orders were given for all the ships to proceed immediately to Alexandria; but so little care had been taken at Corke, in the stowage of the cloathing, arms, and camp necessaries belonging to the regiments of Shirley and Pepperell, that some was put on board almost every ship; they were removed into one vessel, and dispatched immediately to New York and Boston, which caused a delay of four or five days.

★★★★★★

"*The Conduct of Major General Shirley*," etc., which was perhaps prepared from materials furnished by himself, states that these two regiments were the 50th and 51st. But the Army lists do not indicate that Shirley or Pepperell were ever colonels of these regiments. Shirley was indeed of the rank of a colonel in the line since August 31, 1745; but I cannot learn of what regiment he was an actual leader. On 26th February, 1755, he was made a major-general; and on 30th January, 1759, a lieutenant-general. The uniform of the 50th, hereabove alluded to, was red faced with red, with white linings and white lace, which soiled so readily as to give the regiment the sobriquet of "the dirty half-hundred." That of the 51st differed but in having white buttons in lieu of white linings.

Under convoy of the *Syren*, Captain Proby, a transport, with the clothing, etc., of Shirley's regiment on board, sailed from Hampton Roads about March 10th; arriving at Boston in four days. Pepperell's clothing did not follow till about the 20th. *Penn. Gaz.*, No. 1371.

✶✶✶✶✶✶

Everything seemed to promise so far the greatest success. The transports were all arrived safe, and the men in health. Provisions, Indians, carriages and horses were already provided; at least were to be esteemed so; considering the authorities on which they were promised to the general.

The 22nd of March the general set out for Alexandria, accompanied by the governor and Mr. Keppel, where they arrived the 26th. The next day the general named his *aide-de-camps*, and the major of brigade and provost mareschal, and gave out the following orders, for the better regulation of the camp.

ORDERS GIVEN OUT AT ALEXANDRIA.

As the two regiments now employed have served under His Royal Highness the Duke, they are consequently very well acquainted with military discipline.

✶✶✶✶✶✶

In the Scottish campaign of 1746. It may be noticed that these regiments were of the youngest in the service: only dating from 1741. The 49th was at this time the single regiment junior to the 48th. The uniform of the 44th was red faced with yellow; that of the 48th, red faced with buff.

✶✶✶✶✶✶

The general therefore expects their behaviour should be so conformable to good order, as to set the most soldierlike example to the new levies of this country.

As an encouragement to the men, they shall be supplied with a daily allowance of provision gratis; but if any man be found negligent or disorderly, besides corporal punishment, this gratuity shall be stopped.

The articles of war are to be immediately and frequently read, and all orders relating to the men are to be read to them by an officer of a company.

Any soldier that deserts, though he return again, shall be hanged without mercy.

The commanding officers of companies are to be answerable that their men's arms are kept in constant good order. Every man is to be provided with a brush, picker and two good spare flints, and kept always completed with twenty-four rounds.

The roll of each company is to be called over, by an officer, every morning, noon and night, and a return of the absent and disorderly men is to be given to the commanding officer of the regiment, who is to see them properly punished.

Each regiment is to have Divine Service performed at the head of their respective colours every Sunday.

The two regiments are to find the general's guard alternately, which is to consist of a lieutenant and thirty men, and the regiment which finds the general's guard is to find also the adjutant of the day.

All guards are to be relieved in the morning at eight of the clock. Guards, though ever so small, to be told off into two divisions.

All reports and returns to be made at nine of the clock.

Guards, ordered at orderly time, are to remain for that day; and a new detachment is to be made for any ordered afterwards.

All returns are to be signed by the commanding officers of the regiments.

Each regiment, troop, or company, is to make a daily return to the major of brigade, specifying their numbers wanting to complete, who is to make a general return for his Excellency.

A daily return of the sick is to be made to the general, through an *aide de camp*.

In case of any alarum, the Virginia troops are to parade before the church.

The line is to find daily one field-officer, who is to be relieved at nine of the clock. This duty is to be done by the two lieutenant colonels and the two majors. The field officer of the day is to visit all guards and out-parties, except the general's, and to go the rounds of the picket, which as well as the other guards and out-parties, are to report to him. He is to make his report of the whole at nine of the clock to the general, and in case of any alarum, the field officer is to repair with all expedition to the place where it is, and to send for any necessary assistance to the two regiments which are immediately to comply with his orders.

The eldest battalion company is to act as a second grenadier company, and to be posted upon the left of the battalion, leaving the same interval as the grenadiers upon the right.

This company is to be kept complete of officers, and two of them, as well as of the other grenadier companies are to be posted in the front, and the other in the rear.

The eight battalion companies are each of them to be told off into two divisions, that they may either form eight firings, or sixteen platoons, and are always to be commanded by their own officers, who are to be posted in the same manner as the grenadier officers, and that every company might be complete of officers, the general made three ensigns to each regiment, without pay.

Each regiment is to mount a picket guard, consisting of one captain, two subalterns and fifty men which are to report to the field officer of the day.

Upon any application from Sir John St. Clair to either of the regiments for men, they are immediately to furnish them.

Sir Peter Halket is to regulate all affairs relative to the provisions.

★★★★★★

Sir Peter Halkett of Pitferran, Fifeshire, a baronet of Nova Scotia, was the son of Sir Peter Wedderburne of Grosford, who, marrying the heiress of the ancient family of Halkett, assumed her name. In 1734, he sate in the Commons for Dunfermline, and was Lieutenant-Colonel of the 44th at Sir John Cope's defeat in 1745. Being released on his parole by Charles Edward, he was ordered by Cumberland to rejoin his regiment and serve again against the Jacobites. With great propriety, he refused such a dishonourable duty, saying that "His Royal Highness was master of his commission, but not of his honour." The king approved of Sir Peter's course, and he retained his rank. On the 26th Feb., 1751, he succeeded to the colonelcy of his regiment. He was married to the Lady Amelia Stewart, second daughter of Francis, 8th Earl of Moray, by whom he had three sons: Sir Peter, his successor, who would also appear to have been in the army; Francis, major in the Black Watch; and James, a subaltern in his own regiment, who died with him on the 9th July, 1755. (Burke's Peerage, etc.) High and generous talents seem to have been hereditary in Sir Peter's family. His father's sister, Mrs. Elizabeth Wardlaw (whom Dr. Percy thought he had sufficiently introduced to the public when he announced her as the aunt of the officer "killed in America, along with General Braddock"), was the authoress of what Coleridge would have styled "the grand old ballad" of Hardiknute.

Let Scots, while Scots, praise Hardiknute.

What little we know of the good and noble hero who died on the banks of the Monongahela, irresistibly leads us to the conclusion that in painting her sketches of character Mrs. Wardlaw need not have gone (and perhaps did not go), beyond the circle of her own fireside. It is discouraging to reflect upon the fate of such a man: loyal, honourable, and sagacious, an experienced soldier and a worthy gentleman, he died in the arms of defeat, and the traditions of a foreign land alone preserve the memory of his virtues. In another place we have recorded the horrid circumstances of his death and the tardy burial of his bones. We would that we could here do justice to the spirit which animated his living frame. Notices of Mrs. Wardlaw will be found in II. Percy's *Reliques*; and I. *Blackwood's Mag.*, 380.

******

The Commissary of Provisions is to make two weekly returns; one for the general, the other for Sir Peter Halket.

When any man is sent to the General Hospital, he is to carry with him a certificate, signed by an officer of his company, setting forth his name, regiment, and company, to what day he is subsisted, and what arms and accoutrements he carries with him, which are to be bundled up and marked with the man's name, regiment, and company.

Each regiment is to send to the artillery for twenty-five thousand flints, out of which they are to choose five thousand and send the remainder back; and where any of the troops have occasion for ammunition, or any military stores, the commanding officers are to send to the train for them, giving proper receipts.

The captains of the two regiments are to account with their men for their sea pay, giving them credit for their subsistence to the first of April, and for their arrears to the 24th of February; and they are to stop for the watchcoats, blankets, and flannel waistcoats.

The men enlisted or incorporated into the 44th and 48th regiments are to have credit for twenty shillings and are to be charged with the above necessaries.

All casualties, or remarkable occurrences in camp, are to be reported, immediately, to the general, through an *aid de camp*.

Whenever Sir John St. Clair has occasion for tools, the commissary of the train is to supply them on proper receipts.

Those officers of companies, who call the evening roll, are to inspect the ammunition of their respective companies, and report the deficiencies to the commanding officer.

No man, upon a march, is on any account to fasten his tent pole, to his firelock, or by any means encumber it.

The quartermasters of each regiment are to apply to the assistant quartermaster-general, who will show them their store-houses, in which their regimental stores are immediately to be lodged.

The soldiers are to leave in the store, their shoulder-belts, waist-belts and swords, the sergeants their halberts, and those officers that can provide themselves with fusils, their espontons. (Spontoons; or a sort of half-pikes; carried by infantry officers.)

The general enquired of Sir John St. Clair the nature and condition of the roads through which the troops and artillery were to march, and also if he had provided the waggons for the Ohio. Sir John informed the general that a new road was near completed from Winchester to Fort Cumberland, the old one being impassable, and that another was cutting from Conegogee to the same place, and that if the general approved of making two divisions of the troops and train, he might reach Will's Creek with more ease and expedition. He proposed that one regiment with all the powder and ordnance should go by Winchester, and the other regiment with the ammunition, military and hospital stores by Frederick in Maryland. That these should be carried ten miles up the Potomack to Rock Creek, and then up the Potomack to Fort Cumberland.

Sir John assured the general that boats, *batteaux*, canoes and waggons were prepared for the service, and also that provisions were laid in at Frederick for the troops. A return was called for of the waggons and teams wanted to remove the train from Alexandria, which Sir

John went up the country to provide.

He told the general two men had undertaken to furnish two hundred waggons and fifteen hundred carrying horses at Fort Cumberland early in May.

Before the general reached Alexandria, the troops were all disembarked, but, very little of the ordnance stores or provisions were (being?) yet on shore, the properest places and methods of unlading them were settled, and they were landed with the utmost dispatch.

On the 3rd of April, the general, governor and commodore went to Annapolis to meet the eastern governors. (They arrived there the afternoon of April 3rd, *Penn. Gaz.*, No. 1373.) The general found no waggons were provided for the Maryland side of the Potomack. He applied to Governor Sharpe, who promised above one hundred, which he said should attend at Rock Creek to carry away the stores as fast as they could be landed.

The general was very impatient to remove the troops from Alexandria, as the greatest care and severest punishments could not prevent the immediate (immoderate?), use of spirituous liquors, and as he was likewise informed the water of that place was very unwholsome: Therefore, as the governors were not arrived, the general returned the 7th to Alexandria for the Congress. (With him, on Monday morning, went Dinwiddie and Keppel, Orme and W. Shirley. *Penn. Gaz.*, No. 1373.)

The Virginia troops being cloathed were ordered to march immediately to Winchester, to be armed, and the general appointed ensign Allen of the 44th to make them as like soldiers as it was possible.

Captain Lewis was ordered with his company of Rangers to Green Briar River, there to build two stockade forts, in one of which he was to remain himself, and to detach to the other a subaltern and fifteen men.

★★★★★★

Probably Andrew Lewis of Augusta Co., appointed Captain of the Virginia troops, March 18th, 1754, whose five brothers were enlisted in his company. It would seem that he rejoined the main army and was with the working-party at the opening of the action. This was the respectable Brigadier General Lewis, whom Washington at the commencement of the Revolution had fixed upon as the foremost soldier in all America. (Howe's *Virg.*; Sharpe's *MS. Corr.*)

★★★★★★

These forts were to cover the western settlers of Virginia from any inroads of Indians.

The soldiers were ordered to be furnished with one new spare shirt, one new pair of stockings, and one new pair of shoes; and Osnabrig waistcoats and breeches were provided for them, as the excessive heat would have made the others insupportable, and the commanding officers of companies were desired to provide leather or bladders for the men's hats.

Sir Peter Halket with six companies of the 44th marched on the 9th to Winchester and was to remain there till the roads were completed from thence to Fort Cumberland, and Lieutenant Colonel Gage was left with the other four companies to escort the artillery.

******

Thomas Gage was the 2nd son of Thomas, 8th Baronet and 1st Viscount Gage. His family, though noble, was poor. His father once remarking in a political dispute that he always gave his sons their own way:—"Yes," said Winnington, "but that is the only thing you ever do give them!" Gage rose to high rank in the army and was long employed and conspicuous in American affairs. He married Margaret, daughter of Peter Kemble, Esq., of the Coldspring (N.Y.), family of that name, and their son subsequently succeeded his uncle in the peerage. Gen. Gage died in 1788.

******

As boats were not provided for the conveying of the stores to Rock Creek, the general was obliged to press vessels, and to apply to the commodore for seamen to navigate them. At length with the greatest difficulty they were all sent up to Rock Creek, and an officer with thirty men of the 48th was sent thither with orders to load and dispatch all the waggons as fast as they came in, and to report every morning and evening to the general the number he had forwarded. He was directed to send a party with every division, and to apply for more men as the others marched: and all the boats upon that part of the river were ordered to assist in transporting over the Potomack the 48th Regiment.

On the 18th, the 48th Regiment marched to Frederick in Maryland. Colonel Dunbar was ordered to send one company to Conegogee to assist in forwarding the stores from thence to Fort Cumberland, and to remain with the corps at Frederick till further orders. Thirty more men were ordered to be left with the officer at Rock Creek.

The sick men of the two regiments. Artillery, and Virginia Companies, were left in the hospital at Alexandria, and an officer and twenty men were ordered for its guard and escort. At this place a general court martial was held, of which Lieutenant Colonel Gage was president; the prisoner was ordered one thousand lashes, part of which was remitted, and at this place the troops were also mustered.

On the 13th of April, the governors arrived at Alexandria, and with them Colonel Johnston; and on the 14th a councell was held at which was present General Braddock, Commodore Keppel, Governor Shirley, Lieut. Governor Delancy, Lieut. Governor Dinwiddie, Lieut. Governor Sharpe, Lieut.-Governor Morris. (The minutes of this Council are in II. *Doc. Hist. N.Y.*; VI. *C. R.*)

At this Council the general declared to them His Majesty's pleasure that the several assemblies should constitute a common fund for defraying in part the expences of the expedition.

He showed them the necessity of cultivating a friendship and alliance with the Six Nations of Indians and asked their opinion if Colonel Johnson was not a proper person to be employed as negotiator, also what presents they judged proper, and how they should be furnished.

The general also acquainted them with his intention of attacking Crown Point and Niagara at the same time with Fort Du Quesne, and desired they would inform him if they thought it advisable to attempt the reduction of Crown Point with the forces agreed to be supplied by the Provinces of New York, New Jersey, Connecticutt, Rhode Island, Massachusetts, and New Hampshire, amounting to four thousand four hundred men; and whether, as they were all Irregulars, they did not think Colonel Johnson a proper man to command this expedition.

The general told the Council his intention to reinforce the fort at Oswego with two companies of Sir William Pepperell's and one independant company of New York, as this fort commanded the south east side of the Lake Ontario, and was a post of great consequence to facilitate the attack, or to secure the retreat of the troops destined to Niagara, and as the entire command of the lake was of the greatest consequence to cutt off the French communication with the western countries, and could only be obtained by Vessels, he was of opinion two or more should be built for that purpose, and desired their advice as to the burthen and force of them.

The governors said, they had severally applied to their respective assemblies to establish a common fund but could not prevail.

They were of opinion it was necessary to make a treaty with the Six Nations. That Mr. Johnson was the properest man to negotiate it, and that eight hundred pounds should be furnished by the several governments to be laid out in presents for them. (For the details of Johnson's employments, see the Johnson MSS., II. *Doc. Hist. N.Y.*)

They approved of the attack of Crown Point by the Irregulars, and also of Colonel Johnson's having the command of that expedition.

It was agreed two vessels of sixty tons should be built upon the Lake Ontario, of which Commodore Keppel undertook to furnish draughts, and to defray the expence and the direction thereof was given to Governor Shirley.

★★★★★★

"The scheme for a naval armament at Oswego was first proposed by the Honourable Thomas Pownall to the Congress of Commissioners of the several colonies, met at Albany in June, 1754. Copies were sent to England and taken by the commissioners for the perusal of their respective governments." Lewis Evans' *Essays*, No. II. The vessels were not finished till Sept. 1755, and cost £22,000.

★★★★★★

The three Governments of Virginia, Maryland, and Pennsylvania were to bear the expence of any additional works at Fort Du Quesne, they were to maintain the garrison, and also to pay for any vessels that it should be found necessary to construct upon the Lake Erie.

★★★★★★

When he had captured Du Quesne, Braddock proposed to march thence to Niagara, reducing all the French posts on his way. A garrison of at least 200 of the Maryland and Virginia provincials was to be left at the fort and anticipating that should the enemy evacuate it at his approach, they would destroy as much as they could of its defences, he designed that the provinces most concerned in the business should furnish its provisions and artillery. He certainly would not be able to spare any from his own train.

Morris anticipated from the first that the furnishing of cannon and stores of war would be repugnant to 'the non-resisting principles of his Quaking Assembly;' and he came to no understanding with them on this point. Virginia sent ten ship-cannon, mounted on trucks, with all the appurtenances, by way of Rock Creek and Conocochcague, to Will's Creek; thence, when the time arrived, to be transported to Fort Du Quesne. (VI. *C. R.*; II. *P. A.*) The general anticipated an easy though an important capture, and already looked forward after all his victories, to spending a merry Christmas with Morris at Philadelphia. (VI. *C. R.*)

★★★★★★

Orders were immediately sent to the commanding officer of Sir William Pepperell's regiment to detach two complete companies with all dispatch to Oswego, and also Capt. King's Independent Company, (this was the remaining Independent Company of New York), was ordered to that fort, and the commanding officer was instructed to put the works into the best repair the nature of them would admit of, and Governor Delancey gave four thousand pounds out of the money that was voted by the Assembly of New York to be employed in the victualling of Oswego; directions were sent to New York to prepare ship carpenters and proper persons of all sorts for constructing and completing the vessels intended for the lake, and directions were given to fell with all diligence proper timber for that purpose, and circular letters were written to the several Eastern Governments to raise and assemble as fast as possible the troops designed for the Crown Point expedition.

It was proposed to Mr. Johnson to employ him as Plenipotentiary to the Six Nations, which he at first declined, as the promises made in the year 1746 in regard to these Indians were not fulfilled, by which means he was then laid under the disagreeable necessity of deceiving them. And the French had made use of this neglect very much to our disadvantage and their own Interest; However, the universal and deserved opinion of the general's integrity prevailed upon him to undertake their negotiation. (This is but one of the many testimonials to Braddock's character for public honesty and truthfulness borne by the records of the time.)

A speech was prepared for Mr. Johnson to deliver to the Indians in the general's name, setting forth that His Majesty had sent a very considerable body of troops to drive the French from the encroachments they had from time to time made on his dominions, and on their lands and hunting-grounds, which in the treaty of 1726, between the English and them, they had given us in trust to be guarantied to them for their use and benefit. And that His Majesty had invested him with the supreme command upon the Continent, with orders to strengthen and confirm the amity which had so long subsisted be-

23

tween the English and them. And that His Majesty had also ordered him to fulfil the spirit of that treaty by building proper fortresses and securing to them those lands and hunting-grounds which were given in trust by the said treaty.

The general also told them, that as his distance from them made it impossible for him to meet them himself, and finding their uneasiness at the improper appointment and ill-treatment from the Commissioners of the Indian affairs at Albany, and being also informed that they had expressed a great desire to have Colonel Johnson, one of their own *sachems*, intrusted with that business, he had therefore given him a commission appointing him whole and sole director and manager of Indian affairs; That he had also impowered Colonel Johnson to call them together, to give them presents and to confirm, treat and conclude with them the strictest and most lasting Treaty of Friendship and alliance; and the general engaged to confirm and ratify all such promises as should be made to them by Mr. Johnson, and desired they would confirm and conclude with him, as if the general himself was present.

A commission was given to Colonel Johnson appointing him whole and sole manager and director of Indian affairs, and also empowering him to convene, confer and conclude any treaties with the Six Nations and their allies, at such times, and in such places, as he should think proper for the good of His Majesty's service and interest in America.

Colonel Johnson was also instructed to call them immediately together to give them presents, and prevail upon them to declare against the French, and also to prevail upon the Six Nations to send messengers forthwith to the Southern and Western Indians to forbid them acting with the French and to order them immediately to take up the hatchet and join the general upon his march or before. He was to take especial care that in all meetings, conferences, agreements, or treaties with the Indians, he was always to have in view His Majesty's honour, service and interest.

And he was by the most early and frequent opportunities to remit to the general copies of all transactions of every kind with the Indians, and also of the progress, situation, and success relating to the expedition in which he was employed.

Governor Shirley had orders to supply him with a sum of two thousand pounds at such times, and in such proportions, as he should choose to draw for it; of which sum, as well as all others, he might hereafter be entrusted with, he was to dispose in the best manner for the most effectual gaining and preserving the Indians to His Majesty's interest, and he was to keep regular and exact accounts of the nature of the disbursements; as it was apprehended it might more readily induce the Six Nations to take up arms in our favour if they were employed upon a service immediately under him, he was permitted to take with him such as would declare upon the expedition against Crown point.

This commission and instructions bearing throughout the whole a regard to the integrity of Colonel Johnson's character engaged him to undertake and to proceed upon this negotiation with the greatest spirit and zeal for the service.

Colonel Shirley having much interest in and being extremely well acquainted in the Eastern Governments was supposed most capable of removing the principal difficulties attending the expedition to Niagara, which would arise from procuring provision and artillery, and from transporting them and the troops. And Mr. Shirley expressing the greatest desire to be employed upon that service, he was appointed by the general to that command.

Letters of credit were accordingly given to him, and instructions for that service, whereby he was directed to take his own and Sir William Pepperell's regiments and the companies of New York under his command; and to proceed with the greatest diligence and dispatch to Niagara; taking care to see the vessels designed for the Lake Ontario built and equipt. He was also to order the works of Oswego to be put in the best repair, and to leave a proper garrison for its defence.

He was directed to give frequent accounts to the general of his situation, and proper marks were agreed between them to render any letters useless which might be intercepted by the enemy.

As the general judged the success of the several expeditions would very much depend upon their being carried into execution at or near the same time, and as the very great distance at which they were to act, made it impossible to be agreed by letter, he desired Colonel Shirley and Colonel Johnson would fix the time in which they would be able to appear before Niagara and Crown point. They both agreed upon the end of June, nearly in July, and the general assured them he would use his utmost endeavours to be at Fort Du Quesne by that time.

The general dispatched a courier to Lieutenant Colonel Monkton to take upon him the command of the troops destined for the attack of Beau Sejour upon the Isthmus of Nova Scotia.

The business of the Congress being now over, the general would have set out for Frederick, but few waggons or teams were yet come to remove the artillery; He then sent an express to Sir John St. Clair informing him of it, and in a few days set out for Frederick in Maryland leaving Lieutenant Colonel Gage with four companies of the 44th regiment, who was ordered to dispatch the powder and artillery as fast as any horses or waggons should arrive, taking care to send proper escorts with them.

The general at Rock Creek called for a return of the stores and gave orders for such as were most necessary to be first transported, and for some of the provisions, ordnance, and hospital stores to be left there, the waggons coming in so slow as to render it impossible to convey the whole to Fort Cumberland in proper time.

Upon the general's arrival at Frederick, he found the troops in great want of provision; no cattle was laid in there; The general applied to Governor Sharpe, who was then present, for provision and waggons, but so little is the authority of a governor in that province, that he afforded the general no assistance; upon which the general was obliged to send round the country to buy cattle for the subsistence of the troops.

It was above a month before the necessary ammunition and stores could be transported from Rock Creek to Conegogee, and as the Potomack was not then navigable, even by the smallest Canoes, new difficulties arose in providing Waggons to send them to Fort Cumberland; proper persons were sent to the justices of peace of those counties, and at last by entreaties, threats, and money, the stores were removed.

As the general had met with frequent disappointments, he took the opportunity of Mr. Franklin's being at Frederick to desire he would contract in Pensylvania for one hundred and fifty waggons and fifteen hundred carrying horses upon the easiest terms, to join him at Fort Cumberland by the 10th of May, if possible; Mr. Franklin procured the number of waggons, and about five hundred horses.

★★★★★★

In Jan. 1756, Governor Morris, under the instructions of General Shirley, appointed a commission to audit, settle and adjust the claims of Franklin and others upon the Crown for the hire of these waggons and horses. In conjunction with Robert Leake, Esq., the King's Commissary General, the board sate ten days in Lancaster to decide upon the accounts of the Pennsylvania creditors, and then met in Philadelphia and passed upon those from Maryland and Virginia. By their action, a saving of seven thousand pounds accrued to the Government. II. P.A.

★★★★★★

As those carriages were to pass through Conegogee in their way to Fort Cumberland, the general sent orders to Cressop the agent at that place to make use of that opportunity of conveying to Fort Cumberland the flour which the Government of Pensylvania had delivered there, it being much wanted at the Fort.

As no road had been made to Will's Creek on the Maryland side of the Potomack, the 48th Regiment was obliged to cross that river at Conegogee, and to fall into the Virginia road near Winchester. The general ordered a bridge to be built over the Antietum, which being furnished, and provision laid in on the road. Colonel Dunbar marched with his regiment from Frederick on the 28th of April, and about this time the bridge over the Opeccon was finished for the passage of the artillery, and floats were built on all the rivers and creeks.

The 31st of April the general set out for Winchester hoping to meet the Indians, but as none were, or had been there, he proceeded to Fort Cumberland, where he arrived the 10th of May, and also the 48th Regiment. Sir Peter Halket with six companies of the 44th, two independant companies and the Virginia troops were already encamped at this place.

The general had applied to Governor Morris for some Indians who lived upon the Susquehannah; about thirty of them met him at this place.

★★★★★★

These were the Aughquick Indians brought by George Croghan, whom Braddock formally commissioned their captain for the campaign. Having been long settled as a trader among the savages, he had acquired the languages of several of their nations and possessed great influence over them. By occasion of the war, he was unable to collect a great number of debts due to him by the Indians and became bankrupt. But the Pennsylvania Assembly considering his value on the frontier, passed an act granting him a freedom from arrest for ten years; and he was soon made a captain in the service of the colony. In 1756, he went to Onondaga, and probably died in New York, as his will (dated 12th June, 1782) is recorded in the Court of Appeals at Albany. He is styled as "late of Passyunk, Pa.;" and appears to have left but one child, Susannah, who married Lieutenant Augustine Prevost. (II. *P.A.*; IV. *Doc. Hist., N.Y.*)

★★★★★★

The general shewed them the greatest marks of attention and esteem, and the next day called them to his tent, and conferred with them agreeably to their forms and customs.

The general told them of the troops and artillery His Majesty had sent to their assistance and made use of every argument to persuade them to take up the hatchet against the French, and to act with spirit and fidelity under him.

A few days after, at another Congress, they informed him of their resolutions to serve with him and declared war against the French according to their own ceremonies. They desired leave to return to the Susquehannah with their wives and children (to whom the general made considerable presents) and promised to rejoin him in a few days, only eight of them remaining with him, who were immediately employed in getting intelligence.

★★★★★★

None who left ever returned. Of the eight who remained one was Scarroyaddy (or Monacatootha), already noticed; another was his son, killed on the march. The names of the remainder we find in the proceedings of a Council at Philadelphia on the 15th of August, 1755, where, after condoling with Scarroyaddy on his loss, Morris thanks individually and by name all the savages who fought with Braddock: *viz.*, Cashuwayon, Froson, Kahuktodon, Attscheehokatha, Kash-wugh-daniunto, and Dyoquario; all Iroquois. (VI. *C R.*; Du Simitiere *MSS.*) Doubtless these were their formal and genuine names; but they were known to the whites by other titles, and nothing was more usual than for an Indian to have two names; so that it is now perhaps impossible to identify them all.

I take it, however, that Kash-wugh-daniunto was the Belt of Wampum (VII. *C. R.*); a Seneca, who had contended with Scarroyaddy for the succession to the Half-King. Cashuwayon, we are fortunately able to say with certainty, was the well-known Captain Newcastle.

In January 1756, one Thomas Graeme being adopted by the Indians, he received Newcastle's old name; the warrior thenceforth being called Ah Knoyis (VII. *C. R.*). He died at Philadelphia, of smallpox, during the same year. Perhaps Aroas (or Silver-Heels), a Seneca; Iagrea, Scarroyaddy's son-in-law; and the Mohawks Esras and Moses (or the Song), his wife's brothers, may have been of the others. This last was one of Stobo's messengers from Du Quesne. An inventory of the morrice-bells, tobacco, knives, cloths, powder, etc., presented to these savages by Morris in August, 1755, may be found in VI. *C. R.* They were all constant and active allies of the English; but it is not within the compass of this design to dilate upon their exploits.

★★★★★★

The others never returned to the general, but about sixteen of them advanced as far as Colonel Dunbar's Camp. The general sent messengers to the Delawar and Shawnoe Indians to invite them to join him.

We had been promised the greatest plenty of all kinds of provisions at this place, but none fresh could be procured. The general was greatly concerned to see the want of all refreshments begin so early, fearing it would disable the men from undergoing the fatigues and hardships they were to meet with on their march to the Ohio. They had already marched two hundred miles through an uninhabited wilderness without any other but the salt provision that they had carried with them, or that had been laid in for them upon the road.

The general offered large rewards and lent several people his own money to enable them to provide the camp and gave all manner of encouragement to such as would bring provision. Everything brought to camp was to be sold at a particular place, and any person was to suffer death who should dare to interupt or molest anybody bringing provision or should offer to buy of them before it was carried to the publick market, which was put under the care and inspection of the captains of the picket, and a sergeant with a small guard of the picket attended the market to prevent all quarrels or confusion.

As a further encouragement, the price of provisions was raised a penny in the pound, and no good meat was to be sold at less than the fixed price, lest the peasants should be distressed when they had brought it many miles. These regulations and encouragements produced some supplies, though by the nature of the country inadequate to the wants of the camp.

About the 20th of May, the artillery, which marched in two divisions, arrived. They had remained at Alexandria a fortnight after the general had left it, through the want of waggons and horses, nor could they at last have marched without press parties, which Lieutenant Colonel Gage sent for many miles round, and he was obliged to continue this method the whole march, having neither pasture nor forage on the road, not even at those places where it had been said to have been provided. This march was over a prodigious chain of mountains, and through deep and rocky roads. The troops were now joined, except a North Carolina company, commanded by Captain Dobbs, (son of the governor of the colony), which was daily expected.

The general had now frequent opportunities of seeing and hearing of the appearance and disposition of the Virginia recruits and companies. Mr. Allen had taken the greatest pains with them, and they performed their evolutions and firings as well as could be expected, but their languid, spiritless, and unsoldierlike appearance considered with the lowness and ignorance of most of their officers, gave little hopes of their future good behaviour.

Guards were posted upon the Potomack and Will's Creek, and two other guards were ordered for the security of the horses that were grazing in the woods; and detachments of the picket lay advanced from retreat beating till daylight, having been informed some Indians had been seen near the camp.

About the latter end of May, the Pensylvania waggons came up to us, but brought very little flour from Conegogee, occasioned by the infamous neglect of Cressop the agent at that place, who suffered almost all the waggons to pass without giving them the order before mentioned. Much about the same time this man's father was employed by Governor Sharpe to salt a quantity of beef for the use of the Maryland troops; which beef had been reckoned in the estimate of those provisions designed for the march; it was no sooner brought to camp but it was condemned to be buried by a survey. The surveyors reported that it had no pickle, and that it was put into dry casks, which could never have contained any. (These men were Colonel Thomas and Captain Michael Cresap. See Mr. Brantz Mayer's paper, read before Md. Hist. Soc., May, 1851.)

Being thus disappointed in flour and beef, the general sent away that night thirty waggons with a captain's detachment to Winchester for provisions over sixty miles of mountainous and rocky country; and also three hundred carrying horses for flour, with part of the troop of light horse, to Conegogee, ninety miles distance, with orders to bring up Cressop, another commissary being appointed.

Most of the horses which brought up the train were either lost, or carried home by their owners, the nature of the country making it impossible to avoid this fatal inconvenience, the whole being a continued forrest for several hundred miles without enclosures or bounds by which horses can be secured: they must be turned into the woods for their subsistance, and feed upon leaves and young shoots of trees. Many projects, such as belts, hobles, etc., were tried, but none of these were a security against the wildness of the country and the knavery of the people we were obliged to employ: by these means we lost our horses almost as fast as we could collect them, and those which remained grew very weak, so we found ourselves every day less able to undertake the extraordinary march we were to perform.

The general, to obviate as much as possible these difficulties, appointed a waggon master general, and under him waggon masters over every forty waggons; and horse masters over every hundred horses, and also a drover to every seven horses; the waggon and horse masters with the drovers were to go into the woods with their respective divisions, to muster their horses every night and morning, and to make a daily report to the waggon master general, who was to report to the general.

These regulations remedied in a great measure that evil.

Some Indians arrived from the Delawars, with whom the general conferred, and to whom he made presents. They promised to join him with their Nation upon the march, which they never performed.

Of all the Indians promised by Governor Dinwiddie, none had joined the general; and a few days before we marched the person sent to the Catawbers and Cherokees returned; He informed the general that three hundred of their warriors had marched three or four days with him in their way to the camp; but one Pearus, (perhaps Paris, who commanded at the defeat of Donville in 1756), an Indian Trader had by means of a quantity of liquor diverted them from their undertaking; advising them to call upon Gist (who was the person employed) to shew some written and sealed authority by which he acted; who not being provided with any instrument of this nature from the Government of Virginia, they judged him an imposter, and returned to their towns.

The general wondered that the Governments of Carolina had not been applied to for obtaining these Indians, as being their natural allies.

While these disappointments were still fresh, one Hile a Virginian, with whom the commissaries appointed by Governor Dinwiddie had made a contract for five hundred beeves to be delivered at Fort Cumberland, came to the camp and informed the general, the Committee of the Virginia Assembly would not confirm the contract, and that it was consequently void. He had already received a part of the money, and the general offered to pay him the ballance, but he said he had recalled his factors from Carolina and would not make another contract without an advanced price; and even then, would not engage to perform 'till September. The general therefore resolved to supply himself elsewhere.

General Braddock had applied to the Governor of Pensylvania, soon after his arrival in America, to open a road from that country towards the Ohio, to fall into his road to that place from Fort Cumberland, either at the great meadows, or at the Yoxhio Geni, that he might keep open a communication with Pensylvania either for reinforcements, or convoys. The governor had laid this before his Assembly and had represented to them in the strongest terms the use, and indeed necessity, of such a measure; but they would pay no regard to it.

Upon a farther acquaintance with the nature and state of Virginia, and the frequent disappointments the general experienced from that province, he thought it would be imprudent to depend entirely upon contracts made with or promises received from them; he therefore wrote again to Governor Morris to desire he would once more apply to his Assembly to open a road, and as he was every day the more convinced of the necessity of such a communication, he desired that it might immediately be begun and carried on with all possible expedition, and that he would undertake to defray the expence of it, in case they should again refuse it. The governor through his zeal for His Majesty's service, had it carried into great forwardness in a very short time.

Mr. Peters the Secretary of Pensylvania, who had been to inspect the road, waited upon the general at Fort Cumberland to inform him of its progress; The general desired Mr. Peters would in conjunction with Governor Morris make a contract in his name for a magazine of provisions to be formed at Shippensburgh, sufficient to subsist three thousand men for three months, and to be completed by the beginning of July; he desired they would appoint some proper person to forward the whole or part with all expedition when demanded.

This contract was concluded, and the deposit made agreeable to the time mentioned. The general also fixed with Mr. Peters that the junction of the two roads should be at the Crow foot of the Yoxhio Geni. (The union of the Yougbiogeny proper, the Laurel Hill Creek, and Castleman's River, in Somerset County, is commonly called the Turkey Foot, or the Crow Foot of the Youghiogeny.)

The general called a Council of War consisting of:

Colonel Sir Peter Halket.
Colonel Dunbar.

Lieutenant Colonel Gage.
Lieutenant Colonel Burton.
Major Chapman.
Major Sparks.
Major Sir John St. Clair, D. Q. G.

★★★★★★

Ralph Burton, lieutenant-colonel of the 48th, seems to have been a favourite of Braddock's. In January, 1748, he received the local rank of a colonel in North America and commanded the right wing at the capture of Quebec. After its fall, he was made governor of the department of Trois-Rivières. (II. Garneau.) He was a colonel in the line, December 10, 1760, and of the 3rd Foot (Buffs), 22nd Nov., 1764. He was created major-general 10th July, 1762.

On 7th March, 1751, Russel Chapman was appointed major of the 44th, and on 20th March, 1750, was gazetted lieutenant-colonel of the 62nd regiment.

All I can learn of the officer, Major Sparks, is that he marched with Dunbar to Philadelphia, and that his name was William Sparkes. (VI. *C. R.*)

★★★★★★

The general acquainted the Council he had formed a plan of march and encampment upon the nature of the service, country, and enemy he was engaged in and expected to be opposed by; That he offered it to them for their opinions, in which he desired they would be very explicit, and make such objections, and offer such amendments, as they should judge proper, by which some general plan might be formed which would effectually answer the end proposed, of marching and encamping with the greater security. He said he should be very much encumbred with a vast number of carriages and horses, which it was absolutely necessary to secure from the insults of the Indians from whom he apprehended frequent annoyance.

It would be therefore necessary to divide the troops into small parties to cover as much as possible the baggage, which would be obliged to march in one line through a road about twelve foot wide, and that it appeared to him also necessary to extend small parties very well upon the flanks, in the front, and in the rear, to prevent any surprise which the nature of the country made them very liable to; and he proposed, as it would be impracticable to have a regular parade, that every commanding officer of a company should regulate that compa-

ny's duty by detaching always upon his flanks a third of the effectives with a sergeant, which sergeant was to detach a third of his men upon his flanks with a corporal; these out parties were to be relieved every night at retreat beating, and to form the advanced pickets.

Each regiment was to find one captain and three subalterns for the picket of each flank; and the independent companies, Virginia, Maryland, and Carolina Rangers, One captain and two subalterns for each of the flanks of their division; and the field officer of the day was to command the whole. The officers of the pickets were to march upon their respective flanks. The waggons. Artillery, and carrying horses were formed into three divisions, and the provisions disposed of in such a manner as that each division was to be victualled from that part of the line it covered, and a commissary was appointed to each. The waggon masters were to attend their respective divisions to proportion the goodness of teams, and to assist at every steep ascent by adding any number of horses from other waggons, till their respective divisions had passed.

The waggons were subdivided again into smaller divisions, every company having a certain number which they were to endeavour to keep together, however the line might be broke: The companies were to march two deep that they might extend the more, be more at liberty to act, and less liable to confusion.

A field officer was to march with a van, and another with a rear guard. Sir Peter Halket was to lead the column, and Colonel Dunbar to bring up the rear. The field officer of the picket had no fixed posts. There was also an advanced party of three hundred men to precede the line to cut and make the roads, commanded by a field officer or the quartermaster general. This detachment was to be either a day's march before the line or to move earlier every morning, according to the country we were to pass through, or the intelligence we could get of the enemy.

The form of the encampment differed very little from that of the march. Upon coming to the ground, the waggons were to draw up in close order in one line, the road not admitting more, care being taken to leave an interval in the front of every company. When this was done the whole was to halt and face outward.

The serjeants' flank parties were to divide, facing to the right and left, and to open a free communication by cutting down saplings and underwood, till they met the divisions of the other serjeants' parties: they were then to open a communication with the corporal in front, who was to keep his men under arms. The serjeant was then to advance half of his party, which was to remain under arms whilst the corporal opened his communications to the right and left. All this was carried on under the inspection of the picket officers of the respective flanks.

Whilst this was executing, half of each company remained under arms, whilst the other half opened the communication to the right and left, and to the serjeants in front, and also cleared ground for the tents, which were pitched by them, and placed in a single row along the line of baggage, facing outwards. These parties were then to be re-lieved, and the corporal's party was all posted in centinels, which made a chain of centinels round the camp. The grenadiers were to encamp across the road, and each company to advance a serjeant's party.

Upon beating the general, the men were to turn out, but not to strike their tents till they received orders; upon the Assembly the hors-es were to be loaded; and upon beating the march the corporals were to join their parties, and the whole was to face upon the right and left.

When the waggons were all closed up, the waggon and horse-masters were to assemble in some particular place their respective di-visions, and to give their orders to the waggoners and drovers. The horses were then to be turned out within the centinels, every centinel having orders not to suffer any horse to pass him.

It was the opinion of the Council this line of march and plan of encampment would answer extremely well for the service we were engaged in; every field officer was to have a copy of it, and they were desired to assemble the captains and explain to them fully the duty they were to perform.

Some Indians returned from a reconnoitring party and informed the general about a hundred soldiers were then in garrison at Fort Du Quesne, but that they soon expected greater reinforcements from Montreal and Quebec.

Two days after, the general called another Council of War. He in-formed them of the present state of the garrison, and read to them some letters of intelligence, that he had received from the governors of New York and Pennsylvania.

The general told the Council, that he found by his returns, that he had not above forty waggons over and above the hundred and fifty he had got from Pensylvania, and that the number of carrying horses did not exceed six hundred, which were insufficient to carry seventy days flour and fifty days meat, which he was of opinion was the least he could march with without running great risques of being reduced to the utmost distress before the convoy could be brought to him if he should meet with any opposition at the fort. And he desired to know their opinions of a measure he had formed for carrying eight days more provision and for saving some days in the march.

The general reminded the Council of the waggons sent to Winchester for provisions, which could not return in less than seven days, and this time would absolutely be lost if the march of the whole was delayed for their return. The general therefore proposed the sending forwards of a party of six hundred men, workers and coverers, with a field officer, and the quartermaster-general; that they should take with them two six-pounders, with a full proportion of ammunition; that they should also take with them eight days provision for three thousand two hundred men; that they should make the road as good as possible, and march five days towards the first crossing of the Yoxhio Geni, which was about thirty miles from the camp, at which place they were to make a deposit of the provisions, building proper sheds for its security, and also a place of arms for its defence and the security of the men.

If they could not in five days advance so far, they were at the expiration of that time to choose an advantageous spot and to secure the provisions and men as before. When the waggons were unloaded, the field officer with three hundred men was to return to camp, and Sir John St. Clair with the first engineer was to remain and carry on the works with the other three hundred. The general proposed marching from Fort Cumberland to the first camp in three divisions, as it would be impossible for the whole line with the baggage to move off the ground in one day.

Sir Peter Halket with the 44th Regiment was to march with the first division, taking with him about a hundred waggons of provisions, stores and powder.

Lieutenant Colonel Burton with the independent companies, Virginia, Maryland, and Carolina Rangers, was to march with the artillery, ammunition, some stores and provision, and to form the second division.

Colonel Dunbar, with the 48th, was to make the third division, and to take with him the provision waggons from Winchester, the returned waggons from the advanced party, and all the carrying horses.

The whole of the general's plan was universally approved of and agreed to; and the resolutions of the first, and of this Council of War were signed by the members.

★★★★★★'

The following sketch of the character and condition of the army at this moment will not be out of place here. I cite from

W. Shirley's letter to Gov. Morris, dated at Fort Cumberland, 23rd May, 1755. (VI. *C. R.*)

It is a joke to suppose that secondary officers can make amends for the defects of the first. The main spring must be the mover; others in many cases can do no more than follow and correct a little its motions. As to them, I don't think we have much to boast. Some are insolent and ignorant; others capable, but rather aiming at showing their own abilities than making a proper use of them. I have a very great love for my friend Orme and think it uncommonly fortunate for our leader that he is under the influence of so honest and capable a man, but I wish, for the sake of the publick, he had some more experience of business, particularly in America.

As to myself, I came out of England expecting that I might be taught the business of a military secretary, but I am already convinced of my mistake. I would willingly hope my time may not be quite lost to me. You will think me out of humour. I own I am so. I am greatly disgusted at seeing an expedition (as it is called), so ill-concerted originally in England and so ill-appointed, so improperly conducted in America; and so much fatigue and expense incurred for a purpose which, if attended with success, might better have been left alone. I speak with regard to our particular share.

However, so much experience I have had of the injudiciousness of public opinion, that I have no little expectation, when we return to England, of being received with great applause. I am likewise further chagrined at seeing the prospect of affairs in America which, when we were at Alexandria I looked upon to be very great and promising, through delays and disappointments which might have been prevented, grown cloudy and in danger of ending in little or nothing.

The writer was destined never to enjoy his country's predicted applause. He was shot through the head at the first fire on the fatal 9th of July, just six weeks after the date of this letter.

★★★★★★

This detachment of six hundred men commanded by Major Chapman marched the 30th of May at daybreak, and it was night before the whole baggage had got over a mountain about two miles from the camp. The ascent and descent were almost a perpendicular rock; three waggons were entirely destroyed, which were replaced from the camp; and many more were extremely shattered. Three hundred men, with the miners (of whom the general had formed a company), had already been employed several days upon that hill.

The general reconnoitred this mountain and determined to set the engineers and three hundred more men at work upon it, as he thought it impassable by howitzers. (A howitzer is a short gun for throwing shells and is mounted on a field carriage. It differs from a mortar mainly in having its trunnions in the middle.) He did not imagine any other road could be made, as a reconnoitring party had already been to explore the country; nevertheless, Mr. Spendelow, lieutenant of the seamen, a young man of great discernment and abilities, acquainted the general, that, in passing that mountain, he had discovered a valley which led quite round the foot of it.

A party of a hundred men, with an engineer, was ordered to cut a road there, and an extreme good one was made in two days, which fell into the other road about a mile on the other side of the mountain.

From this place the general wrote to Colonel Shirley and Colonel Johnson, desiring them to use all possible dispatch in the carrying their expeditions into execution, and he wrote also to the Governor of New York, to desire he would afford them all possible assistance in his Government, as they must necessarily depend entirely upon it for their subsistance.

Mr. Shirley represented to the general the weakness of Sir William Pepperell's regiment, and applied for the five hundred men under the command of Colonel Schyler, who were raised in New Jersey for the Crown Point expedition; which men the governor, Assembly, and Colonel Schyler, were willing should join Mr. Shirley. The general therefore acquiesced and wrote to that purpose to Governor Belchier.

★★★★★★

Pepperell's regiment was not more than half-filled when, on the 26th May, he wrote from New York to his old friend Gov. Morris, asking permission for his recruiting officers to 'raise a hundred or two of brave men' in Pennsylvania. (II. P.A.) It has already been observed how many hundreds from this province were enlisted in the northern campaigns of the war. The New Jersey troops alluded to in the text were commanded by Colonel Peter Schuyler, of whose family was Philip Schuyler of the Revolution. John Belcher was governor of this latter colony.

★★★★★★

The Governor of South Carolina sent the general bills for four thousand pounds, being part of six thousand which was voted by that Assembly towards a common fund. These bills were remitted to Governor Morris to pay in part for the magazine at Shippensburgh. (VI. *C.R.*) This was the only money raised by the provinces which ever passed through the general's hands.

The general wrote to the governors of Virginia, Maryland, and Pensylvania, desiring the two former to have their militia ready to escort his convoys, if he should not be able to detach a sufficient number of men from his own body; and also desired the three governments to provide artillery for the fort, in case he should make himself master of it, as he could not leave any of his ordnance in that place. He also informed them that the French had threatned to fall with their Indians upon the back inhabitants as soon as the army should march, and the general desired they would make the best use of that information. (See VI. *C. R.* This threat was considered a mere bravado.)

A proper commissary was appointed at Conegogee, with orders to send up all the flour to Fort Cumberland, and directions were given for gathering to that place all the provision which had been left for want of carriages at Alexandria, Rock Creek, Frederick, and Winchester. Thus, two magazines were formed in different parts of the country, from either of which the general might supply himself as he should find most convenient.

It appearing to the general absolutely necessary to leave some proper person to superintend the commissaries, and to dispatch the convoys, and also to command at the fort, Colonel Innys was appointed governor of it. Instructions were given to him, and money was left with him for contingent expences, lest the service should for want of it meet with any checks. The general fixed with the several governors of Virginia, Maryland, and Pensylvania proper places for laying horses for the more ready conveyance of their expresses: men were also employed with proper badges; and orders were given in the several governments to supply them with horses upon a proper application.

A company of guides were established under two chiefs; each regiment had three guides. The general had one, and the quartermaster general three.

An hospital was left at this place, and the most infirm officers and men remained in garrison.

Everything being now settled, Sir Peter Halket with the 44th regiment marched the 7th of June.

Lieutenant Colonel Burton with the independent companies and Rangers on the 8th, and Colonel Dunbar with the 48th regiment on the 10th, with the proportions of baggage, as was settled by the Council of War.

The same day the general left Fort Cumberland, and joined the whole at Spendelow camp, about five miles from the fort.

ORDERS GIVEN AT FORT CUMBERLAND.

None of the men that came with the regiments from Ireland to be suffered to act as bat-man.

All the troops to be under arms, and to have the articles of war read to them, at which time the servants and followers are to attend.

A return to be made of such men as understand mining, to whom proper encouragement shall be given.

The troops to begin immediately their field days, each man to have twelve rounds of powder.

The troops are to be immediately brigaded in the following manner:

The first Brigade, Commanded by Sir Peter Halket.

		Compliment.	Effective.
44th Regiment of Foot		700 ...	700
Capt. Rutherford's[1] } ...... Independaut Comp[r] } Capt. Gates } of New York }	...... 100 ...		95
Capt. Polson's[2] .... Carpenters		50 ...	48

[1] Capt. John Rutherford was stationed at Will's Creek in March, 1755; an interesting letter from him will be found in II. P. A., 277. At the end of the year, he held the rank of major under Shirley at New York. (VII. C. R., 23.)

[2] William Polson was probably a Scot who had been concerned in the rebellion of 1745; since, early in 1755, he writes to James Burd complaining bitterly of a report that assigned him in that affair "such a low station as I detest as much as the author of such a falsehood." (I. Shippen MSS. 18.) In 1754, he served under Washington, and received the thanks of the Virginia Burgesses and Governor for his good conduct. His captaincy in the Virginia services dated from 21st July, 1754. (Sharpe's MS. Corr.) Being killed in 1755, an annual pension of £26 was bestowed by Virginia upon his widow. (VII. Sp. Wash., 87.) I believe, too, a lieutenant's commission in the 60th, of which Gage was commandant and Gates major, was given to his son John on 5th May, 1756. (II. Sp. Wash., 127.) He was made captain June 16th, 1773, which rank he held in 1778.

			Compliment.		Effective.
Capt. Peronnee's [1] ⎫	....	Virginia Rangers............	50	...	47
Capt. Wagner's [2] ⎰		Virginia Rangers............	50	...	45
Capt. Dagworthy's [3]		Maryland Rangers...........	50	...	49

Second Brigade, Commanded by Colonel Dunbar.

48th Regiment of Foot	700	...	650
Capt. Demerie's [4] .... South Carolina Detach[t]	100	...	97

[1] William, Chevalier de Peyronie, was a French Protestant, settled in Virginia, and highly esteemed. At Fort Necessity he was an ensign under Washington, whose warm favor he enjoyed. Being desperately wounded in that action, he obtained leave to wait upon the Assembly to petition for some recompense for his personal losses of clothes, &c. On 30th Aug., 1754, the Burgesses voted him their thanks, and especially desired the Governor to promote him; and he accordingly received a captain's commission to date from 25th August, 1754. He died unmarried. (II. Sp. Wash. Sharpe's MS. Corr.)

[2] Thomas Waggener (Capt. Virg. troops, July 20th, 1754), was a lieutenant in the campaign of 1754, and was slightly wounded at Jumonville's defeat. He had previously served under Gov. Shirley, in the projected Canada expedition of 1746. At Fort Necessity he was a lieutenant, and was one of those thanked by the Virginia legislature. His gallant conduct in Braddock's campaign has been noticed : it may be added, that so late as 1757, he continued actively engaged in the war. (II. Sp. Wash. II Belknap's Hist. N. H. Sharpe's MS. Corr.)

[3] Ely Dagworthy had held the King's commission in the previous French war, and was engaged in Shirley's Canada design. For this reason, he esteemed himself superior to any mere provincial officer, though he was himself considered in that very light by Braddock, insomuch as he had no other command than that of a Maryland company. In the fall of 1756, his impudent assumptions of superiority to Washington were summarily put down by Gen. Shirley (II. Sp. Wash.); and not long after he seems to have obtained one of the lieutenancies in the 44th, made vacant by the action of 9th July. His commission dated from 15th July, 1755. In 1765, he had risen no higher.

[4] Paul Demerie, who was killed by the Cherokees in 1760, during the Indian war of South Carolina. I. Ramsay's S. C., 182.

			Compliment.		Effective.
Capt. Dobb's	North Carolina Rangers ...	100	...	80
Capt. Mercer's [1]	Company of Carpenters	50	...	35
Capt. Stevens's [2] ⎫	Virginia Rangers...........	50	...	48
Capt. Hogg's [3] ⎰	Virginia Rangers...........	50	...	40
Capt. Cox's [4] ⎰	Virginia Rangers...........	50	...	43

[1] I do not know if this was George or John Mercer. Both were at Fort Necessity, and thanked by the Burgesses : the former was a Virginia captain, June 4th, 1754, and in 1760, agent of the Ohio Company at London. The latter was a lieutenant, 21st July, 1754, and Washington's aid in 1756; in which year he was killed by the enemy.

[2] Adam Stephen was, in 1754, perhaps the senior captain in Frey's regiment. He rose to be colonel of the Virginia troops, and was a general officer in the Revolution.

[3] Peter Hogg was a captain, March 9th, 1754; and so late as the end of 1757 was still in the Virginia service. Being detached on the march, he and his command escaped the dangers of the 9th of July.

[4] Probably Thomas Cocke, commissioned as captain in the Virginia troops, Dec. 13th, 1754.

★★★★★★

The detachment of seamen to encamp with the second brigade and the troop of light horse separately.

The general is to be acquainted through an *aid de camp* the night before the regiments are to exercise.

Prohibitory orders were given against spirituous liquors being sold to the Indians, or any soldiers going into their camp.

Proper victualling returns were ordered to be given in to the commissary general of the stores, signed by the commanding officers of the regiments and artillery, the several companies, detachment of seamen and troop of light horse, the Director of the hospital, waggonmaster general, and Indian manager, specifying the names and qualifications of those persons, who drew provisions under their command or directions.

All the troops were to account to the director of the hospital once in three months for stoppages at the rate of four pence sterling per day for every man that was admitted into the General Hospital.

It was also ordered, that no suttler should dare to sell any more spirits to the men than one gill a day to each, which an officer of the picket was to see delivered out at eleven of the clock and mixed with three gills of water; and any suttler offending against this order was to be sent to the provost.

If any non-commissioned officer or soldier shall be found gaming, he shall immediately receive three hundred lashes, and the standers by shall be deemed principals and punished as such.

If any soldier is seen drunk in camp, he is to be sent immediately to the quarter guard, and to receive two hundred lashes the next morning.

Agreeably to a resolution of a Council of War, it was ordered that every subaltern superintending the work upon the road should receive three shillings per day; each serjeant one shilling; each corporal nine pence; and every drum or private man six pence. But as it was thought this would weaken too much the military chest, and there being no publick markets, the general promised to settle with them in their winter quarters.

Any soldier or follower of the army that shall be detected in stealing or purloyning any of the provisions, shall suffer death.

SPENDELOW CAMP.

Lieutenant Colonel Burton represented to the general that he had been two days in marching about five miles on a better road than we were to expect afterwards, occasioned by the extreme faintness and deficiency of the horses.

The general thereupon called together all the officers, and told them, that through this inconvenience it would be impossible to continue the march without some alterations, which he was convinced they would readily assist in, as they had hitherto expressed the greatest spirit and inclination for the service. He recommended to them to send to Fort Cumberland all such baggage as was not absolutely necessary, and told them, if any of them had able horses, which they could spare to the publick cause, he would take care that such testimonies of their regard to it should not be forgotten and excited them to it by his example; he and his family contributed twenty horses. This had such an effect, that most of the officers sent back their own, and made use of soldiers tents the rest of the campaign, and near a hundred able horses were given to the publick service.

June 11th. The general called a council of war, consisting of:
Colonel Sir Peter Halket,
Colonel Dunbar,
Lieut.-Colonel Gage,
Lieut.-Colonel Burton,
Major Chapman,
Major Sparks.
In which it was agreed to send back two six-pounders, four cohorns, some powder and stores, which cleared near twenty waggons. All the king's waggons were also sent back to the fort, they being too heavy, and requiring large horses for the shafts, which could not be procured; and country waggons were fitted for the powder in their stead.

This day was employed in shifting the powder, fitting the waggons, and making a proper asortment of the stores.

The loads of all the waggons were to be reduced to fourteen hundred weight; seven of the most able horses were chose for the Howitzers, and five to each twelve-pounder, and four to each waggon. The other horses were all to carry flour and bacon. Every horse was by the contract to have carried two hundred weight, but the contractors were so well acquainted with our situation (which did not permit us to reject anything), that most of the horses furnished by them were the offcasts of Indian traders, and scarce able to stand under one hundred weight.

A detachment of a captain, two subalterns, and fifty men, were sent as a covering party to the workers upon the Pensylvania road; and fifty of the worst men from the Independents and Rangers were ordered to reinforce the garrison at Fort Cumberland; and only two women per company were allowed to be victualled upon the march, but proper provision was made for them at the fort, to which place they were sent back. (They were, however, sent to Philadelphia. II. *P.A.*)

Some orders were found necessary for the farther regulation and security of the camp.

We were now encamped according to the plan approved of by the Council of War. When the carriages were closed up, leaving proper intervals of communications, the extent of the camp, from the front to the rear guard, was less than half a mile.

Orders given at Spendelow Camp.

The captains of the picket are to be at the field officer of the day's tent to receive the countersign, which they are to give to the subalterns, the subalterns to the serjeants, the serjeants to the centinels, who are not to suffer any person to come within ten paces without receiving the countersign; and all advanced corporals and centinels are to have their bayonets fixed.

The field officer of the picket is to be received as grand rounds, whenever he goes his rounds either night or day.

No person whatever to fire a piece within a mile of the camp.

No hutts or bowers to be built by the advanced pickets or centinels.

One tumbril with tools is to march in the front and another in the centre of the carriages, and one engineer with part of the pioneers is to march in the front, and another with the rest of the pioneers in the centre.

It required two days to new load the waggons, and put everything in order, which being settled we marched on the 13th to Martin's plantation, being about five miles from Spendelow Camp. The first brigade got to their ground that night, but the second could not get up before the next day at eleven of the clock, the road being excessively mountainous and rocky. This obliged the general to halt one day for the refreshment of the men and horses.

ORDERS GIVEN AT THE CAMP AT MARTIN'S PLANTATION.

Upon the beating of the general, which is to be taken from the 44th Regiment, all the troops are to turn out, accoutre and form two deep at the head of their encampments upon all halts, though ever so small; the pickets and companies are to face outwards. The officers of the pickets are to take care that their pickets keep at a proper distance upon their flanks. Upon the firing of a cannon, either in front, centre or rear, the whole line is to form, to face outwards, and to wait for orders.

The field officers, excepting him that commands the van guard, are to take no particular post, but to see that the men assist in getting up the waggons at any steep ascent, or difficult pass.

In case any waggon should break down, it is immediately to be drawn out on one side of the road, and a report of it with its lading to be sent to the waggon master-general, who is to order it to be repaired and fall in the rear, or the load to be divided among the other waggons, as he shall think proper.

The carrying horses having suffered very much by bearing their loads so long the day before, they were ordered with an escort of two companies upon the right of the 44th to proceed to the little meadows, at which place Sir John St. Clair was encamped with the three hundred men, not having been able to proceed further in the five days.

June 15th. The line began to move from this place at five of the clock; it was twelve before all the carriages had got upon a hill which is about a quarter of a mile from the front of the camp, and it was found necessary to make one-half of the men ground their arms and assist the carriages while the others remained advantageously posted for their security.

We this day passed the Aligany Mountain, which is a rocky ascent of more than two miles, in many places extremely steep; its descent is very rugged and almost perpendicular; in passing which we intirely demolished three waggons and shattered several. (Mr. Atkinson, II. *O.T.*, very justly points out the error of not passing this mountain by the spur since adopted for the National Road.) At the bottom of the mountain runs Savage River, which, when we passed was an insignificant stream; but the Indians assured us that in the winter it is very deep, broad and rapid. This is the last water that empties itself into the Potomack.

The first brigade encamped about three miles to the westward of this river. Near this place was another steep ascent, which the waggons were six hours in passing.

In this day's march, though all possible care was taken, the line was sometimes extended to a length of four or five miles.

June 16th. We marched from the camp near Savage River to the little meadows, which is about ten miles from Martins' Plantations, where the first brigade arrived that evening, but the second did not all arrive till the 18th.

A great part of this day's march was over a bogg which had been very well repaired by Sir John St. Clair's advanced party with infinite labour. (The route this day lay through the region of dense pine forests called the Shades of Death.)

By these four days' marches it was found impossible to proceed with such a number of carriages. The horses grew every day fainter, and many died: and the men would not have been able to have undergone the constant and necessary fatigue, by remaining so many hours under arms; and by the great extent of the baggage the line was extremely weakened.

The general was therefore determined to move forward with a detachment of the best men, and as little incumbrance as possible.

Therefore a detachment of one field-officer with four hundred men and the deputy quarter master general marched on the 18th to cut and make the road to the little crossing of the Yoxhio Geni—taking with them two six-pounders with, their ammunition, three waggons of tools, and thirty five days provision—all on carrying horses. And on the 19th the general marched with a detachment of one colonel, one lieutenant colonel, one major, the two eldest grenadier companies, and five hundred rank and file.

The party of seamen and eighteen light horse, and four howitzers with fifty rounds each, and four twelve pounders with eighty rounds each, and one hundred rounds of ammunition for each man, and one waggon of Indian presents; the whole number of carriages being about thirty. The howitzers had each nine horses, the twelve pounders seven, and the waggons six. There was also thirty-five days provision carried on horses.

This detachment marched and encamped according to the annexed plan.

47

The Indians were ordered to march with the advanced party; this day Monocatuca the Indian chief being at a small distance from the party was surrounded and taken by some French and Indians. The former were desirous of killing him, but the Indians refused, declaring they would abandon them and join with us if they persisted in their design. They agreed at last to tye him to a tree and leave him: But his son who was with him escaped, and informed our Indians, who went soon after and brought him off.

We this day crossed the first branch (Castleman's River: the ford is called the Little Crossings), of the Yoxhio Geni, which is about four score yards over and knee deep. After having marched four miles from the little meadows we came up with the rear of the advanced party, and were obliged to encamp, as they were then at work in cutting a travers-road over an immense mountain, which could not be finished till the next day. Immediately upon coming to our ground, some guides ran into us, extremely frightened, and told us a great body of the enemy were marching to attack our advanced guard.

The general sent forward an *aid de camp* to know the truth of this report, who found Lieutenant Colonel Gage in possession of the top of the mountain, and his men very advantageously posted. Our Indians had discovered the tracks of several men very near the advanced party, which had given rise to this alarm. Lieutenant Colonel Gage remained about two hours under arms, but no enemy appearing he sent parties to scour the neighbouring woods, and upon their return proceeded with the work, leaving proper parties to secure the heights, and encamped there that night.

As the advanced party was to move forward early in the morning, the general ordered a detachment of a captain and one hundred men to march at daybreak, and to occupy that eminence till he should pass it with the artillery and baggage.

Every field-officer had an orderly light horseman by whom they were to inform the general of all accidents, stops or delays in their respective parts of the line; by which means, the extent of the carriages, upon the march, was very seldom above half a mile; and the encampments was but three hundred yards from the front to the rear.

ORDERS AT THE CAMP ON THE WEST SIDE THE LITTLE CROSSING OF THE YOXHIO GENI.

June 19. The quartermasters are constantly to see the; communications opened.

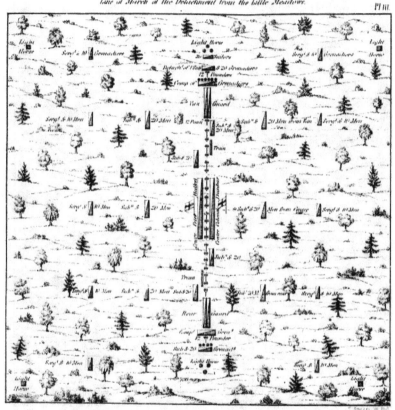

SCALE OF YARDS

Pl. II.

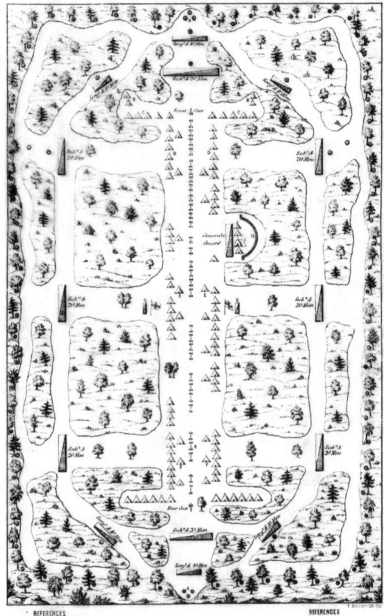

REFERENCES

A Vedet of Light Horse
B Party of Sailors
C Comp.ⁿ of Grenadiers
D Van Guard
E Main Body

SCALE OF YARDS

N.B. — The Dots by the Trees are Sentries

REFERENCES

F. Rear Guard
G. Color Guard
H. One Comp.ⁿ of Light Horse.
I. Generals Tent.
K. Line of Bivouac.

The pickets of the detachment to consist of two captains and the subaltern officers' parties that are advanced upon the flanks in the front and in the rear.

The eldest captain of the picket is to command and visit the pickets of the front grenadiers and the left flank, and the youngest captain the picket and the rear grenadiers and the right flank. The retreat is to beat an hour before sunset, at which time the picket is to be relieved, that the officers may have light to reconnoitre the ground and to post their centinels.

From thence we marched about nine miles to Bear Camp over a chain of very rocky mountains and difficult passes. We could not reach our ground 'till about 7 of the clock, which was three hours later than common, as there was no water, nor even earth enough to fix a tent, between the great mountain and this place. We halted here two days, having a road to cut in the side of a mountain, and some swamps to make passable.

Orders at Bear Camp; June 20th.

The men of the pickets are always to load afresh when they go on duty, and to take particular care to save the ball, which the commanding officers of companies are to see returned to the train.

The troops that are encamped here are to be formed into companies according to the number of captains present.

The Articles of War are to be read to the men, and that article relating to the alarming of camps to be particularly explained to them.

The general having observed upon the march some neglects upon the out detachments, orders that for the future the subalterns' parties, when the ground will possibly admit of it, keep at least one hundred yards distance from the line, and that the serjeants keep their parties within sight of the subaltern's from which they are detached; and upon every halt, though ever so small, the men are to form two deep, face outwards, and stand shouldered.

The officers and serjeants are to be very attentive to the beat of the drum, taking care always to halt when they hear the long roll beat at that part of the line from which 'they are detached, and to march upon beating the long march.

The field officers and all officers commanding any part of the line are to be particularly careful to beat the long roll and long march upon their halting and marching.

Exact victualling returns are to be given in to the commissaries, signed by the commanding officer.

The quarter masters of the two regiments are always to attend at the delivery of provisions, and to receive from the commissary the full quantity for their respective corps, which they are to distribute to the serjeants of the companies, who are to issue it to the men. The artillery, seamen, and light horse, and waggon masters, are to do the same.

On the 23rd of June we marched from this camp to the squaw's fort, making about six miles of very bad road.

Three Mohawk Indians pretending friendship came to the general and told him they were just come from the French fort. They said that some reinforcements were arrived from Montreal, and that they were in expectation of many more: that they had very little provision at the fort, and that they had been disappointed of their supplies by the dryness of the season having stopped the navigation of Buffler River. (The Rivière aux Boeufs, or French Creek, is here signified.)

The general caressed them, and gave them presents, but they nevertheless went off that night, and with them one of our Indians, whom we had very long suspected. This fellow had frequently endeavoured to conceal himself upon the flanks on the march but was always discovered by the flank parties. Notwithstanding this, we could not punish him, as the Indians are so extremely jealous that we feared it would produce a general disaffection.

The 24th of June we marched at five in the morning, and passed the second branch of the Yoxhio Geni, which is about one hundred yards wide, about three feet deep, with a very strong current.

******

This was at the Great Crossings. "The route thence to the Great Meadows or Fort Necessity was well chosen, though over a mountainous tract, conforming very nearly to the ground now occupied by the National Road, and keeping on the dividing ridge between the waters flowing into the Youghiogeny on the one hand, and the Cheat River on the other. II. *O. T.*

******

In the day's march, we discovered an Indian Camp, which they had just abandoned: our Indians informed us that, by their hutts, their number was about one hundred and seventy. They had stripped and painted some trees, upon which they and the French had written many threats and bravados with all kinds of scurrilous language.

We marched this day about six miles, and at night joined the two detachments.

At daybreak the men of the advanced pickets are to examine their panns and to put in fresh priming.

The subalterns upon the advanced parties are to keep one of their men within sight of the line, whom they are to have always in view; and the serjeants are to do the same by the subalterns.

The general is determined to put the first officer under arrest whom he shall find any ways negligent in any of these duties.

On the 25th, at daybreak, three men who went without the centinels, were shot and scalped. Parties were immediately sent out to scour the woods on all sides, and to drive in the stray horses.

This day we passed the Great Meadows and encamped about two miles on the other side. (A mile west of the Great Meadows Braddock must have passed over the very spot destined for his grave. The Mount Braddock Farm occupies a portion of the route.) We this day saw several Indians in the woods; the general sent the light horse, our Indians, and some volunteers, to endeavour to surround them, but they returned without seeing them.

About a quarter of a mile from this camp, we were obliged to let our carriages down a hill with tackles, which made it later than usual before we got to our ground. The soldiers were now so accustomed to open the communications and understood so well the reason and method of our encampment, that they performed this work with great alacrity and dispatch; and the marching through the woods, which they at first looked upon as unnecessary fatigue, they were now convinced to be their only security, and went through it with the greatest cheerfulness.

Some French and, Indians endeavoured to reconnoitre, the camp, but wherever they advanced, they were discovered and fired upon by the advanced centinels. Two captain's detachments of 50 men each, were ordered to march at 10 o'clock in the morning with guides. One party was to march out at the front and the other in the rear. They were to divide the detachments into small parties, and to lie upon their arms about half a mile wide upon each flank of the encampment. At break of day the pickets were to advance, and at the same time these small parties were to move forward towards the camp. By this measure, any Indians who had concealed themselves near the camp must have been taken; but these parties returned without having seen any of the enemy.

The advanced pickets are to take no more blankets than will be sufficient to cover their centinels.

The line is never to turn out upon any account but by order from the general, or the field officer of the picket.

Every soldier or Indian shall receive five pounds for each Indian scalp.

June the 26th. We marched at five o'clock, but by the extreme badness of the road could make but four miles. At our halting place we found another Indian camp, which they had abandoned at our approach, their fires being yet burning. They had marked in triumph upon trees, the scalps they had taken two days before, and a great many French had also written on them their names and many insolent expressions. We picked up a commission on the march, which mentioned the party being under the command of the Sieur Normanville.

This Indian camp was in a strong situation, being upon a high rock with a very narrow and steep ascent to the top; it had a spring in the middle and stood at the termination of the Indian path to the Monongahela, at the confluence of Red-Stone Creek. By this pass the party came which attacked Mr. Washington the year before, and also this which attended us.

By their tracks, they seemed to have divided here, the one part going straight forward to Fort Du Quesne, and the other returning by Red-Stone Creek to the Monongahela. A captain, four subalterns, and ninety volunteers, marched from this camp with proper guides to fall in the night upon that party which we imagined had returned by the Monongahela. They found a small quantity of provisions, and a very large *batteau*, which they destroyed, and the captain according to orders joined the general at Gist's plantation but saw no men.

June 27th. We marched from the camp of Rock Fort to Gist's plantation, which was about six miles; the road still mountainous and rocky. Here the advanced party was relieved, and all the waggons and carrying horses with provision belonging to that detachment joined us, and the men were to be victualled from us.

June the 28th. The troops marched about five miles to a camp on the east side of the Yoxhio Geni.

(From the Great Meadows, the route had diverged in a northwestwardly direction, to gain a pass through Laurel Hill; it then struck the river at Stewart's Crossing, half a mile below Connellsville. See II. O.T.)

Orders at the Camp on the East Side of the Yoxhio Geni, June the 29th.

Whereas by the connivance of some officers several of the men have fired their pieces in a very irregular and unmilitary manner; The general declares that, for the future, if any officer, of whatever rank, shall suffer the men to fire their pieces, he shall be put under arrest. And it is ordered, that whenever it is found necessary to fire any of the men's pieces, that cannot be drawn, the commanding officers of the several troops are to apply to the general for leave, through an *aid de camp*.

The commanding officers of regiments, troops, and companies, are to send to the train all their damaged cartridges, and to apply to the commanding officer of the artillery for fresh ones in the lieu of them.

June the 30th. We crossed the main body of the Yoxhio Geni, which was about two hundred yards broad and about three feet deep. The advanced guard passed, and took post on the other side, till our artillery and baggage got over; which was followed by four hundred men who remained on the east side 'till all the baggage had passed.

We were obliged to encamp about a mile on the west side, where we halted a day to cut a passage over a mountain. This day's march did not exceed two miles.

Part of the flour having been unavoidably damaged by severe rains, the general sent an order to Colonel Dunbar to forward to him with the utmost diligence one hundred carrying horses with flour, and some beeves, with an escort of a captain and one hundred men.

Upon this day's halt the men's arms were all drawn and cleaned, and four days provision served to the men that they might prepare a quantity of bread, and dress victuals to carry with them.

Orders on the West Side of the Yoxhio Geni.

The men's tents are to be pitched in a single line facing outwards, and no officer is to pitch his tent or have his picket of horses in front of the soldiers' tents. And that there may be sufficient room for this, it is the general's order that as soon as the troops come to their ground and the carriages close up, that the commanding officers of each regiment order their several detachments to advance twenty five paces from that part of the line of carriages which they covered, and there to pitch their tents. No fire upon any account to be lighted in front of the pickets.

On the first of July, we marched about five miles, but could advance no further by reason of a great swamp which required much work to make it passable.

On the 2nd July, we marched to Jacob's cabin, about 6 miles from the camp. A field officer was sent from the line to take the command of the advanced guard, and the disposition thereof was settled according to the annexed plan.

ORDERS AT JACOB'S CABIN.

No more bell tents are to be fixed: the men are to take their arms into their tents with them; and an officer of a company is to see at retreat beating that the men fix on their thumb stalls.

July 3rd. The swamp being repaired, we marched about six miles to the Salt Lick Creek. (Now known as Jacob's Creek.)

Sir John St. Clair proposed to the general to halt at this camp, and to send back all our horses to bring up Colonel Dunbar's detachment.

The general upon this called a council of war consisting of:

Colonel Sir Peter Halket,
Lieut.-Colonel Gage,
Lieut.-Colonel Burton,
Major Sparks,
Major Sir John St. Clair, D. Q. G.,

And informed them of the proposition made to him by Sir John and desired their opinions thereof. Then the following circumstances were considered:

That the most advanced party of Colonel Dunbar's detachment was then at Squaws Fort, and the other part a day's march in the rear, from which place with our light detachment we had been eleven days. And though we had met with some delays while the roads were making, yet, when the badness of them was considered, and the number of carriages Colonel Dunbar had with him, it was judged he could not perform the march in less time:

That the horses could not join him in less than two days:

That no advantage seemed to accrue from this junction, as the whole, afterwards, could not move together:

That Colonel Dunbar was unable to spare many men:

That, besides, he would be more liable to be attacked than at his present distance:

That the horses through their weak situation were not judged capable of performing it:

That by the loss of so many days the provision brought with us from Fort Cumberland would have been so near expended, as to have laid us under the necessity of bringing up a convoy, had we met with any opposition at the fort:

That by these delays the French would have time to receive their reinforcements and provisions, and to entrench themselves, or strengthen the fort, or to avail themselves of the strongest passes to interrupt our march:

That it was conjectured they had not many Indians or great strength at the fort, as they had already permitted us to make many passes which might have been defended by a very few men:

Upon these considerations, the council were unanimously of opinion not to halt there for Colonel Dunbar, but to proceed the next morning.

The general sent for the Indian manager and ordered him to endeavour to prevail with the Indians to go towards the fort for intelligence, which the general had often assayed, but could never prevail upon them since the camp at the Great Meadows. They now likewise refused, notwithstanding the presents and promises which he constantly made them.

ORDERS AT SALT LICK CAMP.

The commanding officers of companies are to view their men's arms this evening before retreat beating, and to see them put in the best order.

At the beating of the assembly tomorrow, all the troops are to load with fresh cartridges. The centinels upon the advanced pickets for the future to be doubled at night, by placing two centinels at every post.

The officers upon the advanced pickets during the night time are to have half their men constantly under arms with fixed bayonets and to relieve them every two hours; and the half that is relieved may lye down by their arms but are not to be suffered to quit their pickets.

When the captains of the pickets are not going their rounds, they are to remain at the head of the centre picket of that flank which they are appointed to visit.

Whenever any advanced centinel fires his piece in the night, the captain of the picket of that flank from which the shot is fired is immediately to go a visiting round to that part of the picket, and to send word to the field officer of the occasion of the shot being fired.

July 4th. We marched about six miles to Thickettyrun; the country was now less mountainous and rocky, and the woods rather more open, consisting chiefly of white oak.

★★★★★★

From the crossing of Jacob's Creek, which was at the point where Welchhanse's Mill now stands, about 1½ miles below Mount Pleasant, the route stretched off to the north, crossing the Mount Pleasant turnpike near the village of the same name, and thence, by a more westerly course, passing the Great Sewickley near Painter's Salt Works, thence south and west of the post-office of Madison and Jacksonville, it reached the Brush Fork of Turtle Creek. (II. *O.T.*)

★★★★★★

From this place two of our Indians were prevailed upon to go for intelligence towards the French fort; and also (unknown to them). Gist, the general's guide:

The Indians returned on the 6th, and brought in a French officer's scalp, who was shooting within half a mile of the fort. They informed the general that they saw very few men there, or tracks; nor any additional works. That no pass was possest by them between us and the fort, and that they believed very few men were out upon observation. They saw some boats under the fort, and one with a white flag coming down the Ohio.

Gist returned a little after the same day, whose account corresponded with theirs, except he saw smoke in a valley between our camp and Du Quesne. He had concealed himself with an intent of getting close under the fort in the night, but was discovered and pursued by two Indians, who had very near taken him.

At this camp the provisions from Colonel Dunbar with a detachment of a captain and one hundred men joined us, and we halted here one day.

On the 6th July we marched about six miles to Monakatuca Camp, which was called so from an unhappy accident that happened upon the march.

Three or four people loitering in the rear of the grenadiers were killed by a party of Indians and scalped. Upon hearing the firing, the general sent back the grenadier company, on whose arrival the Indians fled. They were discovered again a little after by our Indians in the front, who were going to fire upon them, but were prevented by some of our out-rangers, who mistaking these our Indians for the enemy, fired upon them and killed Monakatuca's son, notwithstanding they made the agreed countersign, which was holding up a bough and grounding their arms. When we came to our ground, the general sent for the father and the other Indians, condoled with and made them the usual presents, and desired the officers to attend the funeral; and gave an order to fire over the body.

This behaviour of the general was so agreeable to the Indians, that they afterwards were more attached to us, quite contrary to our expectations.

The line of carrying horses extending very often a prodigious length, it was almost impossible to secure them from insults, though they had yet marched without any interruption, every bat-man having been ordered to carry his firelock, and small parties having kept constantly upon the flanks. The disposition of march for these horses had varied almost every day, according to the nature of the country; but the most common was to let them remain upon the ground an hour after the march of the line, under the guard of a captain and one hundred men: by which means there was no confusion in leaving the ground, and the horses were much eased.

They were now ordered, when the woods would permit, to march upon the flanks between the subalterns' picket and the line; but whenever the country was close or rocky, they were then to fall in the rear, and a strong guard marched thither for their security, which was directed to advance or fall back in proportion to the length of the line of carrying horses, taking particular care always to have parties on the flanks.

ORDERS AT MONAKATUCA CAMP.

If it should be ordered to advance the van or send back the rear guard, the advanced parties detached from them are to remain at their posts, facing outwards.

Whenever there is a general halt, half of each of the subalterns' advanced parties are to remain under arms with fixed bayonets, facing outwards, and the other half may sit down by their arms.

On the 7th July we marched from hence, and quitting the Indian path, endeavored to pass the Turtle Creek about 12 miles from the mouth, to avoid the dangerous pass of the narrows. We were led to a precipice which it was impossible to descend. The general ordered Sir John St. Clair to take a captain and one hundred men, with the Indians, guides, and some light horse, to reconnoitre very well the country. In about two hours he returned and informed the general that he had found the ridge which led the whole way to Fort Du Quesne, and avoided the narrows and Frazier's, but that some work which was to be done would make it impossible to move further that day. We therefore encamped here and marched the next morning about eight miles to the camp near the Monongahela.

★★★★★★

Abandoning thus the passage of the Brush Fork of Turtle Creek, Braddock here turned into the valley of Long Run, near where now is Stewartsville, and encamped on the 8th July at two miles distance from the Monongahela. On the 9th, he followed the valley of Crooked Run to the river.

★★★★★★

When we arrived here, Sir John St. Clair mentioned (but not to the general), the sending a detachment that night to invest the fort; but being asked whether the distance was not too great to reinforce that detachment in case of an attack, and whether it would not be more advisable to make the pass of the Monongahela or the narrows, whichever was resolved upon, with our whole force, and then to send the detachment from the next camp, which would be six or seven miles from the fort, Sir John immediately acquiesced, and was of opinion that would be a much more prudent measure.

The guides were sent for, who described the Narrows to be a narrow pass of about two miles, with a river on the left and a very high mountain on the right, and that it would require much repair to make it passable by carriages. They said the Monongehela had two extreme good fords, which were very shallow, and the banks not steep. It was therefore resolved to pass this river the next morning, and Lieutenant-Colonel Gage was ordered to march before break of day with the two companies of grenadiers, one hundred and sixty rank and file of the 44th and 48th, Captain Gates's independent company, and two six-pounders, with proper guides; and he was instructed to pass the fords of the Monongehela and to take post after the second crossing, to secure the passage of that river.

Sir John St. Chair was ordered to march at 4 of the clock with a detachment of two hundred and fifty men to make the roads for the artillery and baggage, which was to march with the remainder of the troops at five.

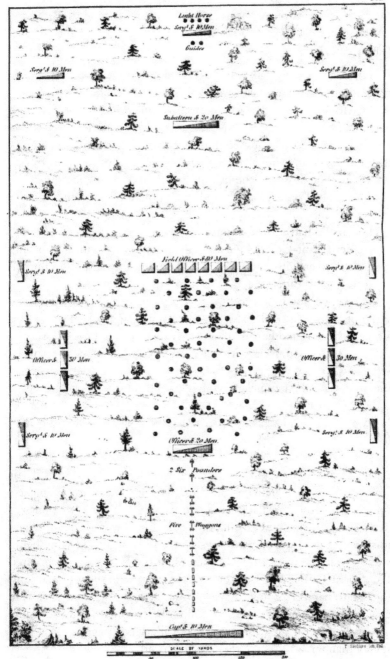

PLAN of the distribution of the advanced party consisting of 400 Men.

PL.II.

All the men are to draw and clean their pieces, and the whole are to load tomorrow on the beating of the general with fresh cartridges.

No tents or baggage are to be taken with Lieutenant-Colonel Gage's party.

July 9th. The whole marched agreeably to the orders before mentioned, and about 8 in the morning the general made the first crossing of the Monongahela by passing over about one hundred and fifty men in the front, to whom followed half the carriages. Another party of one hundred and fifty men headed the second division; the horses and cattle then passed, and after all the baggage was over, the remaining troops, which till then possessed the heights, marched over in good order.

The general ordered a halt, and the whole formed in their proper line of march.

When we had moved about a mile, the general received a note from Lieutenant-Colonel Gage acquainting him with his having passed the river without any interruption and having posted himself agreeably to his orders.

When we got to the other crossing, the bank on the opposite side not being yet made passable, the artillery and baggage drew up along the beach, and halted 'till one, when the general passed over the detachment of the 44th, with the pickets of the right. The artillery waggons and carrying horses followed; and then the detachment of the 48th, with the left pickets, which had been posted during the halt upon the heights.

When the whole had passed, the general again halted, till they formed according to the annexed plan.

It was now near two o'clock, and the advanced party under Lieutenant Colonel Gage and the working party under Sir John St. Clair were ordered to march on 'till three. No sooner were the pickets upon their respective flanks, and the word given to march, but we heard an excessive quick and heavy firing in the front. The general imagining the advanced parties were very warmly attacked and being willing to free himself from the incumbrance of the baggage, ordered Lieutenant-Colonel Burton to reinforce them with the vanguard, and the line to halt. According to this disposition, eight hundred men were detached from the line, free from all embarrassments, and four hundred were left for the defence of the artillery and baggage, posted in such a manner as to secure them from any attack or insults.

The general sent forward an *aid de camp* to bring him an account of the nature of attack, but the fire continuing, he moved forward himself, leaving Sir Peter Halket with the command of the baggage. The advanced detachments soon gave way and fell back upon Lieutenant-Colonel Burton's detachment, who was forming his men to face a rising ground upon the right. The whole were now got together in great confusion. The colours were advanced in different places, to separate the men of the two regiments. The general ordered the officers to endeavour to form the men, and to tell them off into small divisions and to advance with them; but neither entreaties nor threats could prevail.

The advanced flank parties, which were left for the security of the baggage, all but one ran in. The baggage was then warmly attacked; a great many horses, and some drivers were killed; the rest escaped by flight. Two of the cannon flanked the baggage, and for some time kept the Indians off: the other cannon, which were disposed of in the best manner and fired away most of their ammunition, were of some service, but the spot being so woody, they could do little or no execution.

The enemy had spread themselves in such a manner, that they extended from front to rear, and fired upon every part.

The place of action was covered with large trees, and much underwood upon the left, without any opening but the road, which was about twelve foot wide. At the distance of about two hundred yards in front and upon the right were two rising grounds covered with trees.

When the general found it impossible to persuade them to advance, and no enemy appeared in view; and nevertheless, a vast number of officers were killed, by exposing themselves before the men; he endeavored to retreat them in good order; but the panick was so great that he could not succeed. During this time, they were loading as fast as possible and firing in the air. At last Lieutenant-Colonel Burton got together about one hundred of the 48th regiment, and prevailed upon them, by the general's order, to follow him towards the rising ground on the right, but he being disabled by his wounds, they faced about to the right, and returned.

When the men had fired away all their ammunition and the general and most of the officers were wounded, they by one common consent left the field, running off with the greatest precipitation. About fifty Indians pursued us to the river and killed several men in the passage. The officers used all possible endeavours to stop the men, and to prevail upon them to rally; but a great number of them threw away their arms and ammunition, and even their cloaths, to escape the faster.

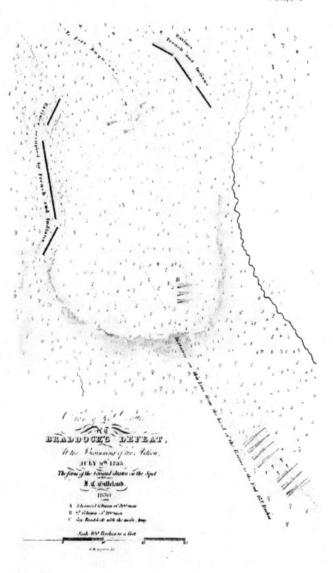

BRADDOCK'S DEFEAT,

At the Beginning of the Action,
JULY 9th 1755.

The form of the ground drawn on the Spot.
J. C. Gilleland.
1830.

A. Advanced column of Britons
B. 2d. Column of Britons
C. The Road &c with the main Army

Scale 100 Perches to a Foot

About a quarter of a mile on the other side the river, we prevailed upon near one hundred of them to take post upon a very advantageous spot, about two hundred yards from the road. Lieutenant-Colonel Burton posted some small parties and centinels. We intended to have kept possession of that ground, 'till we could have been reinforced. The general and some wounded officers remained there about an hour, till most of the men run off.

From that place, the general sent Major Washington to Colonel Dunbar with orders to send waggons for the wounded, some provision, and hospital stores; to be escorted by two youngest grenadier companies, to meet him at Gist's plantation, or nearer, if possible. It was found impracticable to remain here, as the general and officers were left almost alone; we therefore retreated in the best manner we were able. After we had passed the Monongahela the second time, we were joined by Lieutenant-Colonel Gage, who had rallied near 80 men. We marched all that night, and the next day, and about ten o'clock that night we got to Gist's plantation.

GIST'S PLANTATION.

July 11th. Some waggons, provisions, and hospital stores arrived. As soon as the wounded were dressed, and the men had refreshed themselves, we retreated to Colonel Dunbar's Camp, which was near Rock Fort. The general sent a serjeant's party back with provision to be left on the road on the other side of the Yoxhio Geni for the refreshment of any men who might have lost their way in the woods. Upon our arrival at Colonel Dunbar's camp, we found it in the greatest confusion. Some of his men had gone off upon hearing of our defeat, and the rest seemed to have forgot all discipline. Several of our detachment had not stopped 'till they had reached this camp.

It was found necessary to clear some waggons for the wounded, many of whom were in a desperate situation; and as it was impossible to remove the stores, the howitzer shells, some twelve-pound shot, powder, and provision, were destroyed or buried.

July 13th. We marched from hence to the camp, near the Great Meadows, where the general died.

GENERAL COURT MARTIALS.

Alexandria.

Lieutenant Colonel Gage, President.

The prisoner ordered one thousand lashes, but part of punishment remitted.

Fort Cumberland.

12th May. Major Sparks, President.

Luke Woodward, of the 48th regiment, condemned to dye, but pardoned.

★★★★★★

The pardon seems to have made little impression on this fellow. He had been enlisted by Captain Poison, at Shippensburg, and was drafted into Captain Mercer's company of the 48th. Deserting a second time from Dunbar's camp, he was not retaken on 6th Sept., 1755. *Penn. Gaz.*, No. 1394.

★★★★★★

Several other prisoners sentenced to corporal punishment, but part of them remitted.

24th May. Lieutenant Colonel Gage, President.

The punishments put in execution, all corporal ones.

26th May. Sir Peter Halket, President.

To try Lieutenant M'Leod, of the Artillery.

Part of the sentence remitted.

★★★★★★

William McLeod was made a captain of the Royal Regiment of Artillery, Oct. 21st, 1758, which position he held in 1763. In 1765, his name does not appear on the register.

★★★★★★

3rd June. Major Sparks, President.

The punishments put in execution, all corporal ones.

(End of Orme's Journal.)

Royal Navy Officer's Journal

Copy of a Document: Given by Captain Hewitt, R. N., to His Friend Captain Henry Gage Morris, R. N., Whose Father Was an *Aide De Camp* with Washington to Major General Braddock in the Expedition. Winchester, 9th July, 1827.

★★★★★★

I do not know who was the author of this *Journal: possibly* he may have been of the family of Capt. Hewitt. He was clearly one of the naval officers detached for this service by Com. Keppel, whom sickness detained at Fort Cumberland during the expedition. There are two documents from which the ensuing pages are printed. The first, which is the text followed here, appears to have been a revised copy of the second. It is in the possession of the Rev. Francis-Orpen Morris, Nunburnholme Rectory, Yorkshire, to whose father it was given by Capt. Hewitt.

The other and perhaps the original journal is written in a looser and less particular style, and in point of extent is inferior to its companion. It is preserved in the library at Woolwich. What passages of this latter document have seemed to the Editor to differ from the former in any degree save of a clerical error, are appended by way of notes; which are distinguished from his own by alphabetical instead of numeral references, and by being enclosed within brackets. For the rest, so far as the lesser MS. goes, its language is so similar to that of the greater as would render its publication here a mere repetition. It is proper to add that in the summer of 1854 (and since the advertisement of this volume), the *Journal* in the possession of the Rev. Mr. Morris was published in pamphlet form by him for a charitable end: (Lond. Groombridge & Sons, 8vo.)

★★★★★★

From Alexandria to the Little Meadows by this *Journal* 216 miles.

General Braddock was 22 days marching from the Little Meadows to the fatal Monongahela River, which appears to be within eight miles of the French Fort Du Quesne, without a single Indian in his army, or the least suspicion of falling into an ambush, although he was in a country, of all the globe, the most adapted for one to encounter an enemy whose mode of fighting is confined to that method.

List of those officers that were present and of them that was killed and wounded in the action on the banks of ye Monongahela River, ye 9th July, 1755.

List of those Officers that were present and of them that was killed and wounded in the action on the banks of y⁰ Monongohela River, y⁰ 9th July, 1755.

Officers' Names.	Rank.	Killed or Wounded.
His Excellency Edward Braddock, Esqr......	General and comm^r in chief.	Died of his wounds on the 12th.
Robert Orme, Esqr Roger Morris, Esqr George Washington, Esqr	Aia de Camps.	Wounded. "
William Shirley, Esqr	Secretary.	Killed.
Sir John Sinclair, Bart.	D^r. Q^r. M^r. G^l.	Wounded.
M. Leslie, Esqr ¹......	G^l. Assist. do.	"
Fras. Halkett, Esqr...	Major Brigade.	

¹ Lieut. Matthew Leslie of the 44th : promoted to a captaincy, 29 Sept. 1760.

44ᵗʰ *Regiment.*

Officers' Names.	Rank.	Killed or Wounded.
Sir Peter Halkett	Colonel.	Killed.
Gage, Esqr	Lieut. Colonel.	Slightly wounded.
Tatton	Captain.	Killed.
Hobson ¹	"	
Beckworth ²	"	
Githius................	"	"
Falconer ³.............	Lieutenant.	

¹ In the Army Register for 1765, Thomas Hobson ranks as a lieutenant of the 44th from 5 Nov. 1755. This and other instances authorize us to suppose that the above list was made rather from memory than authentic records.

² John Beckwith : major of the 54th, 18 July, 1758 : lieut.-col. in the line, 13 Jan. 1762.

³ Thomas Falconer : captain of the 44th, 5 Nov. 1755.

44th *Regiment.*

Officers' Names.	Rank.	Killed or Wounded.
Sittler	"	Wounded.
Bailey	"	
Dunbar [4]	"	"
Pottenger...............	"	
Halkett...................	"	Killed.
Treby.....................	"	Wounded.
Allen [5]	"	Died of his wounds.
Simpson	"	Wounded.
Lock [6]......	"	"
Disney [7].................	Ensign.	"
Kennedy [8]...............	"	"
Townsend	"	Killed.
Preston..................	"	
Clarke	"	
Nortlow	"	"
Pennington [9]	"	

[4] For an anecdote of Capt. Dunbar, see XVIII. Sparks's Am. Biog., 11.

[5] This may be a mistake. In 1765, James Allen was a lieut. of the 44th; and though his commission dates but from 9 Nov. 1755, it is as old as those of many others who were in the action.

[6] Robert Lock : lieut. of 44th, 27 June, 1755, which rank he held ten years after.

[7] Daniel Disney : capt. in the line, 4 Oct. 1760; of the 44th, 22 Sept. 1764; major in the line, 7 Aug. 1776; of the 38th (which regiment he accompanied to America), 10 March, 1777.

[8] Primrose Kennedy : lieut. of the 44th, 6th June, 1757 ; capt. 15 May, 1772. In 1778, he seems to have been with his regiment in America.

[9] George Penington : a lieut. of the 44th, 6 June, 1755. When he arrived at Philadelphia, after the fight, he sought out the residence of Edward Penington, a leading merchant there, with whom he claimed kindred and resided until his regiment marched for Albany. He was probably of the Dysart family.

48th *Regiment.*

Officers' Names.	Rank.	Killed or Wounded.
Burton, Esqr..........	Lieut. Col.	Slightly wounded.
Sparks, Esqr............	Major.	
Dobson, Esqr..........	Captain.	
Cholmondeley..........	"	Killed.
Bowyer, Esqr	"	Wounded.
Ross, Esqr [1]	"	"
Barbutt, Esqr	Lieut.	
Walsham, Esqr.......	"	
Crymble, Esqr........	"	Killed.
Widman, Esqr	"	"

[1] Robert Ross : lieut.-col. in the line, 6 Jan. 1762 ; of 48th, 2 Sept. 1762.

48th *Regiment.*

Barbutt, Esqr	Lieut.	
Walsham, Esqr	"	
Crymble, Esqr	"	Killed.
Widman, Esqr	"	"
Hansard, Esqr	"	"
Gladwin, Esqr [2]	"	Wounded.
Hotham, Esqr	"	
Edmonstone, Esqr [3] ...	"	"
Cope, Esqr	"	
Brereton, Esqr	"	Killed.
Stuart, Esqr	"	"
Montresore [4]	Ensign.	Wounded.
Dunbar	"	
Harrison	"	
Colebatt	"	
Macmullen	"	"
Crowe	"	"
Stirling [5]	"	"

[2] Henry Gladwyn, who achieved great distinction in the remainder of the war, was made lt.-col. 17 Sept. 1763, and Deputy Adjutant General in America. His gallant defence of Detroit against Pontiac and his leaguering hordes is familiar to the reader in the pages of Parkman. He was made a colonel, 49 Aug. 1777; and maj.-gen. Nov. 26, 1782.

[3] William Edmestone: capt. in the 48th, 23 March, 1758; lt.-col. in the line, 29 Aug., 1777; and in Oct. 1777, was major of the 48th, and a prisoner of war at Easton, Pa.

[4] John Montresor: lt. in the 48th, 4 July, 1755.

[5] Among the officers of the 48th who were left with Dunbar, and therefore do not find a place in this list, were Capts. Gabriel Christie (afterwards lt.-col. of the 60th in 1775), Mercer, Morris, and Boyer; Capt. Lieut. Morris, and Lts. Savage, Caulder, and Hart. (Penn. Gaz., No. 1394.)

LIST OF OFFICERS—*Continued.*

48th *Regiment.*

Independents.

Officers' Names.	Rank.	Killed or Wounded.
Gates	Captain.	Wounded.
Sumain	Lieutenant.	Killed.
Miller	"	
Haworth	"	Wounded.
Grey	"	"
Virginia Officers.		
Stevens	Captain.	Wounded.
Waggoner	"	
Polson	"	Killed.
Perinie..................	"	

48th *Regiment.*

Stewart [1]	"	
Hamilton [2]	Lieutenant.	"
Woodward [3]	"	
Wright [4]	"	"
Spidolf [5]	"	"
Stewart [6]	"	Wounded.
Waggoner [7]	"	Killed.
M'Neal [8]	"	

[1] Robert Stewart; commissioned 1 Nov. 1754. Of his 29 light horse, 25 were killed in the action. See Penn. Gaz., No. 1391: where it is justly observed that " the Virginia officers and troops behaved like men and died like soldiers."

[2] John Hamilton: commissioned Nov. 2, 1754.

[3] Henry Woodward: commissioned Dec. 13, 1754.

[4] John Wright: commissioned Nov. 18, 1754.

[5] Ensign Carolus Gustavus de Spiltdorph: commissioned July 21, 1754. I follow Washington's orthography, under whom he served in 1754. He was the officer selected to escort to Virginia the prisoners captured in Jumonville's affair.

[6] Ensign Walter Stewart: commissioned Aug. 25, 1754. I apprehend him to have been the same who was an additional lieutenant in the 44th during the war, retiring on half-pay in 1763; and who afterwards was conspicuous in our Army of the Revolution.

[7] Ensign Edmond Waggener: commissioned Jan. 1, 1755.

[8] If this was Lt. John M'Neill (Nov. 1, 1754), or Ensign Hector M'Neill (Dec. 12, 1754), I do not know.

LIST OF OFFICERS — *Continued.*

48th *Regiment.*

ARTILLERY.

Officers' Names.	Rank.	Killed or Wounded.
Orde [1]	Captain.	
Smith	Capt. Lieut.	Killed.
Buchanan [2]	Lieutenant.	Wounded.
M'Cloud	"	
M'Culler...............	"	"

ENGINEERS.

M'Keller, Esq[r 3]		Wounded.
Williamson, Esq[r 4] ...	Engineers.	"
Gordon, Esq[r 5]		"

[1] Thomas Orde in 1759 became lt.-col. of the R. R. of Artillery. He was an excellent officer, and stood high in Cumberland's esteem, by whom he was especially selected for this service. Landing in Newfoundland, he hastened to take command of Braddock's artillery, arriving from New York at Philadelphia, June 7, 1755. (II. P. A., 346.) He was accompanied by 13 non-commissioned officers; and was in such an enfeebled condition as to render his joining the army a work of much difficulty. The Assembly's committee not feeling themselves called upon to provide conveniences for his journey, Mr. Morris was compelled to procure him a horse and chaise at his own cost; at the same time issuing a warrant of impressment for waggons for the rest of the party. (Ib. 356, 358. VI. C. R., 417.) Capt. Orde took a conspicuous part in his line of service during the rest of the war.

[2] Sir Fr. Ja. Buchanan: capt. 1 Jan. 1759.

[3] Patrick Mackellar: Sub-Director and Major of Engineers, 4 Jan. 1758; Director and lt.-col. 2 Feb. 1775; col. in the line, 29 Aug. 1777.

[4] Adam Williamson: Engineer Extraordinary and capt. lieut. 4 Jan. 1758.

[5] Harry Gordon: Engineer in Ordinary and captain, 4 Jan. 1758; lt.-col. in the line, 29 Aug. 1777.

LIST OF OFFICERS—*Continued.*

48th *Regiment.*

NAVAL OFFICERS.

Officers' Names.	Rank.	Killed or Wounded.
Spendelowe............	Lieutenant.	Killed.
Haynes	Mid.	
Talbot.................	"	"

VOLUNTEERS.		
Stone...................	Captain.	Killed.
Hayer [1]...............	"	Wounded.

Captain Stone was a captain in Lascelle's, and Hayer in Warburton's Regiment.[2]

[2] Mr. Morris prints this name Flayer.

[1] These were the 45th and 47th reg'ts. The late venerable Bishop White well remembered the corpse of one of Braddock's officers being brought to Philadelphia after the battle, where it lay in state for some days at the old Norris or Penn House at the corner of Second St. and Norris's Alley.

(*a*) A Journal of the proceedings of the seamen (a detachment), ordered by Commodore Keppel to assist on a late expedition to the Ohio, from the 10th of April, 1755, when they received their first orders from the army at Alexandria in Virginia, to the 18th day of August following, when the remaining part of the detachment arrived on board His Majesty's ship *Garland* at Hampton: with an impartial account of the action that happened on the banks of the Monongahela, and defeat of Major General Braddock on the 9th of July, 1755. (*b*)

April 10th, 1755. Moderate and fair but sultry weather; today we received orders to march tomorrow morning, and 6 companies of Sir Peter Halket's Regiment to march in their way to Wills's Creek.

★★★★★★

(*a*) Here begins the lesser MS., previously referred to, as follows:
Journal of M. General Braddock's March, etc., towards Fort Du Quesne, 1755.
Names of the Principal French and Canadian Officers.
Monsieur Beaujeu Captain Commanding the French and Canadians.
Monsieur Dumas Captain and Second in command.
Monsieur Derligniris Captain.
Monsieur Montigny Captain.
Messieurs Montesamble, Normanville, etc., etc., subalterns.
The Canadians say, 600 savages joined the French and Canadians after the attack began two hours.

F. M., Montreal, 1769.

(*b*) Extracts from a Journal of the proceedings of the detachment of seamen, ordered by Commodore Keppel, to assist on the late expedition to the Ohio, with an impartial account of the late action on the banks of the Monongahela the 9th of July, 1755; as related by some of the principal officers that day in the Field, from the 10th April, 1755, to the 18th August, when the detachment of seamen embarked on board His Majesty's ship *Garland* at Hampton in Virginia.

★★★★★★

April 11th:—Our orders were countermanded, and to provide ourselves with 8 days provisions, and to proceed to Rock Creek, 8 miles from Alexandria, in the *Sea Horse* and *Nightingale's* boats tomorrow.

On the 12th:—Agreeably to our orders we proceeded and arrived at Rock Creek at 10 o'clock. This place is 5 miles from the lower falls of Potomack, and 4 from the eastern branch of it. Here our men got quarters, and we pitched our tents: found here Colonel Dunbar, whose orders we put ourselves under.

On the 13th:—We were employed in getting the regimental stores into waggons, in order to march tomorrow: This is a pleasant situation, but provisions and everything dear.

On the 14th:—We began our march at 6, and were ordered with our detachment to go in front, and about 2 o'clock at one Lawrence Owens, 15 miles from Rock Creek, and 8 miles from the upper falls of Potomack; and encamped upon good ground.

On the 15th:—Marched at 5 in our way to one Dowden's a public-house 15 miles from Owen's, and encamped upon very bad ground on the side of a hill. We got our tents pitched by dark, when the wind shifted from the south to the north—from a sultry hot day it became excessively cold, and rained with thunder and lightning till about 5 in the morning, when in 10 minutes it changed to snow, which in 2 hours covered the ground a foot and a half.

On the 16th:—On account of the bad weather, we halted today, though a terrible place, for we could neither get provisions for ourselves, nor fodder for our horses, and as it was wet in the camp it was very disagreeable, and no house to go into.

On the 17th:—Marched at 6 on our way to Frederick's Town, 15 miles from Dowden's; the roads this day were very mountainous. After going 11 miles, we came to a river called Mouskiso, which empties itself into the Potomack; it runs very rapid, and after hard rain is 13 feet deep: we ferried the army over here in a flatt for that purpose, and at 3 o'clock arrived at the town, and put our men and ourselves into quarters, which were very indifferent. This town has not been settled above 7 years, and there are about 200 houses and 2 churches, one English, one Dutch; the inhabitants, chiefly Dutch, are industrious but imposing people: here we got plenty of provisions and forage.

On the 18th:—At 10 the drums beat to arms, when the army encamped at the north end of the town, upon good ground: we got our tents pitched and lay in the camp, and the sutler dieted us here: orders came for us to buy horses to carry our baggage, as there will be no more waggons allowed us. We found here an independent vessel belonging to New York under the command of Captain Goss.

On the 19th:—The weather here is very hot in the day, but the nights are very unwholesome, occasioned by heavy dews.

On the 20th:—A guard turned out to receive the general.

On the 21st:—At noon the general arrived here attended by Captains Orme and Morris his *aids de camp*, and Secretary Shirley, and went to the headquarters, a house provided for him; and Sir John St. Clair arrived here.

★★★★★★

Roger Morris, descended from one of the most ancient families in Britain, was born 28 Jan., 1727. At an early age adopting the profession of arms, he obtained a captaincy in the 17th Foot when but 17 years old. After Braddock's defeat, he continued to serve with reputation in America; and married, 19 Jan., 1758, Mary, daughter of Frederick Philipse, of New York; a great heiress, who is said to have been unsuccessfully wooed by Washington, and whose character is beautifully drawn by Cooper in the heroine of *The Spy*. It affords a curious speculation to consider how circumstances might have moulded the future career of the Father of his Country had his lot been linked with that of Mary Philipse instead of Martha Custis.

The landed possessions of the Philipse family were enormous, embracing much of the site of the city of New York, and covering an area twice as great as all Yorkshire. Morris continued to reside in New York, where he occupied a seat in the Council, till the breaking out of the Revolution. Adhering to the Crown, his estates and those of his wife were confiscated, and he returned to England. By a marriage contract, however, Mrs. Morris's property had been settled on her children, and these being omitted in the act of confiscation, the ministry conceived their rights remained unaffected.

Therefore but £17,000 were granted from the treasury to Mr. Morris in satisfaction of his life-interest. After the peace, it was found impracticable to reinstate the children in their possessions, and in1809 their claims were purchased by the late Mr. John Jacob Astor for £20,000. The estimated value of the property in question was then nearly £1,000,000; at this day, the sum would be incalculable. On 19 May, 1760, Morris was made Lieutenant-Colonel of the 47th Foot and died 13 Sept.,

1794. His widow, who was born 5 July, 1730, survived to 18 July, 1825. Their only surviving son was the late Admiral Henry Gage Morris, R. N., of Keldgate House, Yorkshire. Colonel Morris is sometimes confounded with his cousin, Lieutenant-Colonel Roger Morris, of the Coldstreams, an intimate of the Duke of York, under whose command he fell in Holland.

★★★★★★

On the 24th:—Very hard showers of rain, and from being very hot became excessively cold and blew hard.

On the 25th:—Received orders to be ready to march on Tuesday next. Arrived here 80 recruits and some ordnance stores.

On the 27th:—We sent 3 of our men to the hospital, *viz.*, John Philips, Edward Knowles and James Connor. Employed in getting ready to march.

On the 29th:—We began our march at 6, but found much difficulty in loading our baggage, so that we left several things behind us, particularly the men's hammocks. We arrived at 3 o'clock at one Walker's, 18 miles from Frederick, and encamped there on good ground; this day we passed the South Ridge or Shannandah Mountains, very easy in the ascent. We saw plenty of hares, deer, and partridges: This place is wanting of all refreshments.

On the 30th:—At 6, marched in our way to Connecochieg, where we arrived at 2 o'clock, 16 miles from Walker's: this is a fine situation, close by the Potomack. We found the Artillery Stores going by water to Wills's Creek and left 2 of our men here.

May 1st, 1755. At 5, we went with our people, and began ferrying the army etc. into Virginia, which we completed by 10 o'clock, and marched in our way to one John Evans, where we arrived at 3 o'clock—17 miles from Connecochieg, and 20 from Winchester. We got some provisions and forage here. The roads now begin to be very indifferent.

On the 2nd:—As it is customary in the army to halt a day after 3 days march, we halted today to rest the army. (*May 2nd:*—Halted, and sent the horses to grass.)

On the 3rd:—Marched at 5 on our way to one Widow Barringer's, 18 miles from Evans: this day was so excessively hot that several officers and many men could not get on till the evening, but the body

76

got to their ground at 3 o'clock. This is 5 miles from Winchester, a fine station if properly cleared.

On the 4th:—Marched at 5 in our way to one Potts—9 miles from the Widow's—where we arrived at 10 o'clock. The road this day very bad: we got some wild turkeys here: in the night it came to blow hard at N. W.

On the 5th:—Marched at 5 in our way to one Henry Enock's, being 16 miles from Potts, where we arrived at 2 o'clock. The road this day over prodigious mountains, and between the same we crossed over a run of water 20 times in 3 miles distance. After going 15 miles we came to a river called Kahapetin, where our men ferried the army over and got to our ground, where we found a company of Peter Halket's encamped.

On the 6th:—We halted this day to refresh the army.

★★★★★★

May 5th:—Marched to Mr. Henry Enock's, a place called the forks of Cape Capon. . . . .
May 6th:—Halted, as was the custom to do so every third day. The officers, for passing away the time, made horse races, and agreed that no horse should run over 11 hands and to carry 14 stone.

★★★★★★

On the 7th:—We marched at 5 in our way to one Cox's, 12 miles from Enock's.

★★★★★★

I take this person, Cox, to be the same alluded to in the following paragraph: "There has a strange affair happened in Virginia: one Cox, which, you may remember by the *Gazettes*, behaved gallantly against the Indians some time ago, and another person, thinking their services not taken proper notice of, dressed themselves up like Indians and attacked a house a few miles from Winchester. The in-dwellers were so fortunate as to escape, although Cox and his partner fired on them several times. An officer, being informed that the house was attacked by the Indians, sent a detachment to pursue the enemy, who, finding tracks, pursued by them until they came near the place where the fellows, Cox and the other, were sitting by a fire; fired on them—killed Cox on the spot and wounded the other so mortally that he had scarce time before his departure to disclose

77

who they were." David Jameson to Lieutenant-Colonel Burd.
Philadelphia, April 25, 1758. (Shippen *MSS.*)
★★★★★★

This morning was very cold but by 10 o'clock it was prodigiously
hot. We crossed another run of water 19 times in 2 miles, and got to
our ground at 2 o'clock, and encamped close to the Potomack.

On the 8th:—We began to ferry the army over the river into
Maryland, which was completed at 10, and then we marched on our
way to one Jackson's, 8 miles from Cox's. At noon it rained very hard
and continued so till 2 o'clock, when we got to our ground, and encamped on the banks of the Potomack. A fine situation, with a good
deal of clear ground about it. Here lives one Colonel Cressop, a rattle
snake colonel, and a vile rascal, (there lives Colonel Cressop, a rattle
snake colonel and a d——d rascal); calls himself a Frontier man, as he
thinks he is situated nearest the Ohio of any inhabitants of the country
and is one of the Ohio Company.

He had a summons some time ago to retire from the settlement, as
they said it belonged to them, but he refused, as he don't want resolution; and for his defence has built a log fort round his house. This place
is the track of the Indians and warriors when they go to war, either to
the northward or southward. There we got plenty of provisions, etc.,
and at 6, the general arrived here with his attendants, and a company
of light horse for his guard, and lay at Cressop's. As this was a wet day,
the general ordered the army to halt tomorrow.

On the 10th:—Marched at 5 on our way to Will's Creek, 16 miles
from Cressop's; the road this day very pleasant by the water side. At 12
the general passed by, the drums beating the Grenadier March. At 1
we halted and formed a circle, when Colonel Dunbar told the army
that as there were a number of Indians at Will's Creek, our friends,
it was the general's positive orders that they do not molest them, or
have anything to say to them, directly or indirectly, for fear of affront-
ing them. We marched again and heard 17 guns fired at the fort to
salute the general. At 2 we arrived at Will's Creek and encamped to
the westward of the fort on a hill and found here 6 companies of Sir
Peter Halket's Regiment, 9 companies of Virginians, and a Maryland
company.

Fort Cumberland is situated within 200 yards of Will's Creek, on a
hill, and about 400 from the Potomack; its length from east to west is
about 200 yards, and breadth 46 yards, and is built by logs driven into

the ground, and about 12 feet above it, with embrasures for 12 guns, and 10 mounted, 4 pounders, besides stocks for swivels, and loop holes for small arms.

We found here Indian men, women and children, to the number of about 100, who were greatly surprised at the regular way of our soldiers marching, and the numbers. I would willingly say something of the customs and manners of the Indians, but they are hardly to be described. The men are tall, well made, and active, but not strong, but very dexterous with a rifle barrelled gun, and their tomahawk, which they will throw with great certainty at any mark and at a great distance. The women are not so tall as the men, but well-made and have many children, but had many more before spirits were introduced to them. They paint themselves in an odd manner, red, yellow, and black intermixed.

And the men have the outer rim of their ears cut, which only hangs by a bit top and bottom, and have a tuft of hair left at the top of their heads, which is dressed with feathers. Their watch coat is their chief clothing, which is a thick blanket thrown all round them, and wear moccasins instead of shoes, which are deer skin, thrown round the ankle and foot. Their manner of carrying their infants is odd. They are laid on a board, and tied on with a broad bandage, with a place to rest their feet on, and a board over their head to keep the sun off and are slung to the women's backs. These people have no notion of religion, or any sort of Superior being, as I take them to be the most ignorant people as to the knowledge of the world and other things. In the day they were in our camp, and in the night, they go into their own, where they dance and make a most horrible noise.

On the 11th:—Orders that the general's levee be always in his tent from 10 to 11 every day.

On the 12th:—Orders this morning that there will be a congress at the general's tent at 11 o'clock, at which time all the officers attended the general, and the Indians were brought; the guard received them with their firelocks rested. The interpreter was ordered to tell them that their brothers, the English, who were their old friends, were come to assure them that every misunderstanding that had been in former times should now be buried under that great mountain (a mountain close by).

Then a string of *wampum* was given them; then a belt of *wampum* was held forth with the following speech, *viz.*: that this *wampum* was to assure them of our friendship; that everybody who were their enemies were ours; and that it was not the small force only that we had here, but numbers to the northward under our great war captains, Shirley, Pepperell, Johnston and others that were going to war, and that we would settle them happy in their country, and make the French both ashamed and hungry: But that whatever Indians after this declaration did not come in, would be deemed by us as our enemies, and treated as such. The general then told them he should have presents for them in a few days, when he should have another speech to make to them, so took their leaves after the ceremony of drams round. In the afternoon Mr. Spendlowe and self surveyed 20 casks of beef by order of the general and condemned it, which we reported to the general. This evening we had a gust of wind, with lightning, thunder and rain, which drove several tents down, and made the camp very uncomfortable.

On the 13th:—The weather is now extremely hot. This day as the corporal came to exercise our men in the evening, I went to see the Indian camp, ¼ mile from ours, in the woods. Their houses are 2 stakes driven into the ground, with a ridge pole, and bark of trees laid up and down the sides, but they generally have a fire in them. This is all the shelter they have from the weather when they are from home. (This day's journal in the lesser MS. concludes here thus: "The Americans and seamen exercising.")

As soon as it was dark they began to dance, which they do round a fire in a ring. Their music is a tub with a sheep skin over it, and a hollow thing with peas to rattle.

★★★★★★

The *Tay wa' egun* (struck-sound-instrument) is a tambourine, or one-headed drum, and is made by adjusting a skin to one end of the section of a moderate sized hollow tree. When a heavier sound is required, a tree of larger circumference is chosen, and both ends covered with skins.

The *Sheshegwon*, or rattle, is constructed in various ways, according to the purpose or means of the maker. Sometimes it is made of animal bladder, from which the name is derived; sometimes of a wild gourd; in others, by attaching the dried hoofs of the deer to a stick. This instrument is employed both to mark time, and to produce variety in sound." (*Schoolcraft; Red Race of America.*)

★★★★★★

It is a custom with them, once or twice a year, for the women to dance and all the men sit by. Each woman takes out her man that she likes, dances with him and lies with him for a week, and then return to their former husbands, and live as they did before.

On the 14th:—This day 2 of our men arrived from Frederick hospital, and our men from Connecockieg that were left to assist the artillery. Orders to send the returns of our people to the brigade major every morning.

On the 15th:—Mr. Spendlowe and self surveyed 22 casks of beef, and condemned it, which we reported to the general.

On the 16th:—Arrived here Lieut.-Col. Gage, with 2 companies of Sir Peter Halket's, and the last division of the train, consisting of 3 field pieces, 4 howitzers, a number of cohorns, and 42 waggons with stores. Departed this life Captain Bromley of Sir Peter Halket's.

On the 17th:—Had a survey of our men's arms, and found several of them unserviceable. All the officers are desired to attend Captain Bromley's funeral tomorrow morning, and at the general's tent at 12.

On the 18th:—Excessively hot. At 10 o'clock we all attended the funeral, and the ceremony was a captain's guard marched before the corpse, with the captain of it in the rear, and the fire locks reversed, the drums beating the dead march. When we came near the grave, the guard formed 2 lines facing each other; rested on their arms, muzzles downwards; and leaned their faces on the butts: the corpse was carried between them, the sword and sash on the coffin, and the officers following two and two. After the clergyman had read the service, the guard fired 3 vollies over him and returned. (The chaplain of the 44th was Mr. Philip Hughes: that of the 48th I do not know. One of these gentlemen marched with the expedition and was wounded at the defeat.)

At 12 we attended the general's tent, when all the Indians came, and the general made a speech to them to this purpose. He desired they would immediately send their wives and children into Pensylvania, and take up the hatchet against the French: that the great King of England, their father, had sent them the presents now before them for their families, and that he had ordered arms etc. to be given to their warriors; and expressed concern for the loss of the Half-King killed last year. The presents consisted of strouds, rings, beads, linen, knives, wire, and paint. They received their presents with 3 belts and a string of *wampum* and promised their answer next day. And to show they were pleased, they made a most horrible noise, dancing all night.

On the 19th:—Captain Gate's New York Company arrived here. This evening the Indians met at the general's tent to give their answer, which was, that they were greatly obliged to the Great King their father, who had been so good as to send us all here to fight for them, and that they would all give their attendance, and do what was in their power of reconnoitring the country and bringing intelligence. That they were obliged to the general for his expressing concern for the loss of the Half-King our brother, and for the presents he had given them. Their chief men's names are as follows: Monicotoha, their wise man who always speaks for them, (their mentor);—Belt of Wampum or White Thunder, who has a daughter called Bright Lightning—he keeps the *wampum*: the next is the Great Tree and Silver Heels, (Jerry Smith and Charles), with many others belonging to the Six Nations.

The general told them he was their friend, and never would deceive them, after which they sung the war song, which is shouting and making a terrible noise, declaring the French their perpetual enemies, which they never did before.

After this the general carried them to the artillery, and ordered 3 howitzers, 3 12-pounders, and 3 cohorns to be fired, all the drums and fifes playing, and beating the point of war, which astonished and pleased the Indians greatly. They then retired to their own camp, where they ate a bullock, and danced their war dance, which is droll and odd, showing how they scalp and fight, expressing in their dance the exploits of their ancestors, and warlike actions of themselves.

On the 20th:—Arrived here 80 waggons from Pennsylvania, to assist in the expedition, and eleven waggons from Philadelphia, with presents for the officers of the army. (Arrived 80 waggons from Pennsylvania with stores; and 11 likewise from Philadelphia, with liquors, tea, sugar, coffee, etc., to the amount of £400, with 20 horses, as presents to the officers of the 2 regiments.) An Indian arrived from the French fort in 6 days and said they have only 50 men in the fort but expect 900 more; that when our army appears they will blow it up. I believe this fellow is a villain, as he is a Delaware, who never were our friends.

On the 21st:—There are 100 carpenters employed, under the carpenter of the *Sea-horse*, in building a magazine, completing a flatt, and squaring timber to make a bridge over Will's Creek; the Smiths in making tools; the bakers baking biscuits; and commissaries getting the provisions ready for marching. Arrived here a troop of light horse, and 2 companies of Sir Peter Halket's, (under the command of Major Chapman, came in from Winchester.) On the 22nd, the Indians had arms and clothes given them.

On the 23rd:—Both the regiments exercised and went through their firings, (formings?) Sent 3 of our men to the provost for neglect of duty and disobedience of orders.

On the 24th:—Our force here now consists of 2 regiments of 700 men each; 9 companies (Virginia) of 50 men each; 3 Independent Companies of 100 men each; one Maryland Company of 50 men; 60 of the train, (2 New York, 1 Independent *Carolina* Companies of 100 men,....1 company of artillery of 60), and 30 seamen. This day 2 men were drummed out of Sir Peter Halket's regiment for theft, after receiving 1000 lashes, and preparations making for marching.

On the 27th:—We have now here 100 waggons, which the commissaries are loading with provisions. In the evening a captain's guard marched for Winchester, to escort the provisions to the camp. Some Indians came in here belonging to the Delawares.

On the 28th:—At 11, the Delawares met at the general's tent, and told him that they were come to know his intentions, that they might assist the army. The general thanked them and said he should march in a few days towards Fort De Quesne. The Indians told him they would return home and collect their warriors together and meet him on his march. These people are villains, and always side with the strongest. At noon it blowed and rained hard.

On the 29th:—A detachment of 600 men marched towards Fort de Quesne, under the command of Major Chapman, with 2 field pieces, and 50 waggons with provisions. Sir John St. Clair, 2 Engineers, Mr. Spendlowe, & 6 of our people to cut the road, and some Indians went away likewise, (—and 6 seamen with some Indians were ordered to clear the roads for them.)

On the 30th:—Arrived here a company from North Carolina, under the command of Captain Dobbs.

June 1st:—We hear the detachment is got 15 miles: Mr, Spendlowe and our people returned.

On the 2nd:—Col. Burton, Capt. Orme, Mr. Spendlowe and self went out to reconnoitre the road. Mr. Spendlowe left us, and returned to camp at 2 o'clock, and reported he had found a road to avoid a great mountain. In the afternoon we went out to look at it and found it would be much better than the old road, and not above 2 miles about.

On the 3rd:—This morning an Engineer, (—Mr. Engineer Gordon), and 100 men began working on the new road from Camp, and Mr. Spendlowe and self with 20 of our men went to the place where the new road comes into the old one, and began to clear away, and completed a mile today.

On the 4th:—Went out today, and cleared another mile. (Midshipman and 20 men cleared ¾ of a mile.)

On the 5th:—We went out as before, and at noon, Mr. Spendlowe and I went to the other party to mark the road for them, but at 1, it came to blow, rain, thunder, and lighten so much, that it split several tents, & continued so till night, when we returned to the camp.

On the 6th:—We went out as usual, and at 2 o'clock completed the road, & returned to camp. This evening I was taken ill.

On the 7th:—A rainy day, with thunder and lightning. Sir Peter Halket and his brigade marched with 2 field pieces, and some waggons with provisions. A midshipman and 12 of our people went to assist the train.

On the 9th:—Orders for Col. Dunbar's Brigade to march tomorrow morning.

On the 10th:—The director of the hospital came to see me in camp, and found me so ill of a fever and flux, that he desired me to stay behind, so I went into the hospital, & the army marched with the train etc., and as I was in hopes of being able to follow them in a few days, I sent all my baggage with the army, and in the afternoon the general, his *aids de camp* etc., with a company of light horse, marched.

✶✶✶✶✶✶

The long and fatal delay of the English at Fort Cumberland was undoubtedly produced, in great part, by the necessities of the case: but a different view of the matter was taken by some of the subordinates of the army. Thus, Captain Rutherford, after pointing out the success which crowned Halket's command of the encampment at that place, pictures Braddock arriving there to waste the precious moments like a second Hannibal at Capua. According to his letter (*Philadelphia Evening Bulletin*, Sept 19th, 1849), the general there "spent a month idly with his women and feasting." It will be noticed that the writer was a professed supporter of the inefficient Dunbar, and that the whole burthen of his strain is the laudation of that incompetent man and depreciation of Braddock. The measures adopted by the general upon the suggestion of Washington appear to have elicited his warmest indignation

★★★★★★

On the 24th:—A man came into the fort, and reported that a party of Indians of about 20 had surprised, killed & scalped two families to the number of about 14 or 15 people, and not above 3 miles from this place.

On the 26th:—An account came in of 2 more families being scalped within 2 miles of us. The governor sent out a party to bury the dead, as well as to scour the woods for the Indians. They found a child of about 7 years old, standing in the water scalped & crying; they brought it into the fort and the doctors dressed it: it had 2 holes in its skull, besides being scalped, but was in spirits, and had its skull not been wounded might have lived, but as it was it died in a week. It would be too tedious to recount every little incident here in the fort, therefore will return to the army, and give an account of their proceedings from the time they left us.

June 10th, 1755. The last division of His Majesty's Forces marched from Will's Creek or Fort Cumberland, with General Braddock and his *aides de camp*, etc.

On the 15th.—The general and all the army arrived at the Little Meadows, which is 22 miles from the fort. He found here that the number of carriages, etc., that he had with him occasioned his marches to be very short, and that in all probability if they continued to do so, the French fort would be reinforced before he got before it. He therefore thought proper to take 1200 of the choicest men, besides artillery and sailors, with the most necessary stores that would be wanted to attack the fort, making up in all 51 carriages, and left all the heavy baggage, etc. with Col. Dunbar, and the rest of the forces to follow him as fast as possible, and marched accordingly, and continued so to do without being molested (except now and then losing a scalp, which in the whole amounted to 8 or 9, a number far less than expected), till the 8th of July, when he encamped within 8 miles of the French Fort.

And there held a Council of War, which agreed that as they were to pass over the Monongahela River twice (this river is a ¼ mile broad, and 6 miles from the French Fort), that the advance party should parade at 2 o'clock to secure that pass, as on the contrary if the enemy should have possession of it, they would not be able to get over without a great loss. They likewise agreed that the army should march over the river in the greatest order, with their bayonets fixed, colours flying, and drums and fifes beating and playing, as they supposed the enemy would take a view of them in the crossing.

On the 9th July, 1755.—The advance party consisted of 400 men and upward, under the command of Lieut.-Col. Gage, and marched accordingly; and about 7 o'clock started a party of about 30 Indians, but they got off.

★★★★★★

About 7 o'clock, some Indians rushed out of the bushes, but did no execution. The party went on and secured both passes of the river; and at 11 the main body began to cross, with colours flying, drums beating, and fifes playing the Grenadiers' March, and soon formed: when they thought that the French would not attack them, as they might have done it with such advantage in crossing the Monongahela.

★★★★★★

They marched on and secured both, crossings of the river without interruption. The main body marched about 6 o'clock and about 11 began to cross over as proposed in the Council of War, and got over both passes, when they began to think the French would not attack them, as they might have done with so many advantages a little time before.

The advance party was now about ¼ of a mile before the main body, the rear of which was just over the river when the front was attacked. The 2 grenadier companies formed the 2 flank advance picquets, 2 companies of carpenters cutting the roads, and the rest covering them. The first fire our men received was in front, and on the flank of the flank picquets, which in a few minutes nearly cut off the most part of the grenadiers and a company of carpenters.

★★★★★★

The first fire the enemy gave was in front, and they likewise galled the picquets in flank, so that in a few minutes the grenadiers were nearly cut in pieces, and drove into the greatest confusion, as was Captain Poison's company of carpenters.

★★★★★★

As soon as the general with the main body heard the front was attacked, they hastened to succour them, but found the remains retreating. Immediately the general ordered the cannon to draw up and the batallion to form. By this time the enemy began to fire on the main body, who faced to the right and left and returned it, and the cannon began to play, but could not see at what, for our men were formed in the open road they had just cut, and the enemy kept the trees in front and on the flanks.

On the right they had possession of a hill, which we could never get possession of, though our officers made many attempts to do it: but if the officers dropped, which was generally the case, or that the enemy gave a platoon of ours advancing up the hill a smart fire, they immediately retreated down again. As numbers of our officers declared they never saw above 4 of the enemy at a time the whole day, it struck a panic through our men to see numbers daily falling by them, and even their comrades scalped in their sight. As soon as the general saw this was the case, he ordered that our men should divide into small parties and endeavour to surround the enemy, but by this time the greatest part of the officers were either killed or wounded, and in short the soldiers deaf to the commands of those few that were left alive.

★★★★★★

It was in an open road that the main body were drawn up, but the trees were excessive thick around them, and the enemy had possession of a hill to the right, which consequently was of great advantage to them. Many officers declare that they never saw above 5 of the enemy at one time during the whole affair. Our soldiers were encouraged to make many attempts by the officers (who behaved gloriously), to take the hill, but they had been so intimidated before by seeing their comrades scalped in their sight, and such numbers falling, that as they advanced up towards the hill, and their officers being pict off, which was generally the case; they turned to the right about and retired down the hill.

When the general perceived and was convinced that the soldiers would not fight in a regular manner without officers, he divided them into small parties and endeavoured to surround the enemy, but by this time the major part of the officers were either killed or wounded, and in short, the soldiers were totally deaf to the commands and persuasions of the few officers that were left unhurt. The general had 4 horses shot under him before he was wounded, which was towards the latter part of the action, when he was put into a waggon with great difficulty, as he was very solicitous for being left in the field.

★★★★★★

By this time, too, the greatest part of the train were cut off, having fired between 20 and 30 rounds each cannon, for the enemy made a mark of them and the officers.

The general had 4 horses shot under him before he was wounded, which was towards the latter end of the action, for when the general was put in a waggon the men soon dropped out of the field, and in a little time became too general after standing three hours, and with much difficulty got the general out of the field (for he had desired to be left.)

★★★★★★

According to Geo. Croghan, the grenadiers delivered their fire at 200 yards distance, completely throwing it away. (Chas. Swayne's letter in *Phila. Evening Bulletin*, Sept. 19th, 1849.) The same authority estimates the French in the action at 300, 'clad in stuff's;' besides the naked Indians. 400 Onondagos, he says, came into the fort the day before; and there were also '100 Delawares, 60 Wiandots, 40 Puywaws, 300 Pawwaws, the Shawnees who lived about Logtown, and some of all other tribes.' In conclusion, a curious anecdote of Braddock is given: when Croghan approached him, after he was wounded, the general sought to possess himself of the former's pistols, with a view to self-destruction. The story is given here for what it is worth.

★★★★★★

It was the opinion of most of the officers there, that had greater numbers been there, it would have been the same, as our people had never any hopes of getting the field, for they never got possession of the ground the front was attacked on. But very luckily for us they pursued us no further than the water, and there killed and scalped many. One of our engineers, who was in the front of the carpenters marking the road, saw the enemy first, who were then on the run, which plainly shews they were just come from the fort, and their intention certainly was to secure the pass of the Monongahela, but as soon as they discovered our army, an officer at the head of them dressed as an Indian, with his gorget on, waved his hat, and they immediately dispersed to the right and left, forming a halfmoon.

★★★★★★

Mr. Engineer Gordon was the first man that saw the enemy, being in the front of the carpenters, marking and picketing the roads for them, and he declared when he first discovered them, that they were on the run, which plainly shows they were just come from Fort Du Quesne, and that their principle Intention was to secure the pass of Monongahela River, but the officer who was their leader, dressed like an Indian, with a gorget on, waved his hat by way of signal to disperse to the right and left, forming a half moon.

★★★★★★

It was impossible to judge of their numbers, but it was believed they had at least man for man.

Our remains retreated all night, and got to Col. Dunbar's Camp the next day, which was near 50 miles from the field of action, and then the general ordered Col. Dunbar to prepare for a retreat, in order to which they were obliged to destroy all the ammunition and provisions they could not possibly carry, and the reason of so much was the absolute necessity there was for a number of waggons to carry the wounded officers and men: The general's pains increased in such a manner—for he was shot through the arm into the body—together with the great uneasiness he was under, that on the 12th, at 8 at night, he departed this life, much lamented by the whole army, and was decently, though privately buried next morning.

The number killed, wounded, and left on the field, as appeared by the returns from the different companies, was 896, besides officers, but cannot say any particular company suffered more than another, except the grenadier companies and carpenters; for out of Colonel Dunbar's Grenadiers, who were 79 complete that day, only 9 returned untouched, and out of 70 of Halket's, only 13. (Sir P. Halket's were 69, and only 13 came out of the field.) Amongst the rest, I believe I may say the seamen did their duty, for out of 33, only 15 escaped untouched, (the seamen had 11 killed and wounded out of 33); and every grenadier officer either killed or wounded. Our loss that day consisted of 4 fieldpieces, 3 howitzers, and 2 waggons, with cohorns,

(4 six-pounders, 2 twelve-pounders, 3 howitzers, 8 cohorns), together with the 51 carriages of provisions and ammunition, etc., and hospital stores, and the general's private chest with £1000 in it, (probably a clerical error for £10,000), and about 200 horses with officers' baggage.

Col. Dunbar with the remains of the army continued their retreat, and returned to Will's Creek, or Fort Cumberland, the 20th of July. (On the 21st, the wounded officers and soldiers were brought in.)

August 1st, 1755.—Colonel Dunbar received a letter from Commodore Keppel, desiring the remains of the detachment of seamen might be sent to Hampton in Virginia. Colonel Dunbar gave us our orders, and on the 3rd we left the army, marched down through Virginia, and on the 18th we arrived on board His Majesty's ship *Garland* at Hampton.

★★★★★★

30th July. Orders were given for the army to march the 2nd August.

1st August. Colonel Dunbar received a letter from Commodore Keppel to send the seamen to Hampton, and accordingly the 2nd, they marched with the army, and on the 3rd August left them.

August 5th. Arrived at Winchester.

August 11th. Marched into Fredericksburgh and hired a vessel to carry the seamen to Hampton where they embarked on board His Majesty's ship *Garland* the 18th August, 1755.

★★★★★★

George Croghan's Statement

The Government continued to maintain the Indians that lived at my house till the Spring, when General Braddock arrived. They then desired Governor Morris to let me know that they would not maintain them any longer, at which time Governor Morris desired me to take them at Fort Cumberland to meet General Braddock, which I did. On my arrival at Fort Cumberland, General Braddock asked me where the rest of ye Indians were? I told him I did not know: I had brought with me about 50 men which was all which was at that time under my care and which I had brought there under direction of Gov. Morris. He replied 'Governor Dinwiddie told me at Alexandria that he had sent for 400 which would be here before me.'

I answered I knew nothing of that, but that Capt. Montour the Virginia interpreter was in camp and could inform his Excellency; on which Montour was sent for, who informed the general that Mr. Gist's son was sent off some time ago for some Cheroquees Indians, but whether they would come he couldn't tell: on which the general asked me whether I could not send for some of ye Delawares and Shawnese to Ohio. I told him I could; on which I sent a messenger to Ohio who returned in eight days and brought with him three chiefs of the Delawares. The general had a conference with these chiefs in company with those 50 I had brought with me, and made them a handsome present, and behaved as kindly to them as he possibly could during their stay, ordering me to let them want for nothing.

The Delawares promised in council to meet ye general on the road, as he marched out, with a number of their warriors, but whether the former breaches of faith on the side of the English prevented them, or that they had before engaged to assist the French, I cannot tell: but they disappointed the general and did not meet him.

Two days after the Delaware chiefs had left the camp at Fort Cum-

91

berland, Mr. Gist's son returned from the Southern Indians where he had been sent by Governor Dinwiddie but brought no Indians with him. Soon after the general was preparing for ye march with no more Indians than those I had with me, when Col. Innis told the general that the women and children of the Indians which was to remain at Fort Cumberland would be very troublesome, and that the general need not take above ten men out with him, for if he took more, he would find them very troublesome on the march, and of no service: on which the general ordered me to send all the men, women and children back to my house in Pennsylvania, except eight or ten which I should keep as scouts: which I accordingly did.

But I am yet of opinion that had we had fifty Indians instead of eight, that we might in a great measure have prevented the surprise, that day of our unhappy defeat.

(George Croghan's *Journal* to the Ohio during Mr. Hamilton's and part of Mr. Morris's administration, taken from the original delivered by himself to Mr. Peters. August 18th, 1757.—Du Simitiere MSS., Library Co. of Philadelphia.)

French and Indian Cruelty

Exemplified in the Life And various Vicissitudes of Fortune,
of Peter Williamson, a Disbanded Soldier
Written by Himself

PREFACE

The following short tract is humbly offered to the public in hopes
of gaining by their generous contribution in the sale thereof a small
matter, to enable me to settle in some industrious way, and provide in
my old age against the malevolence of fortune who hitherto for the
space of twenty-eight years hath with her smiles and frowns alternately chequered my life. My situation, after my arrival in America,
was not, I confess, unhappy, 'till the year 1754, when the Indians began
their depredations in the province of Pennsylvania; but, since that time,
the reader will find few happy minutes to have been in my possession,

Could I be reinstated in the like circumstances, I enjoyed before,
my utmost wishes would be obtained. Thousands, who have gone
to these parts, have met with more unpleasing fortune than myself;
many (who are not kidnapped as I was) being ignorant what measures
to take, on going thither, contract themselves with some merchant
or factor here, to serve a certain number of years in the plantations,
where, when arrived, they often meet with very bad, and I may say,
cruel masters, through whose barbarous treatment, they are often induced to elope, to avoid servitude, or (more properly) slavery under
much tyrants.

If this happens, their case is worse, for they are almost certain of being taken again, as none are allowed to travel without a pass, and then,
for every day they have been absent, they must after the expiration of
their contract, serve a week, and pay such sums of money as the master
shall advertise for taking and bringing them back, or serve a certain

93

time in lieu thereof. But, those, who go at their own expense, find it much more to their satisfaction and interest; for as soon as they arrive, they are sure of employment, particularly tradesmen in any branch, at great wages in all parts of Pennsylvania, and the other provinces.

If any go to better their fortunes, and have money enough to enable them to live there without service, they are almost sure, with industry, to obtain their ends; for, in whatever place they first reside, there, have they a settlement, by the laws of the several provinces; and land may be obtained very cheap, as thousands of acres near all our settlements still lie uncultivated, that with some trouble, and little expense, may be made to produce all sorts of grain in great plenty, This they sell to the West-India merchants, and in times of peace, to the French, for rum, sugar, blankets, and cloathing of all sorts, which they again exchange with the Indians for deer-skins, and furs of all kinds to great advantage; and such trade seldom fails, in a few years, of gratifying the most avaricious in their thirst after wealth.

INTRODUCTION

The reader is not here to expect a large and useless detail of the transactions of late years, in that part of the world, where, ever since my infancy, it has been my misfortune to have lived. Was it in my power indeed, to set off with pompous diction, and embellish with artificial descriptions, what has so engrossed the attention of Europe, as well as the scenes of action for some years past, perhaps I might; but, my poor pen, being wholly unfit for much a task, and never otherwise employed than just for my own affairs and amusement, while I had the pleasure of living tranquil and undisturbed; I must beg leave to desist from much an attempt; and if much is expected from me, claim the indulgence of that pardon which is never refused to those incapacitated of performing what may be desired of them.

And, as a plain, impartial, and succinct narrative of my own life and various vicissitudes of fortune, is all I shall aim at, I shall herein confine myself to plain simple truth, and, in the dictates, resulting from an honest heart, give the reader no other entertainment than what shall be matter of fact; and of such things as have actually happened to me, or come to my own knowledge, in the sphere of life, in which it has been my lot to be placed. Not, but I hope, I may be allowed, now and then, to carry on my narrative from the informations I may have received of much things as relate to my design though they have not been done or transacted in my presence.

It being usual in narratives like this, to give a short account of the author's birth education, and juvenile exploits, the same being looked upon as a necessary, or at least satisfactory piece of information to the curious and inquisitive reader; I shall, without boasting of a family I am no way intitled to, or recounting adventures in my youth, to which I was intirely a stranger, in a short manner, will gratify such curiosity; not expecting, as I said before, to be admired for that elegance of stile and profusion of words, so universally made use of in the details and histories of those adventurers, who have of late years obliged the world with their anecdotes and memoirs; and which have had scarce any other existence than in the brains of a bookseller's or printer's garretteer; who, from fewer incidents, and less surprising matter than will be found in this short narrative, have been, and are daily enabled, to spin and work out their elaborate performances to three or four volumes.

That I, like them, publish this for support, is true, but as I am too sensible, the major part of mankind will give much more to a bookseller, to be in the fashion, or satisfy their curiosity, in having or reading a new puffed-off history or novel, than to a real object of distress, for an accurate and faithful account of a series of misfortunes, I have thought it more advisable to confine myself as to size and price, than by making a larger volume miss that assistance and relief, of which I at present am in so great need.

Know, therefore, that I was born within ten miles of the town of Aberdeen, in the North of Scotland; if not of rich, yet of reputable parents, who supported me in the best manner they could, as long as they had the happiness of having me under their inspection; but fatally for me and to their great grief, as it afterwards proved, I was sent to live with an aunt at Aberdeen, where, at eight years of age, playing on the kay, with others of my companions, being of a stout robust constitution, I was taken notice of by two fellows belonging to a vessel in the harbour, employed (as the trade then was) by some of the worthy merchants of the town, in that villainous and execrable practice, called kidnapping; that is stealing young children from their parents and selling them as slaves in the plantations abroad.

Being marked out by those monsters of impiety as their prey, I was easily cajoled on board the ship by them, where I was no sooner got, than they conducted me between the decks, to some others they had kidnapped in the same manner. At that time, I had no sense of the fate that was destined for me and spent the time in childish amusements with my fellow sufferers in the steerage, being never suffered to go upon deck whilst the vessel lay in the harbour; which was 'till such time as they had got in their loading, with a complement of unhappy youths for carrying on their wicked commerce.

In about a month's time the ship set sail for America. The treatment we met with, and the trifling incidents which happened during the voyage, I hope I may be excused from relating, as not being, at that time, of an age sufficient to remark anything more than what must occur to everyone on such an occasion. However, I cannot forget, that when we arrived on the coast, we were destined for, a hard gale of wind sprung up from the S. E. and to the captain's great surprise, (he not thinking he was near land) having been but eleven weeks on the passage, about 12 o'clock at night the ship struck on a sand-bank, off Cape May, near the Capes of De-la-ware, and to the great terror and affright of the whole ship's company, in a small time, was almost full of water.

The boat was then hoisted out, into which the captain and his fellow villains, the crew, got with some difficulty, leaving me and my deluded companions to perish; as they then must naturally conclude inevitable death to be our fate. Often in my distresses and miseries since, have I wished that much had been the consequence, when in a state of innocence! but Providence thought proper to reserve me for future trials of its goodness. Thus, abandoned and deserted, without the least prospect of relief, but threatened every moment with death, did these villains leave us. The cries, the shrieks, and tears of a parcel of infants had no effed on, or caused the least remorse, in the breasts of these merciless wretches.

Scarce can I say, to which to give the preference; whether, to such as these, who have had the opportunity of knowing the Christian religion, or to the savages herein after described, who profane not the Gospel, or boast of humanity; and, if they act in a more brutal and butcherly manner, yet 'tis to their enemies, for the sake of plunder and the rewards offered them; for their principles are alike; the love of sordid gain is in both the same motive. The ship, being on a sand-bank, which did not give way to let her sink deeper, we lay in the same deplorable condition 'till morning; when, though we saw the land of Cape May, at about a mile's distance, we knew not what would be our fate.

The wind at length abated, and the captain (unwilling to lose all his cargo) about 10 o'clock, sent some of his crew in a boat to the ship's side to bring us on shore, where we lay, in a sort of a camp, made of the sails of the vessel, and such other things as they could get. The provisions lasted us 'till we were taken in by a vessel bound to Philadelphia; lying on this island, as well as I can recollect, near three weeks. Very little of the cargo was saved undamaged, and the vessel, though repaired as well as the hands were able, was never fit for sea again.

When arrived and landed at Philadelphia the capital of Pennsylvania, the captain had soon people enough who came to buy us. He making the most of his villainous loading, after his disaster, sold us at about 16*l*. per head. What became of my unhappy companions, I never knew; but it was my lot to be sold to one of my countrymen, a North-Briton, for the term of seven years, who had in his youth undergone the same fate as myself; having been kidnapped from St. Johnston in Scotland, As I shall often have occasion to mention Philadelphia during the course of my adventures, I shall in this place give a short and concise description of the finest city in America, and one of the best laid out in the world.

This city would have been a capital fit for an empire, had it been built and inhabited according to the proprietor's plan. Considering its late foundation, 'tis a large city, and most commodiously situated between the De-la-ware and Schuylkill, two navigable rivers. The former being two miles broad, and navigable 300 miles for small vessels. It extends in length two miles from one river to the other. There are eight long streets two miles in length, cut at right angles by sixteen others, of one mile in length, all strait and spacious. The houses are stately, very numerous, (being near 3000), and still increasing, and all carried on regularly according to the first plan.

It has two fronts on the water, one on the east-side facing the Schuylkill, and that on the west facing the De-la-ware. The Schuylkill being navigable 800 miles above the falls, the eastern part is most populous, where the ware-houses, some three storeys high, and wharfs are numerous and convenient. All the houses have large orchards and gardens belonging to them. The merchants that reside here are numerous and wealthy, many of them keeping their coaches, &c. In the centre of the city there is a space of ten acres, whereon are built the state-house, market-house, and schoolhouse. The former is built of brick and has a prison under it.

The streets have their names from the several sorts of timber, common in Pennsylvania; as Mulberry-street, Sassafras-street, Chesnut-street, Beach-street and Cedar-street. Christ's-Church is the oldest and has a numerous congregation; but the major part of the inhabitants, being at first Quakers, still continue so, who have several meeting-houses, and may not improperly be called the Church, as by law established, being the originals. The kay is beautiful, and 200 feet square, to which a ship of 200 tons may lay her broadside. As the advantages this city may boast of, has rendered it one of the best trading towns out of the British Empire; so, in all probability it will increase in commerce and riches, if not prevented by party faction and religious feuds, which of late years have made it suffer considerably. The assemblies and courts of judicature are held here as in all capitals. The French have no city like it in all America,

Happy was my lot in falling into my countryman's power, as he was, contrary to many others of his calling, a humane, worthy, honest man. Having no children of his own, and commiserating my unhappy condition, he took great care of me 'till I was fit for business; and about the 12th year of my age set me about little trifles; in which state I continued 'till my 14th year, when I was more fit for harder work. During much my idle state, seeing my fellow servants often reading and writing, it incited in me an inclination to learn, which I intimated to my master, telling him, I should be very willing to serve a year longer, than the contract by which I was bound obliged me, if he would indulge me in going to school, this he readily agreed to, saying, that winter would be the best time.

It being then summer, I waited with impatience for the other season; but to make some progress in my design, I got a primer and learnt as much from my fellow servants as I could. At school, where I went every winter for five years, I made a tolerable proficiency, and have ever since been improving myself at leisure hours. With this good master, I continued 'till I was seventeen years old, when he died, and as a reward for my faithful service, left me 200*l.* currency, which was then about 120*l.* sterling, his best horse, saddle, and all his wearing apparel.

Being now my own master, having money in my pocket, and all other necessaries, I employed myself in jobbing about the country, working for any that would employ me, for near seven years; when thinking I had money sufficient to follow some better way of life, I resolved to settle; but thought one step necessary thereto, was to be married; for which purpose, I applied to the daughter of a substantial planter, and found my suit was not unacceptable to her, or her father, so that matters were soon concluded upon, and we married. My father-in-law, in order to establish us in the world, in an easy, if not affluent manner, made me a deed of gift of a tract of land that lay (unhappily for me, as it has since proved) on the frontiers of the province of Pennsylvania, near the forks of De-la-ware, in Berks County, containing about 200 Acres, 30 of which were well cleared and fit for immediate use, whereon was a good house and barn. The place pleasing me well, I settled on it; and though it cost me the major part of my money in buying stock, houshold furniture, and implements for outdoor work; and happy as I was in a good wife, yet did my felicity last me not long.

For about the year 1754, the Indians, in the French interest, who had for a long time before ravaged and destroyed other parts of America, unmolested, I may very properly say, began now to be very troublesome on the frontiers of our province, where they generally appeared in small skulking parties, with yellings, shoutings, and antic postures, instead of trumpets and drums; committing great devastations. The Pennsylvanians little imagined at first, that the Indians guilty of such outrages and violences were some of those who pretended to be in the English interest; which alas! proved to be too true to many of us: For like the French in Europe, without regard to faith of treaties, they suddenly break out into furious rapid outrages and devastations, but soon retire precipitately, having no stores or provisions but what they meet with in their incursions; some indeed carry a bag with biscuit, or Indian corn therein, but not unless they have a long march to their destined place of action.

And those French, who were sent to dispossess us in that part of the world, being indefatigable in their duty, and continually contriving, and using all manner of ways and means to win the Indians to their interest, many of whom had been too negligent, and sometimes, I may say, cruelly treated by those who pretended to be their protectors and friends, found it no very difficult matter to get over to their interest, many who belonged to those nations in amity with us: Especially as the rewards they gave them were so great; they paying for every scalp of an English person 15*l.* sterling.

Terrible and shocking to human nature, were the barbarities daily committed by the savages, and are not to be paralleled in all the volumes of history! Scarce did a day pass, but some unhappy family or other fell victims to French chicanery and savage cruelty. Terrible, indeed! it proved to me, as well as to many others; I that was now happy in an easy state of life, blessed with an affectionate and tender wife, who was possessed of all amiable qualities to enable me to go through this world with that peace and serenity of mind, which every Christian wishes to possess, became on a sudden one of the most unhappy, and deplorable of mankind; scarce can I sustain the shock which for ever recoils on me, at thinking on the last time of seeing that good woman; the fatal 2nd of October, 1754, she that day went from home, to visit some of her relations; as I staid up later than usual, expecting her return, none being in the house, besides myself, how great was my surprise, terror and affright, when about 11 o'clock at night, I heard the dismal warcry, or war-whoop of the savages, which they make on such occasions, and may be expressed, *Woach, woach, ha, hach, woach,* and to my inexpressible grief, soon found my house was attacked by them; I flew to the chamber-window, and perceived them to be twelve in number.

They making several attempts to come in, I asked them what they wanted? they gave me no answer, but continued beating, and trying to get the door open. Judge then the condition I must be in, knowing the cruelty and merciless disposition of those savages, should I fall into their hands. To escape which dreadful misfortune, having my gun loaded in my hand, I threatened them with death, if they should not desist. But how vain and fruitless are the efforts of one man against the united force of so many! and of such merciless, undaunted, and bloodthirsty monsters as I had here to deal with.

One of them that could speak a little English, threatened me in return:

"That if I did not come out, they would burn me alive in the house."

Telling me farther, what I unhappily perceived;

"That they were no friends to the English, but if I would come out and surrender myself prisoner, they would not kill me."

My terror and distraction at hearing this is not to be expressed by words, nor easily imagined by any person, unless in the same condition. Little could I depend on the promises of such creatures; and yet, if I did not, inevitable death, by being burnt alive must be my lot. Distracted as I was in much deplorable circumstances, I chose to rely on the uncertainty of their fallacious promises, rather than meet with certain death by rejecting them; and accordingly went out of my house, with my gun in my hand, not knowing what I did, or that I had it. Immediately on my approach they rushed on me, like so many tygers, and instantly disarmed me. Having me thus in their power, the merciless villains bound me to a tree near the door; they then went into the house and plundered and destroyed everything there was in it, carrying off what moveables they could; the rest, together with the house, which they set fire to, was consumed before my eyes. The Barbarians not satisfied with this, set fire to my barn, stable, and outhouses, wherein were about 200 bushels of wheat, six cows, four horses, and five sheep, which underwent the same fate, being all intirely consumed to ashes. During the conflagration, to describe the thoughts, the fears, and misery that I felt, is utterly impossible, as 'tis even now to mention what I feel at the remembrance thereof.

Having thus finished the execrable business, about which they came, one of the monsters came to me with a tomahawk in his hand, threatening me with the worst of deaths if I would not willingly go with them, and be contented with their way of living.

★★★★★★

A tomahawk, is a kind of hatchet, made something like our plaisterers hammers, about two feet long, handle and all. To take up the hatchet (or tomahawk) among them, is to declare war. They generally use it after firing their guns, by rushing on their enemies, and fracturing or cleaving their sculls with it, and very seldom fail of killing at the first blow.

★★★★★★

This I seemingly agreed to, promising to do everything for them that lay in my power; trusting to Providence for the time when I might be delivered out of their hands. Upon this they untied me and gave me a great load to carry on my back, under which I travelled all that night with them, full of the most terrible apprehensions, and oppressed with the greatest anxiety of mind, lest my unhappy wife should likewise have fallen a prey to these cruel monsters. At daybreak, my infernal masters ordered me to lie down my load, when tying my hands again round a tree with a small cord, they forced the blood out at my fingers ends. They then kindled a fire near the tree whereto I was bound, which filled me with the most dreadful agonies concluding I was going to be made a sacrifice to their barbarity.

This narrative, O reader! may seem dry and tedious to you: My miseries and misfortunes, great as they have been, may be considered only as what others have daily met with for years past; yet, on reflection, you can't help indulging me in the recital of them: For to the unfortunate and distressed, recounting our miseries, is, in some sort, an alleviation of them.

Permit me therefore to proceed; not by recounting to you the deplorable condition I then was in, for that is more than can be described to you, by one who thought of nothing less than being immediately put to death in the most excruciating manner these devils could invent. The fire being thus made, they for some time danced round me after their manner, with various odd motions and antic gestures, whooping, hollowing, and crying, in a frightful manner, as is their custom.

Having satisfied themselves in this sort of their mirth, they proceeded in a more tragical manner, taking the burning coals and sticks, flaming with fire at the ends, holding them to my face, head, hands, and feet, with a deal of monstrous pleasure and satisfaction; and at the same time threatening to burn me intirely, if I made the least noise or cried out: Thus tortured as I was, almost to death, I suffered their brutal pleasure without being allowed to vent my inexpressible anguish otherwise than by shedding silent tears; even which, when these inhuman tormentors observed, with a shocking pleasure and alacrity, they would take fresh coals, and apply near my eyes, telling me my face was wet, and that they would dry it for me, which indeed they cruelly did. How I underwent these tortures I have here faintly described, has been matter of wonder to me many times; but God enabled me to wait with more than common patience for a deliverance I daily prayed for.

Having at length satisfied their brutal pleasure, they sat down round the fire, and roasted their meat, of which they had robbed my dwelling. When they had prepared it and satisfied their voracious appetites, they offered some to me; though it is easily imagined I had but little appetite to eat after the tortures and miseries I had undergone; yet, was I forced to seem pleased with what they offered me, lest by refusing it, they had again reassumed their hellish practices. What I could not eat, I contrived to get between the bark and the tree, where I was sixed, they having unbound my hands till they imagined I had eat all they gave me; but, then, they again bound me as before; in which deplorable condition was I forced to continue all that day. When the sun was set, they put out the fire and covered the ashes with leaves, as is their usual custom, that the white people might not discover any traces or signs of their having been there.

Thus, had these barbarous wretches finished their first diabolical piece of work; and shocking as it may seem to the humane English heart, yet what I underwent, was but trifling, in comparison to the torments and miseries which I was afterwards an eye witness of being inflicted on others of my unhappy fellow creatures.

Going from thence along by the River Susquehana, for the space of six miles, loaded as I was before, we arrived at a spot near the Apalatian Mountains, or Blue Hills, where they hid their plunder under logs of wood—And, oh, shocking to relate! from thence did these hellish monsters proceed to a neighbouring house, occupied by one Jacob Snider and his unhappy family, consisting of his wife, five children, and a young man his servant. They soon got admittance into the unfortunate man's house, where they immediately, without the least remorse, and with more than brutal cruelty, scalped the tender parents and the unhappy children.

★★★★★★

Scalping, is taking off the skin from the top of the head; which they perform with a long knife that they hang round their neck, and always carry with them. They cut the skin round as much of the head as they think proper, sometimes quite round from the neck and forehead, then take it in their fingers and pluck it off, and often leave the unhappy creatures so served to die in a most miserable manner. Some who are not cut too deep in the temples or scull, live in horrid torments many hours, and sometimes a day or two after. The scalps, or skins thus taken off, they preserve and carry home in triumph, where they receive, as is said before, a considerable sum for every one.

★★★★★★

Nor could the tears, the shrieks, or cries of these unhappy victims prevent their horrid massacre: For having thus scalped them, and plundered the house of everything that was moveable, they set fire to the same, where the poor creatures met their final doom amidst the flames, the hellish miscreants standing at the door, or as near the house as the flames would permit them, rejoicing, and echoing back in their diabolical manner, the piercing cries, heart-rending groans, and parental and affectionate soothings, which issued from this most horrid sacrifice of an innocent family.

Sacrifice! I think I may properly call it, to the aggrandising the ambition of a king, who wrongly stiles himself Most Christian. For, had these savages been never tempted with the alluring bait of all-powerful gold, myself as well as hundreds of others, might still have lived most happily in our stations. If Christians countenance, nay, hire those wretches, to live in a continual repetition, of plunder, rapine, murder, and conflagration, in vain, are missionaries sent, or sums expended for the propagation of the Gospel. But, these sentiments. with many others, must before the end of this narrative occur to every humane heart—Therefore to proceed. Not contented with what these infernals had already done, they still continued their inordinate villainy, in making a general conflagration of the barn and stables, together, with all the corn, horses, cows, and everything on the place.

Thinking the young man belonging to this unhappy family, would be of some service to them, in carrying part of their hellish acquired plunder, they spared his life, and loaded him and myself with what they had here got, and again marched to the Blue-Hills where, they stowed their goods as before. My fellow sufferer could not long bear the cruel treatment which we were both obliged to suffer, and complaining bitterly to me, of his being unable to proceed any farther, I endeavoured to console him, as much as lay in my power, to bear up under his afflictions, and wait with patience, 'till by the divine assistance, we should be delivered out of their clutches.

But all in vain, for he still continued his moans and tears, which one of the savages perceiving, as we travelled on, instantly came up to us, and with his tomahawk, gave him a blow on the head, which fell the unhappy youth to the ground, where they immediately scalped and left him. The suddenness of this murder, shocked me to that degree, that I was in a manner like a statue, being quite motionless, expecting my fate would soon be the same: However, recovering my distracted thoughts, I dissembled the uneasiness and anguish which I felt as well as I could from the Barbarians; but still, such was the terror I was under, that for some time, I scarce knew the days of the week, or what I did; so that at this period, life did, indeed, become a burthen to me, and I regretted my being saved from my first persecutors, the sailors.

The horrid fact being compleated, they kept on their course near the mountains, where they lay skulking four or five days, rejoicing at the plunder and store they had got. When provisions became scarce, they made their way towards Susquehana; where, still to add to the many Barbarities they had already committed, passing near another house, inhabited by an unhappy old man, whose name was John Adams, with his wife and four small children; and meeting with no resistance, they immediately scalped the unhappy wife, and her four children, before the good old man's eyes, inhuman and horrid as this was! it did not satiate them; for, when they had murdered the poor woman, they acted with her in much a brutal manner, as decency, or the remembrance of the crime, will not permit me to mention; and this even, before the unhappy husband; who, not being able so avoid the sight, and incapable of affording her the lead relief, intreated them to put an end to his miserable being; but they were as deaf, and regardless to the tears, prayers, and intreaties, of this venerable sufferer, as they had been to those of the others, and proceeded in their hellish purpose of burning and destroying his house, barn, corn, hay, cattle, and everything the poor man, a few hours before, was master of.

Having saved what they thought proper from the flames, they gave the old man, feeble, weak, and in the miserable condition he then was, as well as myself, burthens to carry, and loading themselves likewise, with bread and meat, pursued their journey on towards the Great Swamp; where, being arrived, they lay for eight or nine days, sometimes diverting themselves, in exercising the most atrocious and barbarous cruelties on their unhappy victim, the old man: Sometimes they would strip him naked, and paint him all over with various sorts of colours, which they extracted, or made from herbs and roots.

At other times they'd pluck the white hairs from his venerable head, and tauntingly tell him, he was a fool for living so long, and that they should shew him kindness in putting him out of the world; to all which, the poor creature could only vent his sighs, his tears, his moans, and intreaties, that to my affrighted immagination, were enough to penetrate a heart of adamant, and soften the most obdurate savage. In vain, alas! were all his tears, for daily, did they tire themselves with the various means they tried to torment him; sometimes tying him to a tree, and whipping him, at others, scorching his furrowed cheeks, with red-hot coals, and burning his legs, quite to the knees.

But the good old soul, instead of repining, or wickedly arraigning the divine justice, like many others, in much cases; even in the greatest agonies, incessantly offered up his prayers to the Almighty, with the most fervent thanksgivings for his former mercies, and hoping the flames, then surrounding and burning his aged limbs, would soon send him to the blissful mansions of the just, to be a partaker of the blessings there. And, during much his pious ejaculations, his infernal plagues would come round him, mimicking his heart-rending groans, and piteous wailings.

One night after he had been thus tormented, whilst he and I were sitting together, condoling each other at the misfortunes and miseries we daily suffered, twenty-five other Indians arrived, bringing with them twenty scalps and three prisoners, who had unhappily fallen into their hands in Cannocojigge, a small town near the River Susquehanna, chiefly inhabited by the Irish. These prisoners gave us some shocking accounts of the murders and devastations committed in their parts. The various and complicated actions of these Barbarians would intirely fill a large volume; but what I have already written, with a few other instances which I shall select from their information, will enable the reader to guess at the horrid treatment the English and Indians, in their interest, have suffered for years past.

I shall therefore only mention in a brief manner those that suffered near the same time with myself. This party, who now joined us, had it not, I found, in their power, to begin their wickedness as soon as those who visited my habitation; the first of their tragedies being on the 25th Day of October, 1754, when John Lewis, with his wife, and three small children, fell sacrifices to their cruelty, and were miserably scalped and murdered; his house, barn, and everything he possessed, being burnt and destroyed. On the 28th, Jacob Miller, with his wife, and six of his family, together, with everything on his plantation, underwent the same fate.

The 30th, the house, mill, barn, twenty head of cattle, two teems of horses, and everything belonging to the unhappy George Folke, met with the like treatment, himself, wife, and all his miserable family, consisting of nine in number, being inhumanly scalped, then cut in pieces, and given to the swine, which devoured them. I shall give another instance of the numberless and unheard-of barbarities they related of these savages and proceed to their own tragical end. In short, one of the substantial traders, belonging to the province, having business that called him, some miles up the country, fell into the hands of these devils, who not only scalped him, but immediately roasted him, before he was dead; then like canibals, for want of other food, eat his whole body, and of his head, made what they called, an Indian pudding.

From these few instances of savage cruelty, the deplorable situation of the defenceless inhabitants, and what they hourly suffered in that part of the globe, must strike the utmost horror to a human soul, and cause in every breast the utmost detestation, not only, against the authors of much tragic scenes, but, against those, who through perfidy, inattention, or pusillanimous and erroneous principles, suffered these savages at first, unrepelled, or even unmolested, to commit much outrages and incredible depredations and murders. For no torments, no barbarities that can be exercised on the human sacrifices, they get into their power, are left untried or omitted.

The three prisoners that were brought with these additional forces, constantly repining at their lot, and almost dead with their excessive hard treatment, contrived at last to make their escape, but being far from their own settlements, and not knowing the country, were soon after met by some others of the tribes, or nations at war with us, and brought back to their diabolical masters, who greatly rejoiced at having them again in their infernal power. The poor creatures, almost famished for want of sustenance, having had none during the time of their elopement; were no sooner in the clutches of the barbarians, than two of them were tied to a tree, and a great fire made round them, where they remained 'till they were terribly scorched and burnt; when one of the villains with his scalping knife, ript open their bellies, took out their entrails, and burnt them before their eyes, whilst the others were cutting, piercing, and tearing the flesh from their breasts, hands, arms, and legs, with red-hot irons, 'till they were dead.

The third unhappy victim, was reserved a few hours longer, to be, if possible, sacrificed in a more cruel manner; his arms were tied close to his body, and a hole being dug, deep enough for him to stand upright, he was put therein, and earth ramed, and beat in, all round his body up to his neck, so that his head only appeared above ground; they then scalped him, and there let him remain for three or four hours, in the greatest agonies; after which they made a small fire near his head, causing him to suffer the most excruciating torments immaginable; whilst the poor creature could only cry for mercy in killing him immediately, for his brains were boiling in his head.

Inexorable to all his plaints, they continued the fire, whilst, shocking to behold! his eyes gushed out of their sockets; and such agonising torments did the unhappy creature suffer for near two hours, 'till he was quite dead! They then cut off his head and buried it with the other bodies; my task being to dig the graves, which feeble and terrified as I was, the dread of suffering the same fate enabled me to do. I shall not here take up the reader's time, in vainly attempting to describe what I felt on such an occasion, but continue my narrative, as more equal to my abilities.

A great snow now falling, the Barbarians were a little fearful, lest the white people should by their traces, find out their skulking retreats, which obliged them to make the best of their way to their winter-quarters, about 200 miles farther from any plantations or inhabitants; where, after a long and painful journey, being almost starved, I arrived with this infernal crew. The place where we were to rest, in their tongue, is called, *Alamingo*, There I found a number of *wigwams*, full of their women and children.

★★★★★★

Wigwams, are the names they give their houses, which are no more than little huts, made with three or four forked stakes, drove into the ground, and covered with deer or other skins; or for want of them, with large leaves and earth.

★★★★★★

Dancing, singing, and shooting, were their general amusements. And in all their festivals and dances, they relate what successes they have had, and what damages they have sustained in their expeditions: In which I now unhappily became part of their theme. The severity of the cold increasing, they stript me of my cloaths for their own use, and gave me such as they usually wore themselves, being a piece of blanket, and a pair of *mogganes*, or shoes, with a yard of coarse cloth, to put round me instead of breeches. To describe their dress and manner of living may not be altogether unacceptable to some of my readers, but as the size of this book will not permit me to be so particular as I might otherwise be, I shall just obeserve,

"That they in general, wear a white blanket, which in war-time they paint with various figures; but particularly the leaves of trees, in order to deceive their enemies when in the woods. Their *mogganes* are made of deer skins, and the best sort have them bound round the edges with little beads and ribbands. On their legs they wear pieces of blue cloth for stockings, something like our soldiers spatter-dashes, they reach higher than their knees, but not lower than their ancles; they esteem them very easy to run in. Breeches they never wear, but instead thereof, two pieces of linen, one before and another behind.

The better sort have shirts of the finest linen they can get, and to those some wear ruffles; but these they never put on till they have painted them of various colours, which they get from the pecone root, and bark of trees, and never pull them off to wash, but wear them, till they fall in pieces. They are very proud and take great delight in wearing trinkets; such as silver plates round their wrists and necks, with several strings of *wampum* (which is made of cotton, interwove with pebbles, cockle-shells, &c) down their breasts; and from their ears and noses they have rings and beads, which hang dangling an inch or two. The men have no beards, to prevent which, they use certain instruments and tricks as soon as it begins to grow. The hair of their heads is managed differently, some pluck out and destroy all, except a lock

108

hanging from the crown of the head, which they interweave with *wampum* and feathers of various colours. The women wear it very long, twisted down their backs, with beads, feathers, and *wampum*; and on their heads most of them wear little coronets of brass or copper; round their middle they wear a blanket instead of a petticoat. The females are very chaste and constant to their husbands; and if any young maiden should happen to have a child before marriage, she is never esteemed afterwards.

As for their food, they get it chiefly by hunting and shooting, and boil, broil, or roast all the meat they eat. Their standing-dish consists of Indian-corn soaked, then bruised and boiled over a gentle fire, for ten or twelve hours. Their bread is likewise made of this, wild oats or sunflower seeds. Set meals they never regard but eat when they are hungry. Their gun, tomahawk, scalping knife, powder and shot, are all they have to carry with them in time of war; bows and arrows being seldom used by them. They generally in war decline open engagements; bush-fighting or skulking is their discipline; and they are brave when engaged, having great fortitude in enduring tortures and death.

No people have a greater love of liberty, or affection to their relations; but they are the most implacably vindictive people upon the earth, for they revenge the death of any relation, or great affront, whenever occasion presents, let the distance of time or place be never so remote: To all which I may add, what the reader has already observed, that they are inhumanly cruel. But, some other nations might be more happy, if, in some instances, they copied them, and made wise conduct, courage, and personal strength, the chief recommendations for war-captains, or *werowances*, as they call them, in times of peace, they visit the plantations inhabited by the whites, to whom, they sell baskets, ladles, spoons, and other such trifles, which they are very expert in making.

When night comes, if admitted into any house, they beg leave to lie down by the fireside, chusing that place rather than any other, which is seldom refused them, if sober, for then they are very honest; but if drunk, are very dangerous and troublesome, if people enough are not in the house to quell them. Nor would they at any times be guilty of such barbarous depredations as they are, did not those calling themselves Christians, intice them thereto with strong liquors, which they are vastly fond of; as well as by the pecuniary rewards which they give for the scalps if ambition cannot be gratified, or superiority obtained, otherwise than by the deaths of thousands, would it not, in those who seek such airy phantoms, and are so inordinately fond of their fellow creatures lives, favour a little more of humanity, to have them killed instantly, and, (if they must have proofs of murder) scalped afterwards? than by allowing and encouraging much merciless treatment, render themselves as obnoxious, cruel, and barbarous, to a human mind, as the very savages themselves.

However, they sometimes suffer by their plots and chicanery lain for the destruction of others; it often happening that the traders or emissaries sent to allure them to the execution of their schemes, rightly fall victims themselves; for, as they always carry with them horseloads of rum, which the Indians are fond of, they soon get drunk, quarrelsome, and wicked, and, in their fury, often kill and destroy their tempters. A just reward for their wicked designs! Nay, it has much an effect on them, that when so intoxicated, they even burn and consume all their own effects, beating, wounding, and sometimes killing their wives and children: But, in disputes among themselves, when sober, they are very tenacious of decorum, never allowing more than one to speak at a time. Prophane swearing they know not in their own language how to express but are very fond of the French and English oaths.

The old people, who are by age and infirmities rendered incapable of being serviceable to the community, they put out of the world in a barbarous and extraordinary manner; an instance of which, I had, whilst among them, an opportunity of seeing practiced on an old Indian. He being, through age, feeble and weak, and his eyes failing him, so that he was unable to get his living either by hunting or shooting; he was summoned to appear before several of the leading-ones, who were to be his judges. Before whom being come, and having nothing to say for himself, (as how indeed could he prove himself to be young,) they very formally, and with a seeming degree of compassion, passed sentence on him to be put to death This was soon after executed on him in the following manner: He was tied naked to a tree, and a boy who was to be his executioner, stood ready with a tomahawk in his hands, to beat his brains out.

But, when the young monster came to inflict the sentence, he was so short of stature that he could not lift the tomahawk high enough; upon which, he was held up by some others, (a great concourse being present) and then, though the young devil laid on with the utmost of his strength, he was not for some time able to fracture the old man's scull, so that it was near an hour before he was dead. Thus, are they from their youth inured to barbarity!

When they found no remains of life in him, they put him into a hole dug in the ground for that purpose, in which he stood upright. Into his left hand they put an old gun and hung a small powder-horn and shot-bag about his shoulders, and a string of *wampum* round his neck; and into his right hand, a little silk purse with a bit of money in it; then filled the hole round and covered him over with earth. This I found to be the usual manner of treating the old of both sexes, only that the women are killed by young girls, and put into the ground with nothing but a ladle in one hand, and a wooden dish in the other.

They are very strict in punishing offenders, especially much as commit crimes against any of the royal families. They never hang any; but these sentenced to death are generally bound to a stake, and a great fire made round them; but not so near as to burn them immediately, for they sometimes remain roasting in the middle of the flames for two or three days before they are dead.

After this long digression, it is time to return to the detail of my own affairs—At *Alamingo* was I kept near two months, 'till the snow was off the ground. A long time to be amongst much creatures, and naked as I almost was! Whatever thoughts I might have of making my escape, to carry them into execution was impracticable, being so far from any plantations or white people, and the severe weather rendering my limbs in a manner quite stiff and motionless: However; I contrived to defend myself against the inclemency of the weather as well as I could, by making myself a little *wigwam*, with the bark of the trees, covering the same with earth, which made it resemble a cave: And to prevent the ill effects of the cold which penetrated into it, I was forced to keep a good fire always near the door.

Thus, did I for near two months endure much hardships of cold and hunger as had hitherto been unknown to me. My liberty of going about, was, indeed, more than I could have expected, but they well knew the impracticability of my eloping from them. Seeing me outwardly easy and submissive, they would sometimes give me a little meat, but my chief food was Indian-corn, dressed as I have above described. Notwithstanding such their civility, the time passed so tediously on, that I almost began to despair of ever regaining my liberty, or seeing my few relations again; which, with the anxiety and pain I suffered on account of my dear wife, often gave me inexpressible concern.

At length, the time arrived, when they were preparing themselves for another expedition against the planters and white-people; but before they let out, they were joined by many other Indians, from Fort Du Quesne, well stored with powder and ball they had received of the French,

As soon as the snow was quite gone, and no traces of their vile footsteps could be perceived, they set forth on their journey towards the back parts of the province Pennsylvania; all leaving their wives and children behind in their *wigwams*. They were now a terrible and formidable body, amounting to near 150! My duty was to carry what they thought proper to load me with, but they never intrusted me with a gun. We marched on several days without anything particular occurring, almost famished for want of provisions; for my part, I had nothing but a few stalks of Indian-corn, which I was glad to eat dry: Nor, did the Indians themselves fare much better, for as we drew near the plantations they were afraid to kill any game, lest the noise of their guns should alarm the inhabitants.

When we again arrived at the Blue Hills, about 30 miles from Cannocojigge, the Irish settlement before-mentioned, we encamped for three days, though God knows we had neither tents, nor anything else to descend us from the inclemency of the air, having nothing to lie on by night but the grass. Their usual method of lodging, pitching, or encamping, by night, being in parcels of ten or twelve men to a fire, where they lie upon the grass or brush, wrapt up in a blanket, with their feet to the fire.

During our stay here, a fort of Council of War was held, when it was agreed to divide themselves into companies of about twenty men each; after which, every captain marched with his party where he thought proper. I still belonged to my old masters but was left behind on the mountains with ten Indians, to stay 'till the rest should return; not thinking it proper to carry me nearer to Cannocojigge, or the other plantations.

Here, being left, I began to meditate on my escape, and though I knew the country round extremely well, having been often thereabouts, with my companions hunting deer, pole-cats and other beasts; yet, was I, very cautious of giving the least suspicions of much my intentions. However, the third day after the grand body had left us, my companions, or keepers, thought proper to visit the mountains, in search of game for their subsistence, leaving me bound in much a manner that I could not escape: At night when they returned, having unbound me, we all sat down together to supper on what they had

112

killed and soon after (being greatly fatigued, with their day's excursion) they composed themselves to rest, as usual. Observing them to be in that somniferous state, I tried various ways to see whether it was a scheme to prove my intentions or not, but after making a noise and walking about, sometimes touching them with my feet, I found there was no fallacy. My heart then exulted with joy at seeing a time come that I might in all probability be delivered from my captivity.

But this joy was soon damped by the dread of being discovered by them or taken by any other stragling parties. To prevent which, I resolved, if possible, to get one of their guns, and if discovered, to die in my defence, rather than be taken: For that purpose, I made various efforts to get one from under their heads, (where they always secured them), but in vain. Frustrated in this my first essay towards regaining my liberty, I dreaded the thoughts of carrying my design into execution: Yet, after a little consideration, and trusting myself to the Divine Protection, I set forwards naked and defenceless as I was.

A rash and dangerous enterprise! Such was my terror however, that in going from them, I halted, and paused every four or five yards, looking fearfully towards the spot where I had left them lest they should awake and miss me; but when I was 200 yards from them, I mended my pace, and made as much haste as I possibly could to the foot of the mountains; when on a sudden, I was struck with the greatest terror and amaze, at hearing the wood-cry, as 'tis called, and may be expressed *Jo-hau! Jo-hau!* which the savages I had left were making, accompanied with the most hideous cries and howlings they could utter. The bellowing of lyons, the shrieks of hyaenas, or the roaring of tygers, would have been to my ears, in comparison to the sounds that then saluted them.

They having now missed their charge, I concluded that they would soon separate themselves and hie in quest of me. The more my terror increased the faster did I push on, and scarce knowing where I trod, drove through the woods with the utmost precipitation, sometimes falling and bruising myself, cutting my feet and legs against the stones, in a miserable manner I but though faint and maimed, as I was, I continued my flight 'till break of day, when, without having anything to sustain nature, but a little corn left, I crept into a hollow tree, in which I lay very snug, and returned my prayers and thanks to the Divine Being, that had thus far favoured my escape.

But my repose was in a few hours destroyed, at hearing the voices of the savages near the place where I was hid, threatening and talking how they would use me, if they got me again that I was before too sensible of, to have the least rest, either in body or mind since I had left them. However, they at last left the spot, where I heard them, and I remained in my circular asylum all that day without further molestation.

At night, I ventured forwards again, frightened, and trembling at every bush I passed, thinking each twig that touched me to be a savage. The third day I concealed myself in the like manner, and at night I travelled on in the same deplorable condition, keeping off the main road, used by the Indians, as much as possible, which made my journey many miles longer, and more painful and irksome than I can express. But how shall I describe the fear, terror, and shock, that I felt on the fourth night, when, by the rustling I made among the leaves, a party of Indians, that lay round a small fire, which I did not perceive, started from the ground, and seizing their arms, run from the fire, amongst the woods. Whether to move forwards, or rest where I was, I knew not, so distracted was my imagination.

In this melancholy state revolving in my thoughts the now inevitable fate I thought waited on me, to my great consternation and joy, I was relieved by a parcel of swine that made towards the place I guessed the savages to be; who, on seeing the hogs, conjectured that their alarm had been occasioned by them, and very merrily returned to the fire and lay down to sleep, as before. As soon as I perceived my enemies so disposed of with more cautious step and silent tread, I pursued my course, sweating (though winter, and severely cold) with the fear I had been just relieved from. Bruised, cut, mangled, and terrified as was, I still, through the Divine Assistance, was enabled to pursue my journey 'till break of day, when thinking myself far off from any of the miscreants, I so much dreaded, I lay down under a great log, and slept undisturbed, 'till about noon, when, getting up, I reached the summit of a great hill, with some difficulty, and looking out if I could spy any habitations of white people, to my unutterable joy I saw some, which I guessed to be about ten miles distance.

This pleasure was in some measure abated, by not being able to get among them that night. Therefore, when evening approached, I again recommended myself to the Almighty, and composed my wearied mangled limbs to rest. In the morning, as soon as I awoke, I continued my journey towards the nearest cleared lands, I had seen the day before, and about four o'clock in the afternoon, arrived at the house of John Bell, an old acquaintance, where, knocking at the door, his wife, who opened it, seeing me in such a frightful condition, flew from me like lightning, screaming into the house. This alarmed the whole family, who immediately fled to their arms, and I was soon accosted by the master with his gun in his hand. But on my assuring him of my innocence, as to any wicked intentions, and making myself known, (for he before took me to be an Indian) he immediately caressed me, as did all his family, with a deal of friendship at finding me alive; they having all been informed of my being murdered by the savages some months before.

No longer now able to support my fatigued and worn out spirits, I fainted and fell to the ground. From which state having recovered me and perceiving the weak and famished condition I then was in, they soon gave me some refreshment, but let me partake of it very sparingly, fearing the ill effects, too much at once would have on me. They for two days and nights very affectionately supplied me with all necessaries, and carefully attended me 'till my spirits and limbs were pretty well recruited, and I thought myself able to ride, when I borrowed of these good people (whose kindness merits my most grateful returns) a horse and some cloaths, and set forward for my father-in-law's house in Chester County, about 140 miles from thence, where I arrived on the 4th day of January, 1755, but scarce one of the family could credit their eyes, believing with the people I had lately left, that I had fallen a prey to the Indians,

Great was the joy and satisfaction wherewith I was received and embraced by the whole family; but oh, what was my anguish and trouble, when on inquiring for my dear wife, I found she had been dead two months! This fatal news, as every humane reader must imagine, greatly lessened the joy and rapture I otherwise should have felt at my deliverance, from the dreadful state and company I had been in.

The news of my happy arrival at my father-in-law's house, after so long and strange an absence, was soon spread round the neighbouring plantations by the country people, who continually visited me, being very desirous of hearing, and eagerly inquiring an account of my treatment, and manner of living among the Indians. In all which I satisfied them. Soon after this, my arrival, I was sent for by his Excellency Mr. Morris, the governor, who examined me very particularly, as to all incidents relating to my captivity, and especially, in regard to the Indians, who had first taken me away, whether they were French or English parties?

I assured his Excellency, they were of those, who professed themselves to be friends of the latter; and informed him of the many barbarous and inhuman actions, I had been witness to among them, on the frontiers of the province; and also, that they were daily increasing by others of our pretended friends joining them; that they were all well supplied by the French with arms and ammunition, and greatly encouraged by them in their continual excursions and barbarities, not only, in having extraordinary premiums for much scalps as they should take and carry home with them at their return, but great presents of all kinds, besides rum, powder, ball, &c. before they sallied forth. Having satisfied his Excellency in much particulars as he requested, the same being put into writing, I swore to the contents thereof; as may be seen, by those who doubt of my veracity, in the public papers of that time, as well in England as in Philadelphia.

Having done with me, Mr. Morris gave me three guineas, and sent the affidavit to the Assembly, who were then indolently sitting in the state-house at Philadelphia, little regarding, nay even discrediting the various accounts of the incursions and depredations of the savages. Whether much indolence proceeded from the pacific principles professed by those who are called Quakers, (and mostly constitute that assembly) to be part of their religion, or from any other sinister motive, it behoves not me to hint at, or conjecture.

However, on receiving this intelligence from his Excellency, they immediately sent for me. When I arrived, I was conducted into the lower-house, where the Assembly then sate, and was there interrogated by the speaker, very particularly as to all I had before given the governor an account of; this my first examination lasted three hours. The next day, I underwent a second, for about an hour and a half, when I was courteously dismissed, with a promise (never thought on afterwards) that all proper methods should be taken, not only to accommodate and reimburse all those who had suffered by the savages; but to prevent them from committing the like hostilities for the future. How well the latter part of their promise has been completed, the whole world are as sensible of, as I am of the non-performance of the former.

Now returned, and once more at liberty to pursue my own inclinations, I was persuaded by my father-in-law and friends to follow some employment or other; but the plantation, from whence I was taken, though an exceeding good one, could not tempt me to settle on it again. What my fate would have been if I had, may easily be conceived. And there being at this time (as the Assembly, too late for many of us sound) a necessity for raising men to check those barbarians in

116

their ravaging depredations, I inlisted myself as one, with the greatest alacrity and most determined resolution, to exert the utmost of my power, in being revenged on the hellish authors of my ruin. General Shirley, a gentleman of the law, was the weak instrument pitched upon to direct the operations of war in that part of the world; a man as unfitly qualified for such an undertaking as ever the legislature could employ.

A man never bred or inured to the hardships of war; and never in the least acquainted with the arts and designs of military discipline: True, it is, indeed, that he resided and practiced law in New-England for some years, and in 1741, succeeded Mr. Belcher as Governor-General of New-York, Massachusett's-Bay and New-Hampshire; in which post he continued 'till 1748; when, being still in the good graces of his first patrons at home, (for some reasons not here to be mentioned) he was supposed as being a lawyer, to have a good deal of chicane and art in his composition.

He was accordingly sent to the Court of France, in order to settle the boundaries of Arcadia, or Nova-Scotia, and at a great charge, though to little purpose, there kept for some years; for how weak the artifice, elocution and penetration, of an English lawyer, proved against French perfidy, specious promises, and more deep laid stratagems; that long tedious and expansive negociation, and the disastrous consequences attending the same, have been too fatally experienced by thousands of Europe as well as America. But, I may, perhaps, by some, be thought to venture too far out of my sphere, and that the hidden secrets of cabinets are impervious to, and ought not to be descanted on, by vulgar minds. I shall go on therefore, with my own affairs.

Into a regiment, immediately under the command of this *experienced* general, and in his son, Capt. Shirley's Company, was it my lot to be placed for three years. This regiment was intended for the frontiers, to destroy the forts erected by the French, as soon as it should be completely furnished with arms, &c. at Boston, in New-England, where it was ordered for that purpose. Being then very weak and infirm in body, though possessed of my usual resolution, it was thought advisable to leave me for two months in winter-quarters. At the end of which, being pretty well recruited in strength, I set out for Boston, to join the regiment with some others, likewise left behind; and after crossing the River De-la-ware, we arrived at New-Jersey, and from thence proceeded through the same by New-York, Middletowne,

117

Mendon, in Connecticut to Boston, where we arrived about the end of March and found the regiment ready to receive us,

Boston, being the capital of New-England, and the biggest city in America, except two or three on the Spanish Continent, I shall here subjoin a short account of it.

'Tis pleasantly situated, and about four miles in compass, at the bottom of Massachusets' Bay, into which there is but one common and safe passage, and not very broad, there being scarce room for three ships to come in abreast; but once in, there's room for the anchorage of 500 sail. It's guarded by several rocks, and above a dozen islands; the most remarkable of these islands is Castle-Island, which stands about a league from the town, and so situated, that no ship of burthen can approach the town, without the hazard of being shattered in pieces by its cannon.

It's now called, Fort-William, and mounted with 100 pieces of ordnance; 200 more which were given to the province by Queen Anne are placed on a platform, so as to take a ship fore and aft, before she can bring about her broadsides to bear against the castle. Some of these cannon are 42 pounders; 500 able men are exempted from all military duty in times of war, to be ready at an hour's warning to attend the service of the castle, upon a signal of the approach of an enemy, which there seems to be no great danger of at Boston; where, in 24 hours time, 10,000 effective men, well armed, might be ready for their defence. According to a computation of the collectors of the light-house, it appeared that there were 24,000 tons of shipping cleared annually.

The pier is at the bottom of the bay 2000 feet long, and runs so far into the bay, that ships of the greatest burthen may unload without the help of boats or lighters. At the upper end of the chief street in the town, which comes down to the head of the pier, is town-house or Exchange a fine building, containing, besides the walk for merchants, the council-chamber, the House of Commons, and a factious room for the Courts of Justice. The Exchange is surrounded with bookseller's shops that have a good trade: Here being five printing-houses, and the presses generally full of work, which is in a great measure owing to the colleges and schools in New-England; whereas at New-York there are but two or three little bookseller's shops, and none at all in Virginia, Maryland, Carolina, Barbadoes and the Sugar Islands.

The town lies in the form of an half-moon round the harbour, and consisting of about 4000 houses, must make an agreeably prospect, the surrounding shore being high, the streets long, and the buildings beautiful. The pavement is kept in so good order, that to gallop an horse on it is 3*s*. 4*d*. forfeit. The number of inhabitants is computed at about 24,000.

There are eight churches, the chief of which is called the Church-of-England-Church; besides the Baptist Meeting, and the Quaker's Meeting.

The conversation in this town is as polite as in most of the cities and towns in England. A gentleman of London would fancy himself at home at Boston, when he observes the number of people, their furniture, their tables, and dress, which, perhaps, is as splendid and showy as that of most tradesmen in London.

In this city, learning military discipline, and waiting for an opportunity of carrying our schemes into execution, we lay 'till the 1st of July, during all which time great outrages and devastations were committed by the savages in the back parts of the province. One instance of which in particular I shall relate, as being concerned in rewarding according to desert, the wicked authors thereof.

Joseph Long, Esq; a gentleman of large fortune in these parts, who had in his time been a great warrior among the Indians, and frequently joined in expeditions with those in our interest against the others. His many exploits and great influence among several of the nations were too well known, to pass unrevenged by the savages against whom he had exerted his abilities. Accordingly, in April 1756, a body of them came down on his plantation, about 30 miles from Boston, and skulking in the woods for some time, at last seized an opportunity to attack his house, in which, unhappily proving successful, they scalped, mangled, and cut to pieces, the unfortunate gentleman, his wife, and nine servants, and then made a general conflagration of his houses, barns. cattle, and everything he possessed, with the mangled bodies; all suffered together in one great blaze!

But his more unfortunate son and daughter were made prisoners, and carried off by them, to be reserved for greater tortures. Alarmed and terrified at this inhuman butchery, the neighbourhood, as well as the people of Boston, quickly assembled themselves, to think of proper measures to be revenged on these execrable monsters, Among the first of those who offered themselves to go against the savages, was James Crawford, Esq., who was then at Boston and heard of this tragedy; he was a young gentleman who had for some years paid his addresses to Miss Long and was in a very little time to have been married to her. Distracted, raving, and shocked, as he was, he lost no time, but instantly raised 100 resolute and bold young fellows to go in quest of the villains.

As I had been so long among them, and pretty well acquainted with their manners and customs, and particularly their skulking places in the woods, I was recommended to him as one proper for his expedition; he immediately applied to my officers and got liberty for me. Never did I go on any enterprise with half that alacrity and chearfulness I now went with this party. My wrongs and sufferings were too recent in my memory, to suffer me to hesitate a moment in taking an opportunity of being revenged to the utmost of my power.

Being quickly armed and provided, we hastened forwards for Mr. Long's Plantation on the 29th, and after travelling the most remote and intricate paths through the woods, arrived there the 2nd of May, dubious of our success, and almost despairing of meeting with the savages, as we had heard or could discover nothing of them in our march. In the afternoon some of our men being sent to the top of a hill to look out for them, soon perceived a great smoak in a part of the low grounds. This we immediately and rightly conjectured to proceed from a fire made by them. We accordingly put ourselves into regular order, and marched forwards, resolved, let their number have been what it might, to give them battle.

Arriving within a mile of the place, Captain Crawford, whose anxiety and pain made him quicker lighted than any of the rest, soon perceived them, and guessed their number to be about 50. Upon this we halted and secreted ourselves as well as we could 'till twelve o'clock at night. At which time, supposing them to be at rest, we divided our men into two divisions, 50 in each, and marched on; when, coming within twenty yards of them, the captain fired his gun, which was immediately followed by both divisions in succession, who instantly rushing on them with bayonets fixed, killed, every man of them.

Great as our joy was, and flushed with success as we were, at this sudden victory, no heart among us but was ready to burst at the sight of the unhappy young lady. What must the thoughts, torments, and sensations, of our brave captain then be, if even we, who knew her not, were so sensibly affected! For, oh! what breast, though of the brutal savage race we had just destroyed, could, without feeling the most exquisite grief and pain, behold in such infernal power, a lady in the bloom of youth, blessed with every female accomplishment that could set off the most exquisite beauty! Beauty, which rendered her the envy of her own sex, and the delight of ours, enduring the severity of a windy, rainy night! Behold one nurtured in the most tender manner, and by the most indulgent parents, quite naked, and in the open woods, encircling with her alabaster arms and hands a cold rough tree, whereto she was bound with cords so straitly pulled, that the blood trickled from her fingers ends! Her lovely tender body, and delicate limbs, cut, bruised, and torn with stones and boughs of trees as she had been dragged along, and all besmeared with blood! What heart can even now, unmoved, think of her distress, in such a deplorable condition? having no creature with the least sensations of humanity near to succour or relieve her, or even pity or regard her flowing tears and lamentable wailings!

The very remembrance of the sight, has at this instant much an effect upon me, that I almost want words to go on—Such then was the condition in which we found this wretched fair, but faint and speechless with the shock our firing had given her tender frame. The captain for a long time could do nothing but gaze upon, and clasp her to his bosom, crying, raving, and tearing his hair, like one bereft of his senses; nor did he for some time perceive the lifeless condition she was in, 'till one of the men had untied her lovely mangled arms, and she fell to the ground. Finding among the villain's plunder the unhappy lady's cloaths, he gently put some of them about her; and after various trials and much time spent, recovered her dissipated spirits, the repossession of which she first manifested by eagerly fixing her eyes on her dear deliverer, and smiling with the most complaisant joy, blessed the Almighty and him for her miraculous deliverance.

During; this pleasing, painful interview, our men were busily employed in cutting, hacking, and scalping the dead Indians; and so desirous was every man to have a share in reaking his revenge on them, that disputes happened among ourselves who should be the instruments of further shewing it on their lifeless trunks, there not being enough for every man to have one wherewith to satiate himself: the captain observing the animosity between us, on this occasion, ordered, that the two divisions should cast lots for this bloody, though agreeable piece of work; which being accordingly done, the party, whose lot it was to be excluded from this business, stood by with half-pleased countenances, looking on the rest; who with the utmost chearfulness and activity pursued their revenge in scalping, and otherwise treating their dead bodies as the most inveterate hatred and detestation could suggest.

The work being done, we thought of steering homewards trium-phant with the 50 scalps; but how to get the lady forwards, who was in such a condition, as rendered her incapable of walking further, gave us some pain, and retarded us a little, 'till we made a sort of carriage to seat her on; and then, with the greatest readiness, we took our turns, four at a time, and carried her along. This, in some measure, made the captain chearful, who all the way endeavoured to comfort and revive his desponding afflicted mistress: But alas! in vain; for the miseries she had lately felt, and the terrible fate of her poor brother, of whom, I doubt not, but the tender-hearted reader is anxious to hear, rendered even her most pleasing thoughts, notwithstanding his soothing words, corroding and insufferable.

The account she gave of their disastrous fate and dire catastro-phe, besides what I have already mentioned, was, that the savages had no sooner seen all consumed, but they hurried off with her and her brother, pushing, and sometimes dragging them on, for four or five miles, when they stopt; and stripping her naked, treated her in a shock-ing manner, whilst others were stripping and cruelly whipping her unhappy brother. After which, they in the same manner pursued their journey, regardless of the tears, prayers, or entreaties of this wretched pair; but, with the most infernal pleasure, laughed and rejoiced at the calamities and distresses they had brought them to, and saw them suf-fer, 'till they arrived at the place we found them; as here, they had that day butchered her beloved brother in the following execrable and cruel manner:

They first scalped him alive, and after mocking his agonising groans and torments, for some hours, ripped open his belly, into which they put splinters, and chips of pine-trees, and set fire thereto; the same (on account of the turpentine wherewith these trees abound) burnt with great quickness and fury for a little time, during which, he remained in a manner alive, as she could sometimes perceive him to move his head, and groan. They then piled a great quantity of wood all round his body, and most inhumanly consumed it to ashes.

Thus, did these Barbarians put an end to the being of this unhappy young gentleman, who was only 22 years of age when he met his ca-lamitous fate. She continued her relation, by acquainting us, that the next day, was to have seen her perish in the like manner, after suffering worse, than even such a terrible death, the satisfying these diabolical miscreants in their brutal lust. But it pleased the Almighty to permit us to rescue her, and entirely extirpate this crew of devils!

Marching easily on her account, we returned to the captain's plantation the 6th of May, where, as well as at Boston, we were joyfully received, and rewarded handsomely for the scalps of those savages we had brought with us. Mr. Crawford and Miss Long, were soon after married, and in gratitude to the services we had done them, the whole party were invited to the wedding, and nobly entertained, but no riotous or noisy mirth was allowed, the young lady, as we may well imagine, being still under great affliction, and in a weak state of health.

Nothing further material, that I now remember, happened during my stay at Boston; to proceed therefore, with the continuation of our intended expedition.

On the 1st of July the regiment began their march for Oswego. The 21st we arrived at Albany, in New-York. through Cambridge, Northampton, and Hadfield, in New-England. From thence, marching about twenty miles farther, we incamped near the mouth of the Mohawk River, by a town called Schenectady, not far from the Endless-Mountains. Here did we lye some time, 'till *batteaux* (a sort of flat-bottomed boats, very small, and sharp at both ends) could be got to carry our stores and provisions to Oswego; each of which, would contain about six barrels of pork, or in proportion thereto; Two men belonged to every *batteau*, who made use of strong scutting poles, with iron at the ends, to prevent their being too soon destroyed by the stones in the river (one of the sources of the Ohio) which abounded with many, and large ones, and in some places was so shallow, that the men were forced to wade and drag their *batteaux* after them.

Which, together, with some cataracts, or great falls of water, rendered this duty very hard and fatiguing, not being able to travel more than seven or eight English miles a day, 'till they came to the Great-Carrying place at Wood's Creek, where the provisions and *batteaux* were taken out, and carried about four miles, to Alliganey, or Ohio great river, that ran quite to Oswego, to which place, General Shirley got with part of the forces on the 8th of August; but Colonel Mercer with the remainder, did not arrive 'till the 31st. Here we found Colonel Schuyler with his regiment of New-Jersey Provincials, who had arrived there some time before. A short description of a place, which has afforded so much occasion for animadversion, may not here be altogether disagreeable to those unacquainted with our settlements in that part of the world.

Oswego is situated N. lat. 43 Deg. 10 min. near the mouth of the River Onondaga, on the South-side of the Lake Ontario, or Cataraquie. There was generally a fort and constant garrison of regular troops kept before our arrival. In the proper seasons, a fair for the Indian trade is kept here: Indians of above twenty different nations have been observed here at a time. The greatest part of the trade between Canada and the Indians, of the Great Lakes, and some parts of the Mississippi, pass near this fort; the nearest and fastest way of carrying goods upon this lake being along the south-side of it. The distance from Albany to Oswego Fort is about 300 miles west; to render which march more comfortable, we met with many good farms and settlements in the way. The *Outawaes*, a great and powerful nation, living upon the Outawae River, which joins the Catarique River, (the outlet of the Great Lakes) deal considerably with the New-York trading houses here.

The different nations trading to Oswego are distinguishable by the variety and different fashions of their canoes; the very remote Indians are cloathed in skins of various sorts, and have all fire-arms: Some come from so far north at Port Nelson, in Hudson's Bay, N. lat. 57 deg. And some from the Chirakees, west of South-Carolina, in N. lat. 32 deg. This seems indeed to be a vast extent of inland water-carriage, but it is only for canoes, and the smallest of craft.

Nor will it in this place be improper to give some account of our friends in those parts, whom we call the Mohawks, *viz.* The Iroquois, commonly called the Mohawks; the Oneiadaes, the Onondagues, the Cayugaes, and the Senekeas. In all accounts they are lately called the Six Nations of the New-York, friendly-Indians; the Tuscararoes, straglers from the old Tuscararoes of North-Carolina, lately are reckoned as the sixth—I shall here reckon them as I have been informed they were formerly, 1. The Mohawks: they live upon the Mohawk's or Schenectady River, and head, or lye north of New-York, Pennsylvania, Maryland and some part of Virginia; having a castle or village, westward from Albany forty miles, and another sixty-live miles west, and about 160 sensible men. 2. The Oneiadaes, about eighty miles from the Mohawk's second village, consisting of near 200 fighting men. 3. The Onondagues, about twenty-five miles further, (the famous Oswego trading place on the Lake Ontario, is in their country) consist of about 250 men. 4. The Cayugaes, about seventy miles further, of about 130 men; and 5. The Senekeas, who reach a great way down the River Susquehanna, consist of about 700 marching, fighting men:

So that the fighting men of the five or six nations of Mohawks, may be reckoned at 1500 men, and extend from Albany, west 400 miles, lying in about thirty tribes or governments. Besides these, there is settled above Montreal, which lies N. E. of Oswego, a tribe of scoundrel run-a ways from the Mohawks; they are called Kahnuages, consisting of about eighty men—This short account of these nations, I think it necessary to make the English reader acquainted with, as I may have occasion to mention things concerning some of them.

★★★★★★

It may not be improper here also to give a succinct detail of the education, manners, religion, &c., of the natives. The Indians are born tolerably white, but they take a great deal of pains to darken their complexions by anointing themselves with grease and lying in the sun. Their features are good, especially those of the women. Their limbs clean, straight, and well proportioned, and a crooked or deformed person is a great rarity amongst them. They are very ingenious in their way, being neither so ignorant nor so innocent as some people imagine. On the contrary, a very understanding generation are they, quick of apprehension, sudden in despatch, subtle in their dealings, exquisite in their inventions, and in labour assiduous. The world has no better marksmen with guns or bows and arrows, than the natives, who can kill birds flying, fishes swimming, and wild beasts running; nay, with such prodigious force do they discharge their arrows, that one of them will shoot a man quite through, and nail both his arms to his body with the same arrow.

As to their religion, in order to reconcile the different accounts exhibited by travellers, we must suppose that different tribes may have different notions and different rites; and though I do not think myself capable of determining the case with the precision and accuracy I could wish, yet, with what I have collected from my own observation when among them, and the information of my brother captives, who have been longer conversant with the Indians than I was, I shall readily give the public all the satisfaction I can.

Some assure us the Indians worship the images of some inferior deities, whose anger they seem to dread; on which account the generality of our travellers denominate the object of their devotion devils; though, at the same time, it is allowed they pray to their inferior duties for success in all their undertakings, for plenty of food and other necessaries of life. It appears too that they acknowledge one Supreme Being; but him they adore not, because they believe he is too far exalted above them and too happy in himself to be concerned about the trifling affairs of poor mortals. They seem, also, to believe in a future state; and that after death, they will be removed to their friends who have gone before them, to an Elysium or Paradise beyond the Western Mountains; others again, allow them either no religion at all, or at least, very faint ideas of a deity, but all agree that they are extravagantly superstitious, and exceedingly afraid of evil spirits. To these demons they make oblations every new moon for the space of seven days; during which time they cast lots, and sacrifices one of themselves, putting the person devoted to the most exquisite misery they can invent in order to satisfy the devil for that moon; for they think if they please but the evil spirit God will do them no hurt.

Certain, however, it is, that those Indians whom the French priests have had an opportunity of ministering unto, are induced to believe, 'That the Son of God came into the world to save all mankind, and destroy all evil spirits that now trouble them; that the English have killed him ; and that, ever since, the evil spirits are permitted to walk on the earth; that, if the English were all destroyed, the Son of the Good Man, who is God, would come again, and banish all evil spirits from their land, and then they would have nothing to fear or disturb them. Cajoled by these false but artful insinuations of the French Jesuits, Indians from that time have endeavoured to massacre all the English, in order that the Son of God might come again on the earth and rid them from their slavish fears and terrible apprehensions, by exterminating the object thereof.

★★★★★★

Being now at Oswego, the principal object that gave at that time any concern to the Americans, I shall, before I continue my own account, give a short recital of what had been done in these parts, in regard to the defence and preservation of the fort and the colonies thereabouts, before I came, upon such authorities as I got from those who had been long at Oswego, and I can well depend upon for truth.

General Shirley, in 1754, having erected two new forts on the River Onondaga, it seemed probable, that he intended to winter at Oswego with his army, that he might the more readily proceed to action in the ensuing spring. What produced his inactivity afterwards, and how it was, that Fort Oswego was not taken by the French in the

Spring of 1755, are things my penetration will not enable me to discuss. But, Oswego is now lost, and would have been so in the Spring of 1755, if more important affairs had not made the French neglect it. At this time the garrison of Oswego consisted only of 100 men, under Captain King. The old fort being their only protection, which mounted only eight four pounders, was incapable of defence, because it was commanded by an eminence directly cross a narrow river, the banks of which were covered with thick wood.

In May, 1755, Oswego being in this condition, and thus garrisoned; thirty French *batteaux* were seen to pass, and two days after 11 more; each *batteau* (being much larger than ours) containing 15 men; so that this fleet consisted of near 600 men: A force, which with a single mortar, might soon have taken possession of the place.

A resolution was now taken to make the fort larger and erect some new ones; to build vessels upon the lake; to encrease the garrison; and provide everything necessary to annoy the enemy, so as they might render the place tenable. Captain Broadstreet arriving on the 27th of May at the fort with two companies, some small swivel guns and the first parcel of workmen, made some imagine that a stop would be put to the French in their carrying men in sight of the garrison; yet, they still permitted 11 more French *batteaux* to pass by, though we were then superior to them in these boats, or at least in number.

The reason our forces could not attack them, was, because they were four miles in the offing, on board large vessels in which the soldiers could stand to fire without being overset; and our *batteaux* in which we must have attacked them were so small that they would contain only six men each, and so ticklish, that the inadvertent motion of one man would overset them. No care, however, was taken to provide larger boats against another emergency of the same kind. At Oswego, indeed, it was impracticable for want of iron-work; such being the provident forecast of those who had the management of affairs, that though there were smiths enough; yet, there was, at this place, but *one* pair of bellows; so that the first accident that should happen to that necessary instrument, would stop all the operations of the forge at once.

The beginning of June, the ship-carpenters arrived from Boston, and on the 28th of the same month, the first vessel we ever had on the Lake Ontario, was launched and fitted out: She was a schooner, 40 feet in the keel, had 14 oars, and 12 swivel guns. This vessel, and 320 men, was all the force we had at Oswego at the beginning of July and was victualled at the expense of the province of New-York. Happy, indeed, it was, that the colony provisions were there; for so little care had been taken to get the king's provisions sent up, that, when we arrived, we must have perished with famine, had we not found a supply which we had little reason to expect.

About the middle of July, an attack was again expected, when we (the forces under General Shirley) were still near 300 miles distant. And, if the attack had then been made, with the force the enemy was known to have had at hand, it must, for the reason I have just before given, have fallen into their possession.

Such was the state of Oswego, when we arrived there: Where we had been but a small time, before provisions began to be very scarce; and the king's allowance being still delayed, the provincial stores were soon exhausted, and we were in danger of being soon famished, being on less than half-allowance. The men being likewise worn out and fatigued with the long march they had suffered and being without rum (or allowed none at least), and other proper nutriment, many fell sick of the flux, and died; so that our regiment was greatly reduced in six weeks time: A party that we left at the important Carrying-place, at Wood's Creek, being absolutely obliged to desert it for want of necessaries.

Sickness, death, and desertion, had, at length, so far reduced us, that we had scarce men enough to perform duty, and protect those who were daily at work. The Indians keeping a strict lookout, rendered everyone who passed the out-guards or centinels, in danger of being scalped or murdered. To prevent consequences like these, a captain's guard of sixty men, with two lieutenants, two serjeants, two corporals, and one drum, besides two flank-guards of a serjeant, corporal, and twelve men, in each, were daily mounted, and did duty as well as able. Scouting-parties were likewise sent out every day: But the sickness still continuing, and having 300 men at work, we were obliged to lessen our guards, 'till General Pepperell's Regiment joined us.

A little diligence being now made use of, about the middle of September, four other vessels were got ready, *viz.* A decked sloop of eight guns, four pounders, and 30 swivels; a decked schooner, eight guns, four pounders, and twenty-eight swivels; one undecked schooner, of fourteen swivels and fourteen oars, and another of twelve swivels and fourteen oars; about 150 tons each.

On the 24th of October, with this armament, and a considerable number of *batteaux*, which were too small to live upon the lake in moderate weather, we were preparing to attack Niagara; though (notwithstanding we had taken all the provisions we could find in Oswego, and had left the garrison behind, with scarce enough for three days) the fleet had not provisions sufficient on board to carry them within sight of the enemy, and supplies were not to be got within 300 miles of the place we were going against. However, the impracticability of succeeding in an expedition undertaken without victuals, was discovered time enough to prevent our march, or embarkation, or whatever it may be called; but not before nine *batteaux* laden with officers baggage, were sent forwards, four men in each *batteau*; in one of which it was my lot to be.

The men being weak and low in spirits, with continual harrassing and low feeding, rendered our progress very tedious and difficult. Add to this, the places we had to pass and ascend; for, in many parts, the cataracts or falls of water, which descended near the head of the River Onondaga (in some places near 100 feet perpendicular), rendered it almost impossible for us to proceed; for the current running from the bottom, was so rapid, that the efforts of twenty or thirty men were sometimes required to drag the boats along, and especially to get them up the hills or cataracts, which we were forced to do with ropes: Sometimes, when with great labour and difficulty, we had got them up, we carried them by land near a quarter of a mile, before we came to any water. In short, we found four men to a *batteau* insufficient; for the men belonging to one *batteau*, were so fatigued and worn out, that they could not manage her, so that she lay behind almost a league.

The captain that was with us, observing this, as soon as we had got the others over the most difficult falls, ordered two besides myself to go and help her forwards; accordingly, I got into her, in order to steer her, whilst my two comrades and her own crew dragged her along. When we got: to any cataracts, I remained in her to fasten the ropes and keep all safe, while they hauled her up, but drawing her to the summit of the last cataract, the ropes gave way, and down she fell into a very rapid and boisterous stream; where, not being able by myself to work her, she stove to pieces on a small rock, on which, some part of her remaining till morning I miraculously saved myself.

Never, was my life in greater danger than in this situation; the night being quite dark, and no assistance to be obtained from any of my comrades; though many of them, as I afterwards learned, made diligent search for me; but the fall of the waters rendered the noise that they, as well as myself made, to be heard by one another, quite ineffectual.

In the morning they indeed found me, but in, a wretched condition, quire benumbed, and almost dead with the cold, having nothing on but my shirt.

After various efforts, having, with great difficulty, got me up, they used all proper means to recover my worn-out spirits: But the fire had a fatal effect to what they intended, for my flesh swelled all over my body and limbs, and caused such a deprivation of my senses, that I fainted, and was thought by all to be dead. However, after some time, they pretty well recovered my scattered senses and fatigued body; and, with proper care, conducted me, with some others (who were weak and ill of the flux), to Albany, where the hospital received our poor, debilitated bodies.

The rest, not able to proceed, or being countermanded, bent their course back again to Oswego. Where, a friendly storm preventing an embarkation, when a stock of provisions was got together (sufficient to prevent them from eating one another, during the first twelve days), all thoughts of attacking Niagara were laid aside.

Thus, ended this formidable campaign. The vessels that we had built (as I afterwards learned) were unrigged and laid up, without having been put to any use; while a French vessel was cruising on the lake, and carrying supplies to Niagara, without interruption; five others as large as ours, being also ready to launch at Frontenac, which lies across the Lake Ontario, north of Oswego,

The general, whatever appearances might have led others, as well as myself, to think otherwise; soon indicated his intention of not wintering at Oswego, for, he left the place before the additional works were compleated, and the garrison, by insensible degrees, decreased to 1100 men; still living in perpetual terror, on the brink of famine, and become mutinous for want of their pay; which, in the hurry of military business, during a year that was crowded with great events, had been forgotten; for, from my first inlisting, to the time I was laid up at Albany, I never had received above six weeks pay,

A little, indeed, may be offered in vindication of the general and his numberless delays, *viz*. That it took some time to raise the two regiments, which were in British pay, as the name of inlisting for life, is somewhat forbidding to the Americans: (a few of whom, as well as myself, made our agreement for three years; but after that time, I doubt, we must have depended on his pleasure for our being discharged, according to our contract, had it not fallen out otherwise).

The unusual dryness of the summer which rendered the rivers down to Oswego in some places impassable, or very difficult for the *batteaux* to proceed; and it was whispered, that a gentleman, lately in an eminent station in New-York, did all in his power to hinder the undertaking, from a pique to the general. By these disadvantages, he was detained at Albany, 'till August, and even when he did reach Oswego, he found himself put to no little difficulty to maintain his ground, for want of provisions; and the men being so reduced, more than once, to short allowance, as you have seen, became troubled with the flux, and had not any thing necessary, not even rum sufficient for the common men, to prevent the fatal effects of that disorder.

In this manner, the summer was spent on our side, and the reason why the French did not this year take Oswego, when they might, with so little trouble, was, as many besides myself conjectured, that they thought it more their interest to pursue their projects on the Ohio, and preserve the friendship of the considerable Indians, which, an attack upon Oswego, at that time, would have destroyed.

How far they succeeded in such their projects, and the reasons of their successes, a little animadversion on our own transactions will let us into the light of. For as appearances on our side, were very favourable in the spring; General Braddock's defeat greatly increased the gloom which sat on the countenances of the Americans.

Great things being expected from him, he arrived early, and Fort Du Quesne, seemed to be ours, if we did but go and demand it. The attacks designed against Niagara and Fort Frederick, at Crown-Pont, were planned in the winter, and the troops employed against the French in Nova-Scotia, embarked at Boston in April. Let us view the events besides those already mentioned. General Braddock was ready to march in April; but through ignorance, or neglect, or a misunderstanding with the governor of Virginia; had neither fresh provisions, horses or waggons provided and so late as the latter-end of May, it was necessary to apply to Pennsylvania for the most part of those.

This neglect, created a most pernicious diffidence and discredit of the Americans, in the mind of the general, and prevented their usefulness where their advice was wanted, and produced very bad effects. He was a man (as 'tis now too well known and believed) by no means, of quick apprehension, and could not conceive that such people could instruct him; and his young counsellors prejudiced him still more, so as to slight his officers. and what was worse, his enemy; as it was treated as an absurdity to suppose the Indians would ever attack regulars: And, of course, no care was taken to instruct the men to resist their peculiar manner of fighting. Had this circumstance been attended to, I am fully persuaded, 400 Indians, about the number that defeated him, would have given him very little annoyance: Sure, I am, 400 of our people rightly managed, would have made no difficulty of driving before them that handful, to whom he owed his defeat and death.

The undertaking of the eastern provinces to reduce the fort at Crown-Point, met that fate, which the jarring counsels of a divided people commonly meet with; for though the plan was concerted in the winter of 1754, it was August before these petty governments could bring together their troops. In short, it must be owned by all, that delays were the banes of our undertakings, except in the Bay of Fundi, in Nova-Scotia, where secrecy and expedition were rewarded with success, and that province reduced.

The general continued inactive, from the time he left Oswego, to March, 1736, when he was about to resume the execution of his scheme to attack Frontenac and Niagara. What would have been the issue of this project, neither myself, nor any other person, can now pretend to say, for just at this crisis, he received orders from England, to attempt nothing, 'till Lord Loudon should arrive, which was said should be early in the spring. However, his Lordship did not get there 'till the middle of July, so that by this delay, time was given to the Marquis de Montcalm (Major-General Dieskau's successor) to arrive from France at Canada with 3000 regular forces and take the field before us.

But to return from this digression to other transactions. When I was pretty well recovered again, I embarked on board a vessel from Albany for New-York; where, when I arrived, I found to my sorrow, my captain, Mr. Shirley, the general's son, had been dead for some time; he was a very promising, worthy, young gentleman, and universally regretted. His company was given to Major James Kinnair, who ordered, that none of his men should go out on the recruiting parties, as was at first intended by his predecessor; but, that the private men should either return to Oswego, or do duty in the fort at New-York. Not liking my station here, I entreated the general, who was now arrived, for a furlow, to see my friends in Pennsylvania, which, he having then no great occasion for me, at New-York, granted for three months.

As I have here mentioned New-York, and before given a short account of the two cities, Philadelphia and Boston, it would be a disrespect to this elegant one, not to take notice of it, as well as in some measure debarring the reader from much information as may not be disagreeable, but not being of that note or consequence with the others, I shall briefly observe; that New-York is a very fine city, and the capital of the province of that name, it contains about 3000 houses, and near 9000 inhabitants. The houses are all well built, and the meanest of them said to be worth 100*l.* which cannot be said of the city of the same name, nor of any other in England. Their conversation is polite, and their furniture, dress, and manner of living, quite elegant. In drinking and gallantry, they exceed any city in America.

The great church is a very handsome edifice and built in 1695. Here are also a Dutch church, a French church, and a Lutheran church. The inhabitants of Dutch extraction, make a considerable part of the town, and most of them speak English.

Having obtained, my furlow, I immediately set out for Pennsylvania, and arriving at Philadelphia, found the consternation and terror of the inhabitants was greatly increased to what it was when I left them They had made several treaties of friendship with the Indians, who, when well supplied with arms, ammunition, cloaths, and other necessaries, through the pacific measures, and defenceless state of the Philadelphians, soon revolted to the French, and committed great outrages on the back parts of the province, destroying and massacring men, women, and children, and everything that unhappily lay in their way. A few instances of which, together, with the behaviour of the Philadelphians on these occasions, I shall here present the reader with, who, of whatever sect or profession, I am well assured, must condemn the pacific disposition and private factions that then reigned, not only in the Assembly, but among the magistrates; themselves; who were a long time, before they could agree on proper petitions, to rouse the indolent Assembly from the lethargic and inactive condition they absolutely remained in.

For about the middle of October, a large body of Indians, chiefly Shawonese, De-la-wares, &c. fell upon this province, from several quarters, almost at the same instant, murdering, burning, and laying waste all where ever they came; so that in the five counties of Cumberland, York, Lancaster, Berks, and Northampton, which compose more than half the province, nothing but scenes of distraction and desolation were to be seen.

The damages which these counties had sustained by the desertion of plantations, is not to be reckoned up; nor are the miseries of the poor inhabitants to be described; many of whom, though escaping with life, were, without a moment's warning driven from those habitations where they enjoyed every necessary of life, and were then exposed to all the severity of an hard winter; and obliged to solicit their very bread at the cold hand of charity, or perish with hunger under the inclement air,

To these barbarities I have already mentioned, I can't pass over the following, as introductory causes, of the Philadelphians at last withstanding the outrages of the barbarians.

At Guadenhutten, a small Moravian settlement, in Northampton County, the poor, unhappy sufferers, were sitting round their peaceful supper, when the inhuman murderers, muffled in the shades of night, dark, and horrid as the infernal purposes of their diabolic souls, stole upon them, butchered them, scalped them, and consumed their bodies, together, with their horses, their stock, and upwards of sixty head of fat cattle, (intended for the subsistence of the brethren at Bethlehem) all in one general flame; so that next morning furnished only a melancholy spectacle of their mingled ashes.

At the Great Cove in Cumberland at Tulpehockin in Berks, and in several other places, their barbarities were still greater, if possible. Men, women, children, and brute-beasts, shared one common destruction; and where they were not burnt to ashes, their mangled limbs were found promiscuously strewed upon the ground, those appertaining to the human form, scarce to be distinguished from the brute!

But of all the instances of the barbarities I heard of, in these parts, I could not help being most affected with the following—One family, consisting of the husband, his wife and a child, only a few hours old, were all found murdered, and scalped in this manner: The mother stretched on the bed with her new-born child, horribly mangled, and put under her head for a pillow, while the husband lay on the ground, hard-by, with his body ript up, and his bowels laid open.

In another place, a woman with her sucking child, finding that she had fallen into the hands of the enemy, fell flat on her face, prompted by the strong call of nature, to cover and shelter her innocent child with her own body. The accursed savage rushed from his lurking place, struck her in the head with his tomahawk, tore off her scalp, and scoured back into the woods, without observing the child, being apprehensive that he was discovered. The child was found sometime afterwards under the body of its mother and was then alive.

Many of their young women were carried by the savages into captivity, reserved, perhaps, for a worse fate, than those who suffered death in all its horrid shape, and no wonder, since they, were reserved by savages, whose tender mercies, might be accounted more cruel than their very cruelty itself.

Yet, even during all this time, this province (had things been properly ordered) need but, in comparison to her strength, have listed her foot, and crushed all the French Force on their borders; but unused to much undertakings, and bound by non-resisting principles from exciting her strength, and involved in disputes with the proprietaries, they stood still; vainly hoping the French would be so moderate, as to be content with their victory, over Braddock, or at least continue their attacks to Virginia: But they then saw, and felt all this was delusion, and the barbarities of the Indian parties headed by French officers: Notwithstanding all which, they continued in domestic debates, without a soldier in pay, or a penny in the treasury. In short, if the enemy had then had, but 1500 men at the Ohio, and would have attempted it, no rashness could have been perceived in their marching down to the city of Philadelphia.

Thus, stood our affairs on the side of the Ohio, when an old captain of the warriors, in the interest of the Philadelphians, and their ever faithful friend, whose name was Scarrooyda, *alias* Monokatoaby, on the first notice of these misfortunes, came hastening to Philadelphia, together, with Col. Weiser, the provincial interpreter, and two other Indian chiefs. Scarrooyda immediately demanded an audience of the Assembly, who were then sitting, to whom he spoke in a very affecting manner, his speeches being printed, and sold about Philadelphia, I procured one of them, which was as follows.

Brethren,
We are once more come among you, and sincerely condole with you on account of the late bloodshed, and the awful cloud that hangs over you, and over us. Brethren, you may be undoubtedly assured, that these horrid actions were committed by none of those nations that have any fellowship with us, but by certain false-hearted and treacherous brethren. It grieves us more than all our other misfortunes, that any of our good friends, the English should suspect us of having false hearts.
Brethren,
If you were not an infatuated people, we are 300 warriors, firm to your interest; and, if you are so unjust to us, as to retain any doubts of our sincerity, we offer to put our wives, our children, and all we have into your hands to deal with them as seemeth

good to you, if we are found in the least to swerve from you. But, brethren, you must support and assist us, for we are not able to fight alone against the powerful nations who are coming against you; and you must this moment resolve and give us an explicit answer what you will do: For, these nations have sent to desire us, as old friends, either to join them, or get out of their way and shift for ourselves. Alas! Brethren, we are sorry to leave you! We remember the many tokens of your friendship to us; But, what shall we do? We cannot stand alone, and you will not stand with us!—

Brethren

The time is precious. While we are here consulting with you, we know not what may be the fate of our brethren at home. We do therefore, once more invite, and request you to act like men, and be no longer as women, pursuing weak measures, that render your names despicable. If you will put the hatchet, (tomahawk) into our hands, and send out a number of your young men in conjunction with our warriors, and provide the necessary arms, ammunition and provisions, and likewise build some strong houses for the protection of our old men, women, and children, while we are absent in war, we shall soon wipe the tears from your eyes, and make these false-hearted brethren repent their treachery and baseness, towards you, and towards us. But we must at the same time, solemnly assure you, that if you delay any longer to act in conjunction with us, or think, to put us off, as usual, with uncertain hopes, you must not expect to see our faces under this roof any more. We must shift for our own safety, and leave you to the mercy of your enemies, as an infatuated people, upon whom we can have no longer dependance.

The tears flood in the old man's eyes, while he delivered this last part; and no wonder, since the very being of his nation depended upon their joining the enemy, or our enabling them immediately to make head against them.

It was some time, however, before the Assembly could be brought to consent to any vigorous measures for their own defence. The back inhabitants lost all patience at their conduct. 'Till at length the governor exerted his utmost power and procured the militia and money bills to pass. By virtue of the former, the freemen of the province were enabled to form themselves into companies, and each company by a majority of votes, by way of ballot, to chuse its own officers; *viz.* a captain, lieutenant, and ensign; who, if approved of, were to be commissioned by the governor. So that the Philadelphians were at last permitted to rise and arm themselves in their own defence. They accordingly formed themselves into companies; the governor signing to all gentlemen qualified, who had been regularly ballotted, commissions for that purpose.

Captain Davis was one of the first who had a company; and, being desirous of my service, in order to instruct the irregulars in their discipline, obtained from the governor, a certificate to indemnify me from any punishment which might be adjudged by the regiment to which I already belonged; for, without that, I had not gone. Our company, which consisted of 100 men, was not compleated 'till the 24th of December, 1755; when, losing no time, we next morning marched from Philadelphia in high Spirits; resolving to shew as little quarter to the savages, as they had to many of us.

Colonel Armstrong had been more expeditious; for he had raised 280 provincial irregulars, and marched a little time before against the Ohio Morians, but, of him, more hereafter.

We arrived the 16th of December, at Bethlehem, in the forks of the River De-la-ware; where, being kindly received by the Moravians, we loaded six waggons with provisions, and proceeded on to the Apalatian Mountains, or Blue Hills, to a town called Kennorton-head, which the Moravians had deserted on account of the Indians. Fifty of our men, of whom I made one, were ordered before the rest, to see whether the town was destroyed or not, disposing them to the best advantage, we marched on, 'till we came within five miles of the place, which we found standing intire.

Having a very uneven, rugged road to get to it, and not above four men able to go a-breast, we were on a sudden alarmed, by the firing of the flank-guards, which were a little in the rear of our van. The savages briskly returned their fire, and killed the ensign and ten of the men, and wounded several others.

Finding this, I being chief in command (having acted as lieutenant, and received pay as much from my first entrance, for my trouble and duty in learning the company), ordered the men to march on with all expedition to the town, and all the way to keep a running fire on the enemy, as they had fallen on our rear.

We should have got there in very good order, had it not been for a river we had to cross, and the weather being so excessive cold, our cloaths froze to our bodies as soon as we got out of the water. However, with great difficulty we reached the town, and got into the church, with the loss of twenty-seven men. There we made as good preparations for our defence as possibly we could, making a great fire of the benches, seats, and what we could find therein, to dry our cloaths; not esteeming it the least sacrilege or crime, upon much an emergency.

The Indians soon followed us into the town, and surrounding us, tried all methods to burn the church; but our continual firing kept them off for about six hours, 'till our powder and ball were all expended. In the night they set several houses on fire; and, we dreading the consequences of being detained there, resolved to make one bold effort, and push ourselves through the savages forces, which was accordingly done with the most undaunted courage. The enemy fired continually on us during our retreat, and killed many of our men, but in their confusion many of themselves as well; it being so very dark that we were not well able to discern our own party; so that only five of us kept together and got into the woods; the rest, whom we left behind, I doubt fell sacrifices to the savages.

The night being so excessive cold and having but few cloaths with us out of the church, two of my comrades froze to death, before we could reach any inhabited place. In short, we did not get any relief till four o'clock in the morning, when we arrived at an house that lay in the gap of the Blue Hills; were our captain had arrived with the remainder of the men and waggons the day before.

The captain enquiring our success, I gave him the melancholy detail of our unfortunate expedition: upon which, an express was immediately sent to the governor, with the account; who ordered 1600 men to march the next morning for the same place, under the command of General Franklin, not only to bury the dead and build a fort there, but to extirpate the savages who infested these parts, and were too powerful for our small number under Captain Davis.

The remainder of our little party were now building a fort at the place where we lay, for our defence, 'till more assistance should arrive; for we were under continual apprehensions of the Indians pursuing and attacking us again.

On the 9th of January, 1756, we were reinforced by General franklin and his body; and the next day set out again for Kennorton-head; where, when we arrived, to our great consternation, we found little occasion to bury our unhappy comrades, the swine (which in that country are vastly numerous in the woods) having devoured their bodies, and nothing but bones strewed up and down were to be seen. We there built a fort in the place where the old church had stood and gave it the name of Fort Allen; this was finished in six days, and in so good a manner, that 100 men would make great resistance against a much greater number of Indians.

On the 18th, 1400 of us were ordered about fifteen miles distant from thence, on the frontiers of the province; where we built another fort called, Fort-Norris. In our way thither, we found six men scalped and murdered in a most cruel manner. By what we could discern, they had made a vigorous defence, the barrels and stocks of their guns, being broke in pieces, and themselves cut and mangled in a terrible manner.

From thence, we were ordered to march towards a place called, The Minisinkes, but this journey proved longer than we were aware of. The Indians committing great outrages in these parts, having burnt and destroyed all the houses, &c. in our way: These tragic actions caused us to divide ourselves into several parties who were ordered divers ways, to cut off as many of these savages as possible.

The day after this scheme was put into execution, we met with a small party, which we put to the rout, killing fourteen of them. We then made all possible dispatch to save some houses we saw on fire, but on our nearer approach, found our endeavours in vain: John Swisher and his family, having been before scalped, and burnt to ashes in his own house. On the following night, the house of James Wallis underwent the same fate; himself, wife, seven children, and the rest of his family, being scalped and burnt therein.

The houses and families of Philip Green and Abraham Nairn, suffered in the like manner. Nor did the cruelty of these barbarians stop here, but attacked the dwelling-house of George Hunter, Esq; a gentleman of considerable worth, and a Justice of the Peace, who made a brave resistance, and rather than fall into the hands of these miscreants, chose to meet death in the flames; which he, his wife, and all his houshold consisting of sixteen in number, did with the utmost bravery, before any assistance could be received from our general, who had dispatched 500 of us for that purpose, on an express being sent to him that morning.

From thence we marched to the Minisinkes and built Fort-Morris. On the 9th of March we set out with 1000 men to the head of the Minisinkes and built another fort, which we named Franklin, in honour of our general. All which forts we garrisoned with as many men as we could possibly spare.

After this, we were daily employed in scouring the woods from fort to fort, of these noxious creatures, the Indians, and in getting as much of the corn together as we could find, to prevent the savages from having any benefit therefrom.

Notwithstanding our vigilance, these villains on the 15th attacked the house of James Graham, but by Providence, he with his wife, who had just laid in, and her young infant in her arms, (with nothing about her but her shift) made their escape to Fort-Allen, about fifteen miles distant. The child perished by the way, and it was matter of wonder to the whole garrison to find either of them alive; indeed, they were in a deplorable condition, and we imagined they would expire every moment. The wife, however, to our great astonishment, recovered, but the husband did not survive above six hours after their arrival.

The house of Isaac Cook suffered by the flames, himself, his wife, and eight children, being scalped and burnt in it.

Tedious and shocking would it be to enumerate half the murders, conflagrations, and outrages, committed by these hellish *infidels*. Let it suffice therefore, that from the year 1753, when they first began their barbarities, they had murdered, burnt, scalped, and destroyed, above 3500 souls; above 1000 whereof, were unhappy inhabitants of the western parts of Philadelphia. Men, women, and children, fell alike a prey to these savages: No regard being had by them to the tender entreaties of an affectionate parent for a beloved child, or the infant's prayers, in behalf of his aged father and mother. Such are the miserable calamities attendant on schemes for gratifying the ambition of a tyrannic monarch, like France, or the weak contrivances and indolent measures, of blundering ministers and negociators—.

The time of my furlow at length expiring, I prepared to set out for my regiment. Having a recommendatory letter from General Franklin to Major Kinnair, as to my services, I marched forward for New-York: Where being arrived, I waited on the major; and, after giving him an account of all our transactions, and the hardships and labours we had gone through, I was dismissed.

After some stay there, I was ordered to proceed on my march for Oswego once more. But, before I go further with my own affairs, I shall just recount the result of those provincials, who went, as I mentioned before, to quell the savages, under the command of Colonel Armstrong.

He having under his command 280 provincials, destined against the Ohio Morians, against whom nothing had been attempted, notwithstanding their frequent incursions and murders, penetrated 140 miles through the woods, from Fort Shirley, on Juniata River, to Kittanning, an Indian town on the Ohio, about twenty-five miles above Fort Du Quesne, belonging to the French. He soon joined the advanced party at the Beaver-dams; and, on the fourth evening after, being within six miles of Kittanning, the scouts discovered a fire in the road, and reported that there were but three or four Indians at it. At that time, it was not thought proper to attempt surprising these Indians, lest, if one should escape, the town might be alarmed: Lieutenant Hogg, therefore, with twelve men, was left to watch them, with orders not to fall upon them 'till daybreak; and our forces turned out of the path, to pass their fire, without disturbing them.

About three in the morning, having been guided by the whooping of the Indian warriors, at a dance in the town, they reached the river at about 100 perches below it. As soon as day appeared, the attack began; Captain Jacobs, chief of the Indians, gave the war-whoop, and defended his house bravely through the loop-holes in the logs. The Indians generally refusing quarter, Colonel Armstrong ordered their houses to be set on fire, which was done by the officers and soldiers with great alacrity. On this, some burst out of the houses, and attempted to reach the river, but were instantly shot down.

Captain Jacobs, in getting out of a window, was shot and scalped, as were also his squaw, and a lad they called the king's son. The Indians had a number of spare arms in their houses loaded, which went off in quick succession, as the fire came to them; and quantities of gunpowder, which had been stored in every house, blew up from time to time, throwing their bodies into the air.

Eleven English prisoners were released, who informed the colonel, that, that very day, two *batteaux* of Frenchmen, with a large party of De-la-ware and French Indians, were to have joined Captain Jacobs, to march and take Fort Shirley, and that twenty-four warriors had set out before them the preceding evening; which proved to be the party that had kindled the fire the preceding night; for our people returning, found Lieutenant Hogg wounded in three places; and learned, that he had attacked the supposed party of three or four at the fire, but found them too strong for him. He killed three of them, however, at the first fire, and fought them an hour; when, having lost three of his men, the rest as he lay wounded, abandoned him and fled, the enemy pursuing.

Lieutenant Hogg died soon after of his wounds.

Enough of these two expeditions has been said; nor, can I well tell which of the two was most successful, both losing more of their own men than they killed of the enemy.

A little retrospections again on the actions and behaviour of the Philadelphians, and the other provinces and places in conjunction with them, may here be something necessary: For, when I arrived at Philadelphia, I found, that however melancholy their situation had been of late, this good effect had been obtained, that the most prejudiced and ignorant individual was feelingly convinced of the necessity of vigorous measures; and, besides national and public views, then, the more prevailing ones of revenge and self-interest gave a spur to their counsels. They were accordingly raising men with the utmost expedition; and had, before the end of the summer, a considerable number, though not equal to what they could furnish, having at least 45,000 men in Pennsylvania able to fight.

And, pursuant to agreement, some months before, the four governments of New-England, in conjunction with New-York (which last furnished 1300) had now assembled 8000 men (for the attack of Fort Frederic) at Albany, 150 miles N. of New-York, and about 130 from Crown-Point, under the command of General Winslow. But many people dreading the cruelty of the French, were not so very eager to join them, this year as the last; an impress therefore of part of the militia, was ordered in New-York Government. To prevent which, subscriptions were set on foot, to engage volunteers by high bounties; so loath were they, that some got nine or twelve pounds sterling to inlist.

The 44th, 48th, 50th, and 51st Regiments of Great Britain were destined for the campaign on the Great Lake Ontario, and mostly marched for Oswego, thence to be carried over in 200 great whale-boats, which were then at the lake, and were built at Schenectady on Mohawk's River, and were long round and light; as the *batteaux*, being flat-bottomed and small, would not answer the navigation of the lake, where the waves were often very high. They were then, alas! intended to attack Fort Frontenac, mentioned before, and the other French forts on the lake. Upwards of 2000 *batteau*-men were employed to navigate the *batteaux*, each a ton burthen, laden with provisions and stores from Albany up the Mohawk's River, then through Oneyda Lake and River, down to Oswego. There were likewise 300 sailors hired and gone up from New-York (as I found, when I arrived there) to navigate the four armed ships on the lake, built there, as I have before-mentioned, the last year, for the king's service, and two others were then building; Smiths, carpenters, and other artificers, having gone there for that purpose some weeks before. Such were the preparations and armaments for this campaign, but how fruitless, to our great disgrace, were soon known all over the world!

I shall not trouble the reader with a long account, of a long march I had to take from New-York to Oswego, to join my regiment, suffice it therefore, that I arrived there about the middle of July) but in my march thither with some recruits, we joined Colonel Broadstreet, at Albany, and on the 6th of May, at the Great Carrying Place, had a skirmish with the French and Indians, wherein several were killed and wounded on both sides; of the latter I made one, receiving a shot through my left-hand, which intirely disabled my third and fourth fingers; and having no hospital, or any conveniences for the sick there, I was after having my hand dressed in a wretched manner, sent with the next *batteaux* to Albany to get it cured.

As soon as I was well, I set forwards for Oswego. And, when arrived there, I began to make what observations I could, as to the alterations that had been made since my departure in the month of October, preceding. The works of Oswego, at this time, consisted of three forts, *viz*. The Old Fort, built many years before, whole chief strength was a weak stone-wall, about two feet thick, so ill cemented, that it could not resist the force of a four pound ball, and situated on the east-side of the harbour; the two other forts called, Fort-Ontario and Fort-George, (or Fort-Rascal a name given the latter by the soldiers, in honour to Lieutenant F-tz-f-m-ds, the commanding officer at the building of it) were each of them at the distance of about 450 yards from the Old Fort, and situated on two eminences, which commanded it; both these, as I have already observed, were begun to be built last year upon plans, which made them defensible against musquetry, and cannon, of three or four pound ball only; the time not allowing works of a stronger nature to be then undertaken.

For our defence against large cannon, we entirely depended on a superior naval force upon the lake, which might have put it in our power to prevent the French from bringing heavy artillery against the place, as that could only be done by water-carriage, which is my opinion as well as many others.(If the naval force had but done their duty Oswego might have been ours to this very day, and intirely cut off communication of the French from Canada to the Ohio; but if I would insist on this as the particulars require, I perhaps should affront someone and injure myself all to no purpose or of any beneficial service to recall our former losses; for that reason I shall deferr enlarging on the subject although at the same time I can give very good circumstances to maintain my argument if required.)

A day or two after being at Oswego, the fort was alarmed by hearing a firing; when on dispatching proper scouts, it was found to be the French and Indians engaging the *batteau*-men and sailors convoying the provisions to Oswego, from one river to another. On this a detachment of 500 men were ordered out in pursuit of them, whereof I was one. We had a narrow pass in the woods to go through where we were attacked by a great number of Indians, when a desperate fight began on both sides, that lasted above two hours. However, at last we gained a compleat victory, and put them intirely to the rout, killing fourteen of them, and wounding above forty. On our side we had but two men killed and six wounded. Many more would have been killed of both parties had it not been for the thickness of the woods.

I cannot here omit recounting a most singular transaction that happened during this my second time of being there, which, though scarce credible, is absolutely true, and can be testified by hundreds, who knew, and have often seen the man. In short. One of the 50th Regiment, an Irishman, being placed as centinel over the rum which had arrived, and being curious to know its goodness, pierced the cask, and drank 'till he was quite intoxicated; when, not knowing what he did, he rambled from his post, and fell asleep a good way from the garrison.

An Indian scouting that way for prey, (as is conjectured) met him, and made free with his scalp, which he plucked and carried off. The serjeant in the morning, finding him prostrate on his face, and seeing his scalp off, imagined him to be dead; but on his nearer approach, and raising him from the ground, the fellow awaked from the found sleep he had been in, and asked the serjeant what he wanted. The serjeant quite surprised at the strange behaviour of the fellow, interrogated him, how he came there in that condition? He replied, He could not tell; but that he got very drunk: and rambled he knew not whither. The serjeant advised him to prepare for death, not having many hours to live, as he had lost his scalp. Arrah, my Dear, now (cries he), and are you joking me? for he really knew nothing of his being served in the manner he was and would not believe any accident had happened to him, 'till seeing his cloaths bloody, he felt his head, and found it to be too true, as well as having a cut from his mouth to his ear. He was immediately carried before the governor, who asking him, how he came to leave his post? He replied, that being very thirsty, he had broached a cask of rum, and drank about a pint, which made him drunk. but if his Honour would forgive him, he'd never be guilty of the like again.

The governor told him, it was very probable he never would, as he was now no better than a dead man. However, the surgeons dressed his head there, as well as they could, and then lent him in a *batteau* to Albany, where he was perfectly cured; and, to the great surprise of every body, was living when I left the country. This, though so extraordinary and unparalelled an affair, I aver to be true having several times seen the man after this accident happened to him. How his life was preserved seems a miracle, as no instance of the like was ever known.

I had forgot to mention, that, before I left Albany the last time, upon Colonel Broadstreet's arrival there, in his way to Oswego, with the provisions and forces, consisting of about 500 whaleboats and *batteaux*, intended for the campaign on the Great Lake Ontario, mentioned before, I joined his corps and proceeded on with the *batteaux*, &c.

Going up the River Onondaga towards Oswego, the *batteau*-men were on the 29th of June, attacked near the falls, about nine miles from Oswego, by 500 French and Indians, who killed and wounded seventy-four of our men, before we could get on shore, which, as soon as we did, the French were routed, with the loss of 130 men killed, and several wounded, whom we took prisoners,

Had we known of their lying in ambush, or of their intent to attack us, the victory would have been much more complete on our side, as the troops, Colonel Broadstreet commanded, were regular, well disciplined and in tolerable health, whereas the French, by a long passage at sea, and living hard after their arrival at Canada, were much harrased and fatigued.

However, we got all safe to Oswego with the *batteaux* and provisions, together, with rigging and stores for the large vessels, excepting twenty-four four cannon, six pounders, that were then at the Great Carrying Place; which Colonel Broadstreet was to bring with him, upon his next Passage, from Schenectady; to which place, as soon as he had delivered to the quarter-master all the stores he had under his care, he was ordered to return with the *batteaux*: and men to receive the orders of Major-General Ambercrombie. In his return from Schenectady, 'twas expected that Halket's and Dunbar's Regiments would have come with him, in order to take Fort Frontenac, and the other French forts on the Lake Ontario. But, alas! as schemes for building castles in the air, always prove abortive, for want of proper architecture and foundation, so did this scheme of ours, for want of a due knowledge of our own situation!

On the arrival of these forces, a new brigantine and sloop were fitted out; and about the same time a large snow was also launched and rigged, and only waited for her guns and some running rigging, which they expected every day by Colonel Broadstreet; and had he returned in time with the cannon and *batteau*-men under his command, the French would not have dared to have appeared on the lake, but Colonel Broadstreet happened to be detained with the *batteaux* at Schenectady for above a month waiting for the Forty-Fourth Regiment to march with him.

★★★★★★

The dilatoriness of this embarkation at Schenectady cannot be imputed to Colonel Broadstreet because General Shirley waited with impatience for the arrival of Lord Louden Campbell from England; and when his Lordship landed at New York, he, in a few days after, proceeded to Albany where his Lordship took the command of the army from General Shirley and upon comparing and considering how bad a situation his forces and the different governments upon the continent were in, his Lordship, with the advice of several other experienced officers, though himself not in a condition to proceed upon any enterprise for that season, no farther than to maintain our ground at Oswego for which purpose Colonel Broadstreet was immediately ordered off with the *batteaux* and provisions as also the aforesaid regiments, but before Broadstreet arrived at the great carrying place, Oswego was taken with all the ships of war, although our naval force was far superior to the French.

★★★★★★

Before I relate the attack on Oswego, I shall review a little what the French were doing during these our dilatory, pompous proceedings.

The Marquis de Vaudreuil, Governor and Lieutenant-General of New-France, whilst he provided for the security of the frontiers of Canada, was principally attentive to the lakes. Being informed that we were making vast preparations at Oswego for attacking Niagara and Frontenac, he took and razed in the month of March, the fort where we had formed our principal magazine, and in June following, destroyed, on the river of Chonegan or Oswego, some of our vessels, and made some prisoners. The success of these two expeditions encouraged him to act offensively and to attack us at Oswego. This settlement they pretended, and still insist on, to be an incroachment, or invasion, which we had made in a time of profound peace, and against which, they said, they had continually remonstrated, during our blundering, negotiating Lawyer's Residence at France. It was at first, say they, only a fortified magazine; but in order to avail themselves of its advantageous situation in the centre almost of the French Colonies, the English added from time to time several new works, and made it consist of three forts as above described.

The troops designed for this expedition by the French amounted to near 5000, men, 1300 of which were regulars. To prevent his design being discovered, M. de Vaudreuil pretended, in order the better to deceive us, who had so long before been blind, that he was providing only for the security of Niagara and Frontenac. The Marquis de Montcalm, who commanded on this occasion, arrived the 29th of July at Fort Frontenac; and having given the necessary directions for securing his retreat, in case it should have been rendered inevitable, by a superior force; sent out two vessel, one of twelve, and the other of sixteen guns, to cruise off Oswego, and posted a chain of Canadians and Indians on the road between Oswego and Albany, to intercept our couriers. All the forces, and the vessels, with the artillery and stores, being arrived in the Bay of Nixoure, the place of general rendezvous, the Marquis de Montcalm ordered his advanced guard to proceed to a creek called, Anse aux Cabannes, three Leagues from Oswego, But,—

To carry on this account the more accurate and intelligible to the reader, I shall recite the actions of the French and ourselves together, as a more clear and succinct manner, of making those unacquainted with the art of war more sensible of this important affair.

Colonel Mercer, who was then commanding officer of the garrison at Oswego, having on the 6th of August, intelligence of a large encampment of French and Indians, about twelve miles off, dispatched one of the schooners, with an account of it to Captain Bradley, who was then on a cruise with the large brigantine and two sloops; at the same time, desiring him to cruise as far to the eastward as he could, and to endeavour to prevent the approach of the French on the lake; but meeting the next day with a most violent gale of wind, the large brigantine was drove on shore near Oswego in attempting to get into the harbour; of which misfortune, the Indians immediately gave M.

de Montcalm, the French general, notice, who took that opportunity of transporting his heavy cannon to within about a mile and a half of the fort, which he could not otherwise have done.

For on the 10th, the first division of the French being arrived at Anse aux Cabannes, at two o'clock in the morning; the van-guard proceeded at four in the afternoon, by land, across woods to another creek within half a league of Oswego, in order to favour the debarkation. At midnight their first division repaired to this creek, and there erected a battery on the Lake Ontario.

Colonel Mercer, in the morning of the10th, on some canoes being seen to the eastward, sent out the small schooner to make discovery of what they were; she was scarce half a mile from the fort, before she discovered a very large encampment, close under the opposite point, being the first division of the French troops above-mentioned. On this, the two sloops (the large brigantine being still on shore) were sent out with orders, if possible, to annoy the enemy; but this was to no purpose; the enemy's cannon being large and well pointed, hulled the vessels almost every shot, while theirs fell short of the shore.

This day and the next, the enemy were employed in making gabions, fancissons, and fascines, and in cutting a road cross the woods, from the place of landing, to the place where the trenches were to be opened; And, the second division of the enemy arriving on the 11th, in the morning, with the artillery and provisions, the same were immediately landed without any opposition. Though dispositions were made for opening the trenches on the 10th at night, it was midnight before they could begin the trench, which was rather a parallel, of about 100 *toisies* in front, and opened at the distance of 90 *toises* from the soss of Fort Ontario, in ground embarassed with trunks of trees. (A *toise* is a French measure and contains about two fathoms or six feet in length.)

About five in the morning, of the 11th, this parallel was finished, and the workmen began to erect the batteries. Thus, was the place invested by about 5000 men and thirty-two pieces of cannon, from twelve to eighteen pounders, besides several large brass mortars and hoyets, (among which artillery, was part of General Braddock's) About noon, they began the attack of Fort Ontario, with small arms, which was briskly returned. All this day the garrison was employed on the west-side of the river in repairing the batteries on the south-side of the Old Fort.

The next morning, (the 12th), at daybreak, a large number of

French *batteaux* were discovered on the lake, in their way to join the enemy's camp; on which, Colonel Mercer ordered the two sloops to be again sent out, with directions to get between the *batteaux* and the camp, but before our vessels came up, the *batteaux* had secured themselves under the fire of their cannon.

In the evening a detachment was made of 100 men of the 50th (General Pepperell's) Regiment, and 126 of the New-Jersey Provincials, under the command of Col. Schuyler to take possession of the fort on the hill, to the west ward of the Old Fort, and under the direction of the engineer, Mr. Mackeller, were to put it into the best state of defence they could; in which work, they were employed all the following night.

The enemy on the east-side continued their approaches to Fort Ontario, but with their utmost efforts for a long time they could not bring their cannon to bear on it. However, drawing their cannon with great expedition, next morning, (the 13th), about ten o'clock, to a battery erected within sixty yards from it; they played them very hotly on the garrison, notwithstanding the constant fire kept on them, and the loss of their principal engineer, who was killed in the trenches.

A Council of War, was immediately held by the officers of General Pepperell's Regiment, who observing the mortars were beginning to play, concluded it most advisable to quit Fort Ontario, and join Col. Schuyler's Regimen: at Fort George, (or Fort Rascal); and an account of this latter battery being sent to Col. Mercer by the *commandant* of the enemy, ordering him to evacuate the fort, they accordingly did, about three in the afternoon, destroying the cannon ammunition, and provisions therein, and managed their retreat so as to pass the river, and join the troops at the west-side without the loss of a man. These troops being about 370, were immediately ordered to join Col. Schuyler, which they accordingly did, and were employed all the following night in completing the works of that fort.

M. Montcalm immediately took possession of Fort Ontario, and ordered the communication of the parallel to be continued to the banks of the river, where, in the beginning of the night, they began a grand-battery, placed in much a manner, that it could not only batter Fort Oswego, and the way from thence to Fort George, but also the intrenchment of Oswego.

In the morning, of the 13th, the large brigantine being off the rocks and repaired, a detachment of eighty men of the garrison was put on board her and the two sloops, in order to go out immediately, but the wind continuing to blow directly into the harbour, rendered it impossible for them to get out before the place was surrendered. This night, as well as the night before, parties of the enemy's irregulars made several attempts to surprise the advanced guards and centinels on the west-side of the river but did not succeed in any of them.

The enemy were employed this night in bringing up their cannon and raising a battery. On our side, we kept a constant fire of cannon and shells from the Old Fort and works about it. The cannon which most annoyed the enemy, were four pieces, which we reversed on the platform of an earthen work, which surrounded the Old Fort, and which was intirely enfiladed by the enemy's battery on the opposite shore: In this situation without the least cover, the train, assisted by a detachment of fifty of Shirley's Regiment behaved remarkably well.

At daybreak, on the 14th, we renewed our fire on that part of the opposite shore, where we had the evening before, observed the enemy at work in raising the battery.

The enemy in three columns, consisting of 2500 Canadians and savages, crossed the river, some by swimming, and others by wading, with the water up to their middles, in order to invest and attack the Old Fort. This bold action, by which they intirely cut off the communication of the two forts; the celerity with which the works were carried on, in ground that we thought impracticable; a continual return of our fire from a battery of ten cannon, twelve pounders; and their preparing a battery of mortars and hoyets, made Colonel Mercer think it adviseable (he not knowing their numbers) to order Colonel Schuyler, with 500 men to oppose them, which would accordingly have been carried into execution, and consequently every man of the 500 cut off, had not Colonel Mercer been killed by a cannon-ball a few minutes after. (The resolution of this valiant colonel seemed to be determined to oppose the French to the last extremity and to maintain his ground at Oswego but his final doom came on so unexpectedly that his loss was universally regretted.)

About ten o'clock, the enemy's battery were ready to play; at which time, all our places of defence were either enfiladed, or ruined by the constant fire of their cannon; Fort Rascal or George, in particular, having at that time no guns, and scarce in a condition to defend itself against small arms; with 2500 irregulars on our backs, ready to storm us on that side and 2000 of their regulars as ready to land in our front, under the fire of their cannon. Whereas—;

Fort Rascal might have been made a very defensible fortress, lying on a hill, and the ascent to it so steep, that had an enemy been ever so numerous, they must have suffered greatly in an attempt to storm it. Why it was not in a better state, it becomes not me to say, but matters were so.

And in this situation, we were, when Colonel Littlehales, who succeeded Colonel Mercer in the command, called a Council of War, who were, with the engineers, unanimously of opinion, that the works were no longer tenable; and that it was by no means prudent to risque a storm with much unequal numbers.

The chamade was accordingly ordered to be beat, and the firing ceased on both sides, yet the French were not idle, but improved this opportunity to bring up more cannon, and advance the main body of their troops within musquet-shot of the garrison and prepared everything for a storm. Two officers were sent to the French general, to know what terms he would give; the Marquis de Montcalm made answer, that they might expect whatever terms were consistent with the service of His Most Christian Majesty: He accordingly agreed to the following:

Article 1. The garrison shall surrender prisoners of war, and shall be concluded from hence to Montreal, where they shall be treated with humanity, and every one shall have treatment agreeable to their respective ranks, according to the custom of war.

Article 2. Officers, and soldiers, and individuals, shall have their baggage and cloaths, and they shall be allowed to carry them along with them.

Article 3. They shall remain prisoners of war until they are exchanged.

Given at the Camp before Oswego,
August 14, 1756,
Montcalm,

By virtue of this capitulation, the garrison surrendered prisoners of war, and the French immediately took possession of Oswego and Fort George, which they intirely destroyed, agreeable to their orders, after removing the artillery, warlike-stores, and provisions.

But, to describe the plunder, havock, and devastation, made by the French, as well as the savages, who rushed in by thousands, is impossible. For notwithstanding the Christian promise made by the general of His Most Christian Majesty, they all behaved more like infernal beings, than creatures in human shapes. In short, not contented with surrendering upon the above terms, they scalped and killed all the sick and wounded in the hospitals; mangling, butchering, cutting, and chopping off their heads, arms, legs, &c. with spades, hatchets, and other such diabolical instruments; treating the whole garrison with the utmost cruelty, notwithstanding the repeated intercessions of the defenceless sick and wounded for mercy; which were, indeed, piteous enough to have softened any heart possessed of the minutest particle of humanity!

Here, I cannot help observing, that, notwithstanding what has been laid of the behaviour of the officers of these (the 50th and 51st) Regiments, I must, with the greatest truth, give them the characters of brave, but, I wish I could say, experienced, men; every one of them, that I had an opportunity of observing, during the siege, behaving with the utmost courage and intrepidity. Nor, in this place, can I omit particularly naming Captain James Campbell, Captain Archibald Hamilton and Ensigns Evern and Hickes, who assisted with the greatest spirit and alacrity, the private men at the great guns. But, for such an handful of men as our garrisons then consisted of, and the works being of such a weak and defenceless nature, to have made a longer defence, or have caused the enemy to raise the siege, would have been much an instance, as England, for many years, never hath experienced; and, I am afraid, will be many more, before it will, for reasons that are too obvious.

The quantity of stores and ammunition we then had in the three forts, is almost incredible. But of what avail are powder and ball, if walls and ramparts are defenceless, and men insufficient to make use of them. In short, the French, by taking this place, made themselves masters of the following things; all which were immediately sent to Frontenac, *viz.* seven pieces of brass cannon, nineteen, fourteen, and twelve pounders; forty-eight iron cannon, of nine, six, five, three, and two pounders; a brass mortar of nine inches four-twelfths, and thirteen others of six and three inches; forty-seven swivel guns; 23,000*lb.* of gun-powder; 8000*lb.* of lead and musket-balls; two thousand nine hundred and fifty cannonballs; one hundred and fifty bombs, of nine inches, and three hundred more, of six inches diameter; one thousand four hundred and seventy-six grenadoes; one thousand and seventy musquets; a vessel pierced for eighteen guns; the brigantine of sixteen, a *goeletta* of ten, a *batteau* of ten, (the sloops already mentioned) another of eight guns, a skiff of eighteen swivels, and another burnt upon the stocks; seven hundred and four barrels of biscuit, one thousand three hundred and eighty-six firkins of bacon and beef; seven hundred and twelve firkins of meal; thirty-two live oxen; fifteen hogs, and a large sum of money in the military chest, amounting, as the French said, to eighteen thousand five hundred: and ninety-four *livres.*

On this 16th, they began to remove us; the officers were first sent in *batteaux,* and two hundred soldiers a day afterwards, 'till the whole were gone; being carried first to Montreal and from thence to Quebec. Our duty in the *batteaux,* 'till we reached the first place, was very hard and slavish: And, during the time we were upon the lake, or River St. Lawrence, it appeared to me, very easy and feasible, for Commodore Bradley, (had he thought proper) to have destroyed all the enemy's *batteaux,* and have prevented them from ever landing their cannon, within forty miles of the fort. But he knew his own reasons for omitting this piece of service best.

Our party arriving at Montreal, in Canada, on the 28th; we were that night secured in the fort, as were the rest as they came in. The French used various means to win some of our troops over to their interest, or at least to do their work in the fields, which many refused, among whom was myself; who were then conduced on board a ship and sent to Quebec, where, on arriving the 5th of September, we were lodged in a jail, and kept for the space of one month.

During this our captivity, many of our men, rather than lye in prison, went out to work and assist the French in getting in their harvest; they having then, scarce any people left in that country, but old men, women, and children, so that the corn was continually falling into the stubble for want of hands to reap it: But, those who did go out, in two or three days, chose confinement again, rather than liberty on such terms, being almost starved, having nothing in the country to live on but dry bread, whereas, we in the prison, were each of us allowed two pounds of bread, and half a pound of meat a day, and otherwise treated with a good deal of humanity.

Eighteen soldiers, were all the guard they had to place over us, who being greatly fatigued with hard duty, and dreading our rising on them, (which had we had any arms, we might easily have done, and ravaged the country round, as it was then entirely defenceless) and the town's people themselves fearing the consequences of having such a number of men in a place where provisions were at that time very scarce and dear, they thought sending us away, the most eligible way of keeping themselves from famine, and accordingly put five hundred of us on board a vessel for England.

But, before I continue the account of our voyage home to our native country, I shall just make a short retrospection on the consequences which attended the loss of Oswego, as appeared to us and the rest of the people at Quebec, who knew that part of America, to which, this important place was a safeguard.

As soon as Oswego was taken, our only communication from the Mohawk's River, to the Lake Oneida, was stopped up, by filling the place at Wood's Creek with great logs and trees for many miles together. A few, days afterwards, the forts at the Great Carrying Place, and then our most advanced post into the country of the Six Nations, which I have before given a short account of, (and where there were at that time above three thousand men, including one thousand two hundred *batteau*-men; and which still gave the Six Nations some hopes that we would defend their country against the French) were abandoned and destroyed, and the troops, which were under the command of General Webb, retreated to Burnet's Field, and left the country and the Six Nations to the mercy of the enemy.

The French, immediately after the taking of Oswego, demolished (as is said before) all the works there, and returned with their prisoners and booty to Trinonderoge, to oppose our provincial army under the command of General Winslow, who had shamefully been kept, in expectation of the dilatory arrival of Lord Loudon, from attacking Crown-Point, while the enemy were weak, and it was easily in our power to have beat them.

The consequences of the destruction of our forts at the Great Carrying Place, and General Webb retreating to Burnet's Field, is now, Alas! too apparent to every one acquainted with American affairs. The Indians of the Six Nations, undoubtedly, looked upon it as abandoning them and their country to the French; for they plainly saw that we had no strong hold near them, and that (by the place at Wood's Creek, being stopped up), we could not, if we would, afford them any assistance at Onondaga, Cayuga, and in the Senekea's Country, which were their chief castles: That, the forts begun by us in those countries, were left unfinished, and therefore could be of no use to them; and which, if we had kept the Carrying Place, we might have finished, and given them still hopes of our being able to defend.

But, despairing of our being further serviceable to them, those Iroquois, who were before our friends, and some of the others, have indeed deserted us, and the consequence of such their junction with the French, has begun already to be felt by us in the loss of Fort-George on Lake Sacrament.

The fine country on the Mohawk's River, down to Albany, was by this step left open to the ravages of the enemy, and an easy passage opened to the French and their Indians, into the provinces of Pennsylvania and New-Jersey, by the way of Susquehanna and De-la-ware Rivers, which were before covered by our settlements on the Mohawk's River, and the Six Nations.

★★★★★★

I shall here give the best description of the Indians, their way of living, &c. in my power

It is difficult to guess what may be the number of the Indians scattered up and down our back settlements; but, if their own account be true, they amount to many thousands. Be this, however, as it will, they are not to be feared merely on account of their numbers; other circumstances conspire to make them formidable. The English inhabitants, though numerous, are extended over a vast tract of land, 500 leagues in length on the sea shore, and, for the most part have fixed habitations, the easiest and shortest passages to which the Indians, by continually hunting in the woods, are perfectly well acquainted with; and, as their way of making war is by sudden attacks upon exposed places, as soon as they have done the mischief at one place they retire, and either go home by different routs, or go to some distant place to renew their attacks.

If they are pursued, it is a chance if they do not ensnare their pursuers; or, if that be not the case, as soon as they have gained the rivers, so dexterous are they in the use of their canoes; that they presently get out of reach. It is to no purpose to follow them to their settlements; for they can, without much disadvantage, quit their old habitations and betake themselves to new ones; add to this, that they can be suddenly drawn together from any distance, as they can find their subsistence, in travailing, from their guns.

No people on earth have a higher sense of liberty or stronger affection for their relations. When offended, they are the implacably vindictive enemies on earth; for no distance place or space of time will abate their resentment but they will watch every opportunity of revenge and when such an opportunity offers, they revenge themselves effectually.

They will sooner sacrifice their own lives for the sake of liberty than humble themselves to the arbitrary control of any person whatsoever. In battle they never submit and will rather die than be taken prisoners.

Our late transactions in America testify that the friendship of the Indians is to be desired; and the only way to maintain a friendly correspondence with them is by making such propositions to them as will secure their liberties, and be agreeable to their expectations; and not only by keeping these propositions inviolable as well in time of peace as in time of war, but also renewing our treaties with them from time to time; for they are very jealous and tenacious of an affront or neglect They are very proud, and love to be esteemed. In time of peace they live upon what they get of the people, for which they barter skins, furs, &c. Their clothing, and everything else they want, such as arms, they get in the same manner. In war time, they live upon what they can procure by their gun, and if that fails, upon roots, fruits, herbs, and other vegetables of the natural produce of the earth.

They have never the foresight to provide necessaries for themselves; they look only to the present moment and leave tomorrow to provide for itself. They eat of every wild beast which they kill, without distinction. They always prefer game to vegetables; but when they cannot get venison, they live on roots, fruits, and herbs. They destroy a great deal of meat at a time, when they have it in their power, and when they leave any, be it ever such a great quantity; it is ten to one if any of them will take the trouble to carry a pound of it, but will rather leave it behind them; yet notwithstanding this extravagance, such are their tempers, and they are so inured to hardships, that, if they cannot conveniently get at food, they can, and actually do fast sometimes for near a week together, and yet are as active as if they had lived regularly.

All their spare time is taken up in contriving schemes to succeed in their intended expeditions. They can never be taken in pursuit by any European. They will travel 70 miles a day, and continue for months together, as I have reason to know from experience; and they are sure to bring their pursuers into a snare, if they are not wary, and have some Indians on their sides to beat the bushes. When they are overtaken with sleep, they light a great fire, which prevents the wild beasts from falling upon them; for wild beasts have a natural aversion to fire; nor is it easy for an enemy to discover them in this condition, for the country is one continued tract of thick wood, overgrown with brushwood, so that you cannot see the fire till you be within a few yards of it. They having nothing covering them from the inclemency of the weather, but a blanket put upon them, something in the shape of a Highlander's plaid.

And further, to prevent their being long observed by their pursuers, or to be seen too soon when they have a mind to attack any plantation, they paint themselves of the same colour with the trees among which they hide themselves.

When they are to attack a plantation, they never come out till night, and then they rush instantly upon the farms, &c., and destroy everything, as well men, women and children, as beasts; then they fall to plunder, and return to their lurking holes till another opportunity of plunder happens, when they renew their attack in the same manner; so that, if some method is not taken to draw them into our interest, our colonies will be in a continual alarm, and the country will soon become desolate; for nobody will venture their lives to settle on the back parts, unless the Indians are our friends.

The Indian manner of fighting is quite different from that of other nations. They industriously avoid all open engagements; and, besides ambushcades, their principal way is bush-fighting, in the exercise of which they are very dexterous; for the back country being one continued wood except some few spots cleared for the purpose of husbandly by our back settlers, the Indians squat themselves down behind the trees, and fire their muskets at the enemy; if the enemy advance, then they retreat behind other trees, and fire in the same manner; and, as they are good marksmen, they never fire in vain, whereas their pursuers seldom bit.

Notwithstanding, the political schemes of France are nearly brought to a period; yet, if the Indians are not satisfied with the conclusion of peace between us and the French as to America; I mean, unless they are fairly dealt with, we shall gain but little by all our conquests; for it is the friendship of the Indians that will make Canada valuable to us. We have already more lands than we are able to manage; but the advantage, nay, the necessity of keeping Canada I have already shown, and therefore I shall go on with my account of the Indians.

When last in London, I remember to have heard some coffee-house politicians, chagrined at the devastations they made on our back settlements, say that it would be an easy matter to root out the savages by clearing the ground. I answer, that the task may seem easy to them, but the execution of such a scheme on such a tract of land would be so difficult, that I doubt whether there are people enough in Great Britain and Ireland to accomplish it in a hundred years' time, were they to meet with no opposition; but where there is such a subtle enemy to deal with, I am afraid we should make but little progress in reducing the Indians, even allowing the country to be all cleared, as there are hills and other fastnesses to which the Indians, can retire and where they would greatly have the better of every attempt to dislodge them. The only way I would advise is, to keep friends with the Indians, and endeavour to prevail on them to settle in the same manner as the planters do, which they will be more easily brought to if the French are excluded from Canada. For, notwithstanding their wandering way of life, I have the greatest reason to believe they have no dislike to an easy life. And they will have no temptation to murder, as they had when stirred up by the subjects of his Most Christian Majesty, they will soon become useful Members of Society.

When first the English arrived in the American colonies, they found the woods inhabited by a race of people uncultivated in their manners, but not quite devoid of humanity. They were strangers to literature, ignorant of the liberal arts, and destitute of almost every conveniency of life.

But, if they were unpractised in the arts of more civilized nations, they were also free from their vices. They seemed perfect in two parts of the ancient Persian education, namely, shooting with the bow and speaking truth. In their dealings, they commonly exchange one commodity for another. Strangers themselves to fraud, they had an entire confidence in others. According to their abilities, they were generous and hospitable. Happy, thrice happy had they been, if, still preserving their native innocence and simplicity, they had only been instructed in the knowledge of God, and the doctrines of Christianity. Had they been taught some of the more useful parts of life, and to lay aside what was wild and savage in their manners!

They received the English upon their first arrival with open arms, treated them kindly, and showed an earnest desire that they should settle and live with them. They freely parted with some of their lands to their new-come brethren, and cheerfully entered into a league of friendship with them. As the English were in immediate want of the assistance of the Indians, they, on their part, endeavoured to make their coming agreeable. Thus, they lived for some years in the mutual exchange of friendly offices. Their houses were open to each other, they treated one another as brothers. But by their different way of living, the English soon acquired property, while the Indians continued in their former indigence; hence the former found they could easily live without the latter, and therefore became less anxious about preserving their friendship. This gave a check to that mutual hospitality that had hitherto subsisted between them; and this, together with the decrease of game for hunting arising from the increase of the English settlements induced the Indians to remove farther back into the woods.

From this time the natives began to be treated as a people of whom an advantage might be taken. As the trade with them was free and open, men of loose and abandoned characters engaged in it, and practised every fraud. Before the coming of the white people, the Indians never tasted spiritous liquors, and, like most barbarians, having once tasted, became immoderately fond thereof, and had no longer any government of themselves. The traders availed themselves of this weakness; instead of carrying our clothes to cover the naked savages, they carried them rum, and thereby debauched their manners, weakened their constitution, introduced disorders unknown to them before, and, in short, corrupted and ruined them.

The Indians, finding the ill effects of this trade, began to complain. Wherefore laws were made, prohibiting any from going to trade with them without a license from the governor, and it was also made lawful for the Indians to stave the casks, and spill what rum was brought among them; but this was to little purpose; the Indians had too little command of themselves to do their duty, and were easily prevailed upon not to execute this law; and the design of the former was totally evaded, by men of some character taking out licenses to trade, and then employing under them persons of no honour or principle, generally servants and convicts transported hither from Britain and Ireland, whom they sent with goods into the Indian country to trade on their account. These getting beyond the reach of the law, executed unheard of villages upon the poor natives, committing crimes which modesty forbids to name, and behaving in a manner too shocking to be related.

At every treaty which the Indians held with the English, they complained of the abuses they suffered from the traders, and trade as then carried on. They requested that the traders might be recalled, but all to no purpose. They begged in the strongest terms that no rum might be suffered to come among them; but were only told they were at liberty to spill all rum brought into their country. At this time, little or no pains was taken to civilize or instruct them in the Christian religion, till at length, the conduct of traders professing themselves of that religion, gave the Indians an almost invincible prejudice against it. Besides, as these traders travelled among distant nations of the Indians and were in some sort the representatives of the English nation, from them the Indians formed a very unfavourable opinion of our whole nation, and easily believed every misrepresentation made of us by our enemies.

There are instances in history where the virtues and disinterested behaviour of one man has prejudiced whole nations of barbarians in favour of the people to whom he belonged; and is it then to be wondered at if the Indians conceived a rooted prejudice against us, when not one, but a whole set of men, namely, all of our nation that they had an opportunity of seeing or conversing with, were persons of a loose and abandoned behaviour, insincere and faithless, without religion virtue, or morality. No one will think I exaggerate these matters, who has either known the traders themselves, or who has read the public treaties.

If to this be added, what I find in the late treaties, that they have been wronged in some of their lands what room will there be any longer to wonder that we have so little interest with them; that their conduct towards us is of late so much changed; that, instead of being a security and protection to us, as they have been hitherto, during the several wars between us and the French, they are now turned against us and become our enemies, principally on account of the fraudulent dealings and immoral conduct of those heretofore employed in our trade with them, who have brought dishonour on our religion, and disgrace on our nation. It nearly concerns us, if possible, to wipe off these reproaches, and to redeem our character, which can only be done by regulating the trade; and this the Indians, with whom the government of Philadelphia lately treated, demanded and expected of us.

At present, a favourable opportunity presents for doing it effectually. All those who were engaged in this trade are, by the present troubles, removed from it; and it is to be hoped that the legislature will fall upon measures to prevent any such from ever being concerned in it again. This is only the foundation upon which we can expect a lasting peace with the natives. It is evident that a great deal depends upon the persons who are to be sent into the Indian country; from those alone the Indians will form a judgment of us, our religion and manners. If these men, who are to be our representatives among the Indians, be men of virtue and integrity, sober in their conversation, honest in their dealings and whose practice corresponds with their profession, the judgment formed of us will be favourable; if, on the contrary they be loose and profane persons, men of wicked lives and profligate morals, we must expect that among the Indians our religion will pass for a jest, and we, in general, for a people faithless and despicable.

I might here add some observations respecting the commodities proper to be carried among the Indians, in kind as well as quality, with a method of carrying on the trade, so as to preserve the native innocence of the Indian and, at the same time confirm immovably in our interest; but these things, as well as some remarks I have in a course of years made upon the Indians, I shall leave for the subject of some future history.

I shall now proceed to give a concise account of the climates, produce, trade, &c. of North America. And, first,

OF NEW ENGLAND.

The province of New England appears to be vastly extensive, being about 400 miles in length, and near 300 in breadth, situated between 69 and 73 deg. W. long., and between 41 and 46 deg. N. lat. It was first settled by the Independents, a little before the commencement of the civil wars in England; they transported themselves thither, rather than they would communicate with the Church of England.

The lands next the sea in New England are generally low and the soil sandy; but further up the country it rises into hills, and on the north east it is rocky and mountainous. The winters are much severer here that in Old England; though it lies 9 or 10 degrees more south, but they have usually a clearer sky and more settled weather both in winter and summer than in Old England; and though their summers are shorter, the air is considerably hotter while it lasts. The winds are very boisterous in the winter season, and the north wind blowing over a long tract of frozen and uncultivated countries with several fresh-water lakes, makes it excessively cold. The rivers are sometimes congealed in a night's time. The climate is generally healthful, and agreeable to English constitutions.

The fruits of Old England come to great perfection here, particularly peaches, which are planted trees; and we have commonly 1200 or 1400 fine peaches on such a tree at one time; nay, of the fruit of one single apple tree at one season, nine barrels of cider have been made. English wheat I find does not thrive here within 40 or 50 miles of Boston; but farther up the country they have it in great abundance and I think it comes to the same perfection as in Britain. Now, why wheat should not grow near this city, I confess I can assign no reason that will fully satisfy the reader's curiosity. The conjectures upon it are various; some venture to say that it was occasioned by the unjust persecution of the Quakers, the Independents having vented their spleen against them in a way the most rigorous, and in flat contradiction to the laws of Christianity. All other grain but wheat thrives in this place with great success; in particular Indian corn, one grain whereof frequently produce 200, and sometimes 2000 grains. This corn is of three different colours, *viz.*, blue, white and yellow.

OF NEW YORK.

The situation of this province is between 72 and 76 W. long., and between 41 and 44 N. lat., being about 200 miles in length, and 100 miles in breadth. The lands in the Jerseys and south part of New York are low and flat; but, as you ascend 20 or 30 miles up the Hudson's River, the country is rocky and mountainous. The air is much milder here in winter than in New England, and in summer it is pretty much the same. The produce and trade of New York and the Jerseys consist in cattle and a good breed of horses. They have plenty of wheat and other grain, such as Indian corn, buck-wheat, oats, barley, and rye. It abounds also, with store of fish. They supply the sugar islands with flour, salt beef, pork, salt fish, and timber planks, in return for the produce raised there.

Of Pennsylvania

The extent of this colony is 200 miles in length, and 200 miles in breadth. The soil is much better than in Jersey, chiefly consisting of a black mould; the country rises gradually as in the adjacent provinces, having the Apalachian mountains on the west, and is divided into six counties. The air, it lying in the 40 deg. of N. lat., it near the same as in New York, and very healthy to English constitutions. The produce and merchandise of Pennsylvania consists in horses, pipe staves, beef, pork, salt fish, skins, furs and all sorts of grain, *viz.*, wheat, rye, peace, oats, barley, buck-wheat, Indian corn, Indian pease, beans, potashes, wax, &c,, and in return for these commodities, they import from the Carribee islands, and other places, rum, sugar, molasses, silver, negroes, salt and clothing of all sorts, hardware, &c. The nature of the soil in Pennsylvania, the Jerseys and New York, is extremely proper to produce hemp, flax, &c.

If the government of Pennsylvania since the death of its first proprietor, William Penn, had taken proper methods to oblige the traders to deal justly with the Indians; whose tempers when exasperated with resentment, are more savage than the hungry lion, these disasters might have been in a good degree prevented.

I intend to conclude this argument in a few words and shall endeavour to do justice on both sides by adhering strictly to truth. Know therefore, that, within these late years, the Indians being tolerably acquainted with the nature of our commerce, have detected the roguery of some of the traders, whereupon they lodged many and grievous complaints to Colonel Weiser the interpreter between them and the English, of the injurious and fraudulent usage they had received for several years, backwards from white people, who had cheated them out of their skins and furs, not giving them one quarter their value for them.

Likewise, they remonstrated, that, whereas hunting was the chief way or art they ever had to earn a livelihood by, game was now become very scarce, because the whites practised it so much on their ground, destroying their prey. Colonel Weiser, their interpreter advised them to bring down their skins and furs to Philadelphia themselves, promising that he would take proper care to see their goods vended to their advantage. Whereupon they did so, in pursuance of his instructions, and finding it their interest, resolved to continue in the way he had chalked out for them; for now they were supplied with everything they wanted from the merchants' shops, at the cheapest rates. And thus, it plainly appeared to the Indians that they had been long imposed on by the traders, and therefore they were determined to have no more dealings with them. This conduct and shyness of the Indians was very disagreeable to several gentleman of the province, who were nearly interested in that species of commerce.

Accordingly, in the year 1753 and 1754, some of the traders had the assurance to renew their friendship with them, when, instead of remitting them clothes and other necessaries as had been usual, and were most proper for them, they, with insidious purposes, carried them large quantities of rum in small casks, which they knew the natives were fond of, under the colour of giving it them *gratis*. In this manner were the savages inveigled into liquor by the whites, who took the opportunity, while they were intoxicated, of going off with their skins and furs; but the natives recovering from the debauch, soon detected the villainy, and in revenge killed many of the traders, and went directly over to the French, who encouraged them to slay every English person they could meet with, and destroyed their houses by fire, giving them orders to spare neither man, women, nor child. Besides, as a farther incitement to diligence in this bloody task, they promised the savages a reward of £15 sterling for every scalp they should take, on producing the same before any of his Most Christian Majesty's officers, civil or military.

Thus, our perfidious enemies instigated those unreasonable barbarians to commence acts of depredation, violence, and murder, on the several inhabitants of North America in 1754, and more especially in Pennsylvania, as knowing it to be the most defenceless province on the continent. This consideration prompted the savage race to exhaust their malicious fury on it in particular.

Of Carolina

This colony is computed to extend 660 miles in length, but its breadth is unknown. The lands here are generally low and flat, and not a hill to be seen from St. Augustine to Virginia, and a great way beyond. It is mostly covered with woods, where the planters have not cleared it. About 100 miles west of the coast, it shoots up into eminences, and continues to rise gradually all along to the Appalachian mountains, which are about 160 miles distant from the ocean. The north parts of Carolina are very uneven; but the ground is extremely proper for producing wheat and all other sorts of grain that grow in Europe will come to great perfection here.

The south parts of Carolina, if properly cultivated, might he made to produce silk, wine and oil. This country yields large quantities of rice of which they yearly ship off to other colonies about 80,000 barrels, each barrel containing 4 cwt.; besides, they make abundance of tar, pitch, and turpentine. They carry on also a great trade with deer skins and furs, to all places of Europe, which the English receive from the Indians in barter for guns, powder, knives, scissors, looking-glasses, beads, rum, tobacco, coarse cloth, &c.

The English chapmen carry their pack horses 500 or 600 miles into the country, west of Charlestown; but most of the commerce is confined within the limits of the Creek and Cherokee nations, which do not lie above 350 miles from the coast. The air is very temperate, and agreeable both summer and winter. Carolina is divided into two distinct provinces, *viz.*, North and South Carolina.

Of Nova Scotia

This place extends about 600 miles in length, and 460 in breadth. The air is pretty much the same as in Old England. The soil is, for the most part, barren; but where it is cleared and cultivated, it affords good corn and pasture. Here is fine timber, and fit for building, from whence pitch and tar may be extracted. Here also hemp and flax will grow, so that this country will be capable of furnishing all manner of naval stores. It abounds likewise with deer, wild fowl, and all sort of game.

On the coast is one of the finest cod-fisheries in the world, European cattle *viz.*, sheep, oxen, swine, horses, &c, they have in great abundance. The winters are very cold, their frosts being sharp and of long duration; their summers moderately hot; so that the climate, in the main, seems to be agreeable to English constitutions.

Of Canada

I shall close the description of the American colonies with a short account of the soil and produce of French Canada. Its extent is, according to their map 1800 miles in length and 1260 in breadth. The soil in the low lands, near the River St. Lawrence will indeed raise wheat, but, withal, I found it so shallow that it would not produce that grain above two years unless it was properly manured. About 20 miles from the said river, so hilly and mountainous is the country that nothing but Indians and wild ravenous beasts resort there. However, they have plenty of Rye, Indian corn, buck-wheat and oats; likewise of horses, cows, sheep, swine, &c. But I have observed that fruits of any kind do not come to such perfection here as in some of the English settlements, which is owing to the long duration and excessive cold of their winters. The summer is short and temperately hot. The climate, in general, is healthy and agreeable to European constitutions. And so much for the provinces in North America.

To conclude, it left the French without the least fear of our being able to give them the least interruption in their passage through Lake Ontario and Lake Erie, to the Frontiers of Pennsylvania, Maryland, Virginia, and all the southern country.

★★★★★★

Whether these my animadversions are true, or not. What has been since transacted in these parts and the present campaign there, will evince—I shall therefore return to our embarkation at Quebec.

Five hundred of us, being to be sent to England, we were put on board *La Renommé*, a French *pacquet*-boat, Capt. Dermis Vitree, commander: We sailed under a flag of truce, and though the French behaved with a good deal of politeness, yet were we almost starved for want of provisions. One biscuit and two ounces of pork a day, being all our allowance, and half-dead with cold, having but few cloaths, and the vessel being so small, that the major part of us were obliged to be upon deck in all weathers, after a passage of six weeks, we at last, to our great joy, arrived at Plymouth on the 6th of November, 1756. But there our troubles and hardships were not as we expected, put a period to for some time; for scruples arising to the commissaries and admiral there about taking us on shore, as there was no cartel agreed on between the French and English, we were still confined on board, 'till the determination of the Lords of the Admiralty should be known; lying there in a miserable condition seven or eight days, before we received orders to disembark, which, when we were permitted to do, being ordered from thence, in different parties to Totnes, Kingsbridge, Newton-Bushel and Newton-Abbot, in Devonshire, I was happy in being quartered at Kingsbridge, where I met with much civility and entertainment, as I had for a long time been a stranger to.

In about four months, we were again ordered to Plymouth Dock, to be draughted into our regiments; where, on being inspected, I was on account of the wound I had received in my hand discharged as incapable of further service.

For want of a certificate from my colonel, or some other necessary qualifications I am ignorant of, I could not get any provision made for me, by pension, or otherwise. Indeed, as a reward for my sufferings and services, I had the favour of a pass allowed, and the sum of six shillings paid, to carry me to Aberdeen, about eight hundred miles only, from the place whereat I was discharged.

But finding that sum insufficient to subsist me half the way, I was obliged to make my application to the honourable gentlemen of the city of York, who, on considering my necessity, and reviewing my manuscript on the transactions of the Indians herein before mentioned, thought proper to have it printed for my own benefit, which they cheerfully subscribed unto. And after disposing of my books through the shire, I took the first opportunity of going in quest of my relations at Aberdeen, where I received very barbarous usage and ill treatment, occasioned by complaining against the illegal practice of kidnapping in the beginning of my book.

Recollections of an Old Soldier the Life of Captain David Perry

Written by Himself

LIFE OF DAVID PERRY.

I was born August 8th, (O. S.) 1741, in the town of Rehoboth, Mass. I was the oldest child of Eliakim and Sarah Perry. The first thing of consequence that occurs to my mind, was the transactions relating to the war between the English and French. An army was raised in the New-England States, to go against Cape Breton, under Gen. Pepperell, at which time I was in my fifth year. My father and one of his brothers, and also one of my mother's brothers, enlisted into this army. And what strengthens my memory with regard to these events, one of my uncles above mentioned, whose name was Abner Perry, was killed at the taking of the Island Battery.

Nothing of consequence took place until the fall after I was seven years old, when my mother died, leaving four small children, *viz*: one brother and two sisters. There was something very singular took place respecting her sickness. She went with my father, to visit his relations at Eastown. They rode on horse-back. While they were there, on Lord's day, I was at play with my brother and two little sisters, and it appeared to me that I saw my mother ride by on the same horse she rode away on and dressed in the same clothes. I mentioned the circumstance to my brother and sisters at the time; but she rode out of my sight immediately.

At this time she was taken sick at Eastown, in which condition they brought her home; and she died a few days afterwards—In consequence of this event, my father broke up housekeeping, and put out his children. Myself and sisters went to live with our uncle David Joy, the brother of my mother who, as I before said, went with my father to Cape Breton. I lived with my uncle, (who treated me very kindly) until my fifteenth year; when I was placed with Mr. David Walker, in Dighton, Mass. to learn the trade of tanner and shoe-maker.

About this time war again broke out between the English and French, and it raged sorely in our part of the country, especially near the lakes. Our people made a stand at the south end of Lake George, where they built a fort, and another about 14 miles below, on the Hudson River, called Fort Edward. In 1755, a bloody battle was fought at the halfway-house, between Fort Edward and Lake George. Gen. Johnson commanded the English forces; and under him Maj. Rodgers commanded the Rangers. They had a number of sore battles with the French and Indians and lost a great many of our best men. In the year 1757, Gen. Mont Calm came against Fort George, with a large army of French and Indians, and obliged the garrison to surrender, after which, contrary to his express agreement, he let loose his Indians upon our men, and massacred a great many of them.

This year, in August, I was sixteen years old; at which age the young lads of that day were called into the training-bands. In the Spring of 1758, I was warned to trainings and there were recruiting officers on the parade-ground,, to enlist men for the next campaign. I enlisted into Capt. Job Winslow's company, of Col. Prebble's regiment, to serve eight months—People said I would not "pass muster," as I was small of my age; but there was no difficulty about that. When the company was full, we marched first to Worcester, staid there a few days, and then marched to Old Hadley. We remained here about a week.

From this place we crossed the river to Northampton, where we drew five days' provisions—left the place in the afternoon, and encamped a few miles out of town, in the woods for the night—In that day there were no human habitations from Northampton, to within ten miles of Albany. There was a small picket fort in what was then called Pantocet Woods, commanded by Col. Williams We had no other road than marked trees to direct our course—no bridges on which to cross the streams; some of which we waded; others we passed on trees felled by our men: and for five successive nights we lay on the ground.

We arrived at Greenbush, and, after a few days' tarry, marched up the North River to a place called Setackuk, where the Indians had driven off, captured, or destroyed the inhabitants. We here took a number of horses to draw the cannon to Lake George, but not having horses enough, some of the cannon were drawn by men. Part of the men went in *batteaus* with the provisions. When we arrived at the Lake, the army, consisting of British and Americans, amounted to about 20,000 men. It was commanded by Gen. Abrecombe, and Lord Howe was second in command. We encamped there until boats and provisions enough were collected to carry us across the lake, with cannon, etc. to attack Ticonderoga. We arrived at the Narrows the second morning after our embarkation, where we expected to be attacked by the enemy.

Major Rodgers, with his Rangers was the first to land. He was joined by Lord Howe and his party; and we had proceeded but a short distance into the woods, before we were met by the enemy, and a brisk fire ensued. It was the first engagement I had ever seen, and the whistling of balls, and roar of musquetry terrified me not a little. At length our regiment formed among the trees, behind which the men kept stepping from their ranks for shelter. Col. Prebble, who, I well remember, was a harsh man, swore he would knock the first man down who should step out of his ranks; which greatly surprised me, to think that I must stand still to be shot at. Pretty soon, however, they brought along some wounded Frenchmen; and when I came to see the blood run so freely, it put new life into me. The battle proved a sore one for us. Lord Howe and a number of other good men, were killed.

The army moved on that day to within a short distance of the enemy, and encamped for the night, in the morning we had orders to move forward again, in a column three deep, in order to storm the enemy's breast-works, known in this country by the name of "the Old French Lines." Our orders were to "run to the breast-work, and get in if we could." But their lines were full, and they killed our men so fast, that we could not gain it. We got behind trees, logs and stumps, and covered ourselves as we could from the enemy's fire. The ground was strewed with the dead and dying.

It happened that I got behind a white-oak stump, which was so small that I had to lay on my side, and stretch myself; the balls striking the ground within a hand's breadth of me every moment, and I could hear the men screaming, and see them dying all around me, I lay there some time. A man could not stand erect, without being hit, any more than he could stand out in a shower, without having drops of rain fall upon him; for the balls come by hands full. It was a clear day—a little air stirring. Once in a while the enemy would cease firing a minute or two, to have the smoke clear away, so that they might take better aim.

In one of these intervals I sprang from my perilous situation and gained a stand which I thought would be more secure, behind a large pine log, where several of my comrades had already taken shelter: but the balls came here as thick as ever. One of the men raised his head a little above the log, and a ball struck him in the centre of the forehead and tore up his scalp clear back to the crown. He darted back, and the blood ran merrily; and, rubbing his face, said it was a bad blow, and no one was disposed to deny it, for he looked bad enough. We lay there till near sunset; and, not receiving orders from any officer, the men crept off, leaving all the dead, and most of the wounded. We had two of our company killed, and a number wounded. Our captain (Winslow) received a ball in his wrist, which passed up the fleshy part of his arm, and he carried it there as long as he lived, which was a number of years: he was afterwards raised to the rank of colonel. Our lieutenant was wounded by a shot in the leg, and one of our sergeants received a ball in his arm, which he carried with him to his grave.

We got away the wounded of our company; but left a great many crying for help, which we were unable to afford them. I suppose, that as soon as we left the ground, the enemy let loose his Indians upon them: for none of those that we left behind were ever heard of afterwards. We started back to our boats without any orders and pushed out on the lake for the night. We left between 6 and 7000, in killed and wounded, on the field of battle, which I believe is a greater number than ever was lost on our side, in one day, in all the battles that have been fought in America. We went over the lake with about 21,000 men, in high spirits, with all kinds of music; but returned back melancholy and still, as from a funeral, and took our old stand at the south end of the lake.

A great deal was said by the subaltern officers and men, at that time, with regard to the conduct of the commanding general. I was but a boy and could have but little judgment about it then; but, from later experience and reflection, I think it looks more like the conduct of a Hull, a Wilkinson, or a Hampton, than like that of an able general and firm patriot. We had artillery enough and might have erected batteries; and it seems as though we might have taken the place. But it was thought by some, that the misfortune happened in consequence of the death of Lord Howe, as he was a more experienced officer.

Nothing of material consequence took place after this, for some time. Hardly a day passed, however, while we lay in camp, in which British and Yorkers did not flog some of their men. We were employed in building a fort.

Not long after, Major Rodgers and Major (afterwards General)

Putnam, took charge of a party of men, on an expedition to a place called South Bay, where they met the enemy, and had a smart engagement. Maj. Putnam was taken and carried to Canada; and Maj. Rodgers returned to Fort Edward with what men they had left. While lying in camp, our water and provisions were very bad, the men grew sickly, and a great many died of the dysentery. But the same Almighty Power that warded off the balls in the day of battle, preserved me from the desolating scourge of disease.

Towards Fall, Maj. Rodgers, with a party of men, went away to the westward, to a place called Cataraqua, and destroyed it.

It was during the Summer of this year, that Generals Wolfe and Amherst came from England with a fleet and army and took Cape Breton; after which Gen. Amherst came and took command of our army, and Abrecombe went off.

When our times were out, we were dismissed, and went home. Our route was back to Albany, through Sharon and the "Green Woods," and over Glascow Mountain to Springfield, and so on to Worcester. I returned to my master and went to work at my trade. In the Spring of 1759, I enlisted under Lieut. John Richmond, expecting to join Capt. Nathan Hogers' company, with the lads that enlisted with me; but when we arrived at Worcester, Lieut. Richmond was transferred to Capt. Samuel Peck's company, of Boston. He (Lt. R.) urged me hard to go with him, as waiter, and told me I should live as well as he did. But Capt. Hogers said I should not go with him, and they contended pretty hard about it, till at last Maj. Caleb Willard, who had the command there, said it should be left to the lad's choice.

I went with the lieutenant, and he was as good as his word as to my fare. We started for Boston: I rode his horse as much as he did until we gained the company. I never saw the captain before, nor any of the company: but he proved to be a fine man, as was the first lieutenant, whose name was Abbot. But the Ensign, (Larkin) was an Irishman, and the company was a pretty rough set: I did not like them much.

This Summer General Wolfe went up the River St. Lawrence with a fleet of about fifty men-of-war, and a great many transport ships. We shipped a-board an English transport, under convoy of a frigate, and the first harbour we made was Cape Breton. The main fleet had sailed before we arrived. We lay there a few days, and sailed up the river after them, and, in forty-one days from the time we left Boston, we arrived at Quebec. Part of the main army had landed at Point Levi, and part on the other side of the river, below Mount Morancy Falls. We were landed on the Island of Orleans.

On our first landing, considerable fighting took place, and many of the Rangers were killed. Two companies, one commanded by Capt. Danks, who was badly wounded, and the other by Captain Hazen, lost so many of their men, that they were put together, and did not then make a full company. They were stationed on that side of the river with General Wolfe: and they came to the Island to see if some of the provincials would go into their company. I turned out for one, and went into Capt. Hazen's company, and went ashore with them, and never saw my company again till after the city was taken, and we had got aboard the ship to return home.

We now had hard fighting enough, as we were scouting over the country nearly all the time, and were shot upon, more or less, nearly every day, and very often had some killed or wounded. We used frequently to get on board large flat-bottomed boats, that would hold eighty men each; to do which we had to wade in the water up to the middle; and, after sitting in our wet clothes all night, jump into the water again, wade ashore, go back into the woods, and scatter into small parties, in order to catch the inhabitants, as they returned from the woods to look after their domestic affairs; and when they had got in among us, one party would rise in their front, and another in their rear, and thus we surrounded and captured a great many of them.

The country was settled on that side of the river, to the distance of about thirty miles below our encampment; and we took the greater part of their cattle and sheep and drove them into camp. We went down there a number of times and found that they had a considerable force stationed back in the woods. One night in particular, I well remember, our company and a company of regulars, took a trip down there in boats, and landed about daybreak—As soon as it was light, Capt. Hazen told his men to stroll back, a few at a time, undiscovered, into the woods.

As soon as we had done this, the regulars marched, by fife and drum, in a body round a point of the woods, in order to draw the enemy there; and we kept still, until they got between us and the regulars, when we rose and fired on them, and put them to flight immediately. Our orders were, to "kill all, and give no quarters." The enemy had a priest with them, who was wounded in the thigh, and begged earnestly for quarters, but the captain told the men to kill him. Upon which, one of them deliberately blew his brains out—We effectually broke up the enemy in this quarter and returned safe to camp.

At another time, we went down the river about forty miles, in the night, and landed in the morning on the opposite side to the place last mentioned, and secreted ourselves in small parties, in the woods, beside the road. I was with the lieutenant's party. We had a man by the name of Frazier in our party, who enlisted under Capt. Peck, in Boston, and he was a pretty unruly fellow. There came along three armed Frenchmen near where we lay concealed, and Frazier saw them, and hallooed to them "boon quarter;" whereupon one of them levelled his piece and shot him through the head and killed him instantly.

The captain hearing the report; came and inquired how it happened. We told him we could not keep Frazier still; "well," said he, "his blood be upon his own head."

We now expected to have some fighting. We left our blankets upon the dead man, and took the road the Frenchmen came in, and, after marching about half a mile, we came into an open field, with a large number of cattle in it; and on the opposite side of the field, just in the edge of the woods, were a great many little huts, full of women and children, with their hasty-pudding for breakfast, of which I partook with them; but their little children scampered into the brush, and could not be got sight of again, any more than so many young partridges. We did not, however, wish to hurt them.

There were three barns in the lot, filled with household goods: we took as many as we could of these, and drove the cattle back the way we came, to where the dead man and blankets were left, which we took up, and were proceeding with our booty to the river, when the enemy fired on us, and killed Lieut. Meachum, of Capt. Dank's company, and wounded one other. In the meantime, the cattle we had taken all ran back; but we drove off the enemy, and got our goods, etc. aboard the boats, and returned to camp.

About this time the French fixed long fire rafts on the banks of the river, near the lower town, and filled them with fuel, and other combustible materials. Our shipping lay below, to the number of about three hundred sail, and nearly filled the river: and in the night, when the wind and tide favoured their project, they communicated fire to this raft, and set it afloat down the river. It was nearly half a mile in length, and so rapidly did the flames extend from one end of it to the other, that it seemed as though the whole river was on fire. The men-of-war despatched their boats with iron hooks and grapples, and fastened one end of it, and so turned it endwise. Some of the vessels, in the meantime weighed anchor—others cut their cables; and in this way they opened a passage and towed this threatening engine of destruction through the fleet, without sustaining much damage.

That part of the army stationed on Point Levi had batteries erected, and threw shells, and shot from them into the town all the time and burnt and demolished a great many of their buildings. On the side of the river where we lay, a large river, which has its rise in the mountains, empties into the St. Lawrence against the Morancy Falls. This river was not fordable back to the mountain; but below the falls, when the tide was out, it spread over the marsh, and was so shallow that men could wade it. The banks of the St. Lawrence are very high, and the French built a strong breastwork on them, to prevent Gen. Wolfe getting to the city that way. And we had a battery against them on the opposite side of the abovementioned river, from which we kept up a pretty constant fire at each other for a long time, but without much effect on either party. At length, Gen. Wolfe ordered a couple of ships up against their breastworks, at high water, with cannon on board, and anchored them, with springs on their cables, in a position to fire on, and with intent to batter down, the enemy's works; but when the tide fell, the vessels grounded, and the crews relinquished the project, set them on fire, and returned in their boats.

Soon after this, at low water, General Wolfe ordered his men to pass down the banks, and cross the river by platoons, in order to storm their breastwork. They formed in solid column, as they reached the opposite shore, to the number of about two thousands The enemy did not fire a single shot until our men had formed, when they opened upon them the most destructive fire I ever witnessed: it appeared to me that nearly four-fifths of them fell at the first discharge, and those who did not fall turned about promiscuously and came back without any order. Our company remained on the bank, with our muskets loaded, as a kind of *corps de reserve*, to follow the detachment, in case it succeeded in making a breach in the enemy's works. Gen. Wolfe stood with us, where we could see the whole manoeuvre; and the tide came and swept them off together—And there arose the most tremendous thundershower I ever witnessed; which, combined with the continual roar of cannon and musketry, conspired to produce a truly sublime and awful scene!

Gen. Wolfe then broke up his encampment on that side of the river and went over to Point Levi. A few nights after, Capt. Warren, commander of a sixty-four man-of-war, was ordered to pass by the town, up the river; and, wind and tide favouring, he went by, under the most tremendous cannonade I ever heard, and we expected she would be blown to atoms, but never a shot hit her. A few nights afterwards two more vessels passed up, under similar circumstances, and had their rigging considerably cut to pieces.

The country this side the river was settled to the distance of about one hundred and sixty miles below. All the rangers, and one company of Light-Infantry of the British, were ordered to go a-board vessels, and to sail down the river as far as it was settled, then to land and march back towards the city, burning and destroying, in our course, all their buildings, killing all their cattle, sheep and horses, and laying waste the country far and near.

The company to which I belonged, landed early one morning, and we went directly to a large house, about a quarter of a mile distant. The people fled at our approach, and we caught plenty of pigs, geese, and fowls; and while part of our men were busied in carrying the squawling and squealing booty to the vessels, there came a Frenchman out of the woods, and ran into the house. We followed after and took him and carried him aboard the vessels. And the officers told him if he would be friendly to us, and pilot us to their back settlements, he should be used well; which he complied with, and he proved true to his engagements.

Having breakfasted aboard the ship, our whole party went up to the house just mentioned, where we found large stores of provisions, of one kind and another, and among the rest a plenty of pickled salmon, which was quite a rarity to most of us; and as we had been several days aboard the vessels, we concluded to stay there the day and night, and went to cooking salmon for dinner, etc. The men strolled about as they pleased, and pretty soon we heard three or four guns fired a short distance from us, and we paraded immediately, to see who was missing. It appeared there were only two absent, *viz*: Lieut. Toot, of Capt. Stark's company, and a private.

******

This is Gen. John Stark, who is now (1822) living at Pembroke, N. Hampshire; and, according to my best recollection as to his age, he is rising of 95 years old. I have frequently been told, within a few years, by intelligent persons, that Gen. S. and myself are the only men now living in New-England, who belonged to the army which took Quebec.

******

We then marched to the place from which the report had been

heard, and found the soldier, who had been shot and scalped, who died soon after. The lieutenant returned unhurt. We marched on a little distance and came to a large opening. Here we surrounded and took a Frenchman, from whom we endeavoured to learn what had become of those who fired the guns, but he would not tell: and the captain told him he would kill him if he did not, at the same time directing us to draw our knives, upon our doing which he fell to saying his prayers upon his knees, firmly refusing to tell. Finding him thus resolute and faithful to his friends, the captain sent him a prisoner to the shipping, and we went to our cooking again.

In the morning our company took the friendly Frenchman for a guide and marched off three or four miles to a back village and got there before it was light. We were divided into small parties, as usual, in order to take what prisoners we could.

I was stationed in a barn with the lieutenant's party, and while we lay there, a Frenchman came along smoking his pipe, and one of our men, an outlandish sort of a fellow, put his gun out of a crack in the barn, and, before we had time to prevent it, fired upon the man; the shot carried away his pipe, but did him no other injury, and he ran off. But when the captain heard of it, he flogged the soldier severely. We burnt the buildings, destroyed everything there, and returned towards the river again. The main party marched up the river, burning and destroying everything before them: and our company followed on some distance in the rear, collecting the cattle, sheep and horses, and burning the scattering buildings, etc.

In this way we continued our march at the rate of about twelve miles a day. Every six miles we found large stone churches, at on& of which we generally halted to dinner, and at the next to supper, and so on. We lived well, but our duty was hard—climbing over hills and fences all day; always starting in the morning before break of day, in order to make prisoners of some of the enemy, in which we were hardly ever disappointed. We were very often fired on by the enemy, and many of our men were killed or wounded, in these excursions. Where there was a stream to cross in our course, they would take up the bridge, secrete themselves on the opposite side, and fire on us unawares.

Our captain was a bold man. I have seen him cock his piece, and walk promptly up to the enemy, face to face; and our men would never shrink from following such an officer, and they seldom followed him without success.

While we were on this tour, Gen. Wolfe landed his main army on the Plains of Abraham; Gen. Mont Calm sallied forth from the city, and a battle took place, the result of which is well known: both the commanding generals were killed, the second in command on the side of the British badly wounded, with the loss of a great many men, on both sides; but the English remained masters of the field.

And we continued our route up the river till we had proceeded about sixty miles, when a vessel came down from the main army, with information of the battle and victory, and with orders for us to "drive on faster and destroy all before us" We continued our march three days more, which brought us to within about sixty miles of headquarters, when a second vessel came down to us, with orders to cease burning and pillaging, for Quebec had given up to the English.

We went a-board our vessels, and sailed up to the city, and landed at the lower town, where we witnessed the destruction made there. From the lower, we went to the upper town, up their dug-way; and it was truly surprising to see the damage done to the buildings, etc. by the shot and shells that were thrown into the town by our artillery. Their houses were principally made of stone and lime—the gable-ends of wood, which were burnt out of a great many of them, and cannon balls stove holes through the buildings in many places, and a great number drove the stones part way out and remained in the walls. The city surrendered to Brigadier General Townsend, as Major General Wolfe was killed, and General Monkton badly wounded. We were sent up the river about four miles above the city, as a vessel guard.

Nothing of consequence took place after this, till our times were out, when we were sent back to our old company, a-board ship, to return home. The ship's crew were very sickly, having lain still all summer on the island.—Lieut. Richmond, with whom I enlisted, was very sick, as also were a great many of the soldiers between decks, and I had to take care of them. Lieut. Richmond kept sending for me to attend on him, and I grew tired of it, and refused to go; upon which Capt. Peck sent for me, to know why I would not, and I told him it was as much as I could do to take care of the sick privates. He then told me to come and live in the cabin, and wait upon Lieut. Richmond, which should be my duty, and I did so. Owing to bad weather, we were a long time getting down the river, and before we arrived at Halifax eight or nine of our men died and were thrown overboard.

When we arrived at Halifax, I went ashore, and found my old captain (Winslow) there, who had been promoted to the rank of major.

He wished me to stay and go home with him before Spring, and I did as he desired, and lived with him and the colonel of the regiment, till about the first of February, when we set sail for Boston, and had a long passage of twenty-one days. On our passage we made the harbours of Penobscot, Portsmouth, and Cohasset, at which last place I left the vessel, and went home on foot.

This year Gen. Amherst went over the lake with an army, where we went the year preceding, and took Crown-Point and Ticonderoga, with the loss of but few men: and in the fall he went back to Albany with his main army, leaving a sufficient force to garrison the places he had taken. In the Spring of 1760, he went up to the head of Mohawk River, and from thence proceeded to Wood-Creek, and on through the western waters to Lake Ontario, and thence down the river St. Lawrence to Montreal, which town surrendered to him without much resistance, and thus terminated the war in that quarter.

After I had been at home about a month, Major Winslow told me, that if I would enlist what men I could, and go back to Halifax with him, I should have a sergeant's berth, as soon as there was a vacancy for one in any of the companies; and if no vacancy occurred, I should be cleared from duty through the season. I accordingly enlisted eight or ten likely young men and went on with them to Boston.

There being no vessel ready at the time we arrived at Boston, we were billeted out at the house of a widow, named Mosely; and while we were here the town took fire in the night. It originated in a tavern, (sign of the Gold Ball) in Main or King's Street, at about midnight, the wind in the north-west and pretty high; and in spite of all we could do with the engines, etc. it spread a great way down King's Street and went across and laid all that part of the town in ashes, down to Fort Hill. We attended through the whole and assisted in carrying water to the engines. The number of buildings burnt was about three hundred.

As soon as the vessel was ready, we sailed for Halifax, and arrived there in four days—There being no vacancy for a sergeant's berth, I lived with the colonel, major and chaplain of the regiment, and fared very well.

During this Summer some of the Connecticut people obtained a grant of a number of towns in the Menus country and moved on to settle them; and as there were a considerable number of French and Indians in that quarter, they wanted a guard to protect them. A draft was made from our regiment, to obtain men for that purpose. I wanted to see that country and turned out for one of the detachment.

Just previous to our departure, a man and woman were executed for murder—— the woman killed a small girl that was living with her.

We set out from Halifax by water and went to the head of the Bason to Fort Sackfield, about twelve miles distant; from that place we went by land about thirty miles through the woods, and then came into a fine open country. There was a fort here, called Fort Pisga, with a considerable number of troops in it. Beside this fort ran a large river, of the same name, (Pisga River) over which we passed in boats, into the Menus country. The people had laid out two towns, one called Horton, and the other Cornwallis. We were stationed at the latter, it being the farthest from Fort Pisga.

We had a very agreeable time of it, among our own country people, and built a picket fort there; but there was not much need of it, for the French and Indians were quite peaceable, and to all appearance friendly. At one time about thirty of the Indians, with their *sachem*, came to see us. I talked with the *sachem* some time; and, among other things, about going a hunting with him. I asked him if he would use me well: he said, if I did as he bid me, he would; if not, that he would kill me. On such terms, I thought it best not to try a new master.

Two French families came to reside with us, who were very friendly and useful to our people, and learned them many useful arts, and among others, how to catch fish, which was of great service to them, as the provisions they brought with them were soon exhausted. But as they could not subsist on fish alone, many of them must in all probability have starved if we had not dealt out to them provisions from the king's stores.

Three large rivers run through the town of Cornwallis. At high water vessels of the largest size could sail up and down them with safety. These rivers made a vast quantity of. marshy land, and the upland between them was not very good. I did not like the country, but staid there till our times were out, and then returned to Halifax, where we remained till a transport could be provided, when about one hundred and fifty of us shipped aboard a large British Snow, for Boston, and had fine weather for a few days; but while our top-sails, etc. were all standing, and everything indicated a short and prosperous voyage, there came on a sudden squall of wind, and stripped our sails all to pieces.

The seas ran mountain high, and every soul of us momently expected to go to the bottom. The captain of the vessel said he had followed the seas fifteen years, and never experienced such a gale before. But being a good new-built vessel, she rode out the storm, which

181

lasted several days, and blowed us so far out of our course that we were obliged to be put on short allowance, of one sea-biscuit and a half, each, per day; or in lieu of the biscuit, a piece of butter of the size of a hen's egg—or a slice of beef as large as one's three fingers. We lived on this allowance about a fortnight, when we arrived at Boston. I went home to my master, to work at my trade again.

This completed the third campaign in which I had served as a private: and I do not remember that in all this time I was ever so unwell as to lose a meal of victuals, or to miss a tour of duty: and I think I have the greatest reason to bless and praise the name of the Lord, that he covered my head in the day of battle and preserved my body from wasting sickness at noonday.

I worked at my trade this year—the war in our part of the country being pretty much over, a few soldiers only being retained for garrison duty.

In 1762, the state raised a regiment of men to go to Halifax. It was commanded by Col. Jonathan Hoar, and Maj. Winslow was lieut. colonel under him. As there was no recruiting officer near him, Col. Winslow persuaded me to enlist once more into the service. I had orders to enlist what men I could; and having obtained a number of recruits, I proceeded with them to join the regiment at the castle, near Boston, and was directed to enter Capt. Abel Cain's company. Here I was appointed a sergeant. We shipped for Halifax, arrived there without any occurrence of note, and encamped a little out of the town, in tents. We were employed in wheeling off the top of Citadel Hill, so called, in order to erect a fort upon it. Our duty was pretty hard, but then we worked without any apprehensions of being fired upon by an enemy.

There is one thing I would here notice, which shows a specimen of British cruelty without a parallel, I could hope, in the history of that nation. Three men, for some trifling offence which I do not recollect, were tied up to be whipped. One of them was to receive eight hundred lashes, the others five hundred a piece. By the time they had received three hundred lashes, the flesh appeared to be entirely whipped from their shoulders, and they hung as mute and motionless as though they had been long since deprived of life. But this was not enough.

The doctor stood by with a vial of sharp stuff, which he would ever and *anon* apply to their noses, and finding, by the pain it gave them, that some signs of life remained, he would tell them, d——mn you, you can bear it yet"—and then the whipping would commence again. It was the most cruel punishment I ever saw inflicted, or had ever conceived of before—by far worse than death. I felt at the time as though I could have taken summary vengeance on those who were the authors of it, on the spot, had it been in my power to do it.

During this year an expedition was fitted out by the English, and American Colonies, against the Havanna, which they succeeded in taking.

In the course of the Summer, the French came and took Newfoundland. In a town called St. Johns, was a very strong fort, built with stone and lime, at the head of the harbour. The French took possession of this fort and distressed the inhabitants very much. After it was ascertained how strong they were by land and by sea, the commander of the British land forces, Col. Amherst, (brother to Gen. Amherst) and Lord Caldwell, commander of the fleet, held a council of war on board the commander's ship. The result of the consultation was, that we had a force sufficient to go and re-take the place, and accordingly immediate preparations were made. It was necessary there should be a company selected out of our regiment for Rangers, of which Capt. William Barron was appointed commander: and as I had become somewhat familiar with a sergeant's duty, he requested me to go into his company, and I complied.

When all things were ready, we set sail with three ships of the line, two or three frigates, and about two thousand five hundred soldiers, British and Americans. We had a good passage. The enemy having possession of the harbour, we could not make the land in that direction, but were compelled to sail round a few miles to Tarpolin Cove, where we landed, though not without much difficulty—the wind blowing strong, and the seas ran so high, that the ships dragged their anchors. But we at length succeeded in landing all our men etc. and marched several miles through the woods, till we came within sight of the fort.

They fired on us with their cannon, but we lay behind the rocks, so that they could do us no harm. It was a fair day. I walked out alone from behind the rocks and saw the men in the fort about firing a cannon in the direction in which I stood. I had heard it remarked that a ball could be seen in the air after it left the cannon's mouth and thought this a good time to ascertain the truth of what appeared so incredible to me. I stood my ground. The piece was fired, and before the ball got half way to me, I could see where it was, by its driving the air together, and forming a blue kind of substance about the size of a barrel.

There were two very high hills near the harbour of St Johns; one was called Flagstaff-Hill, and the other Gibbet-Hill. The enemy had possession of both. These hills commanded the ground on which it was desirable to erect our batteries, to play on the fort. On the Flag-staff-Hill the enemy had placed three hundred men, in a situation very difficult to be got at by an opposing force. After dark our company and a company of British Light Infantry, commanded by Capt. MacDonald, set out under the guidance of one of the inhabitants, and marched in an Indian file round the hill, until we were pretty near the enemy's sentinels. Here we sat down upon the ground, and remained all night without speaking a word, until daybreak, when the word was whispered from the front to the rear, to march forward.

We had a Frenchman in our company, and when we were hailed by the sentinels, he would answer them in French, and by this means we succeeded in taking several of them, without alarming the main force at the top of the hill. But before we had reached the top, one of them fired on us, which gave notice of our approach to their van guard, who immediately opened a brisk fire upon our foremost men. We however rushed on till we came near their main party. In the meantime, Capt. MacDonald was so badly wounded that he died soon after, and about thirty of our party were either killed or wounded.

We killed and took about the same number of the enemy. The lieutenant of the British company and myself, were foremost, and we advanced on and found their stepping-place, and while running up it, the lieut. was shot through the vitals, and he died soon after. Thus I was all alone, the remainder of our party not having gained the summit; the enemy retreated, and I followed them to the other end of the hill—In my route on the hill, I picked up a good French gun, and brought it home with me.

It pretty soon commenced raining exceedingly hard and continued to rain until about midnight of the next night, when it cleared away. We remained masters of the hill, and were obliged to remain on it without a mouthful of food or drink of any sort, until morning of the second day after we started, when a British colonel came on the hill, and applauded us very highly for our exploit and success, and said we should have some refreshment. Gibbet-Hill, before mentioned, was between us and the fort, and we could not tell whether there were any of the enemy's men on it or not. The British col told Capt. Barron to send two men to the top of this hill, and direct them to retreat if they found any body there, if they did not, to swing their hats.

Capt. Barron turned immediately to me, and said "Sergeant Perry, take a man with you, and go to the top of the hill," and before I had time to pick one, he ordered Peter Laford, the Frenchman who deceived the sentry on Flagstaff-hill, to go with me. After we had started, Peter said the captain ought not to have sent him; for they would kill him if they took him. He said "we must throw the priming out of our guns, and if they take us, we will tell them we deserted—and we shall soon be re-taken." I told him he might throw *his* priming out if he chose, but I would not *mine*. The brush were so wet, however, that we could not have used our pieces, if we had occasion. We at length gained the top of the hill, and swung our hats as a signal that there was none of the enemy on it.

We could see into the enemy's fort, which was nearer to us than our own men. They fired a cannon at us, the ball went over our heads, and struck on the other hill within six feet of our men, who were all paraded, but did no injury. Pretty soon the commander, with his men, came to Gibbit-Hill to look out a place for his battery, and set those of his men to work on the battery, who had not been engaged in taking Flagstaff Hill. Our company were much fatigued—The enemy kept up a constant fire upon us, and threw balls and shells on the hill, but did not make very great slaughter, though some of our men were killed.

While a squad of regulars sat eating their breakfast in a tent, a cannon ball passed through it, and killed one man instantly; and another by the name of David Foster, belonging to Capt. Cain's company, was struck on the temple bone by a grape shot, which passed under his forehead, rolled his eyes out, and left a little piece of the lower part of his nose standing; and what I thought was very remarkable, he lived to get home—but how much longer I do not know for a certainty; though, about ten years ago, I was credibly informed that he was then living in the state of Massachusetts.

We landed at the island, on Monday morning—on Tuesday morning took possession of Flagstaff Hill, and on Wednesday broke up the ground for our batteries—so that by Friday they were ready to open upon the enemy. At about 12 o'clock on Friday night, having eleven morters fixed, we commenced throwing shells in great abundance, into the enemy's fort, which caused much screaming and hallooing in their ranks, and did great execution. We kept thein flying the remainder of the night, and until the sun was about two hours high on Saturday morning, when the enemy sent out a flag, with proposals for a capitulation.

But the conditions were such as our commander could not agree to, and we went at it again as hard as ever, and so continued, till the sun was about two hours high at night. They then sent out another flag of truce, bringing word that they had concluded to comply with the terms we offered them in the morning; and about sun-set they marched out of the fort, and we marched in, and took possession.

A few days after this, three men-of-war arrived at the harbour of St. Johns, from Havana, for assistance, and bringing news of the surrender of that place to the English. There was great rejoicing in the fort and on board the vessels, on the occasion of these signal successes. We remained here a short time, and, having put all things to rights, we shipped for Halifax, leaving British soldiers enough to garrison the fort.

After being some time at sea, the men grew sickly, and on our way a great many were taken sick, and I was among the number. I had the nervous fever. When we arrived at Halifax, our times were out; but I was so unwell, that instead of returning home, I was obliged to go to the hospital. I told my friends that were discharged, as we parted, that they would never see me again, for I was very sick and out of my head—and no one thought I could live long. I remained in the hospital some time, but was so deranged that I cannot tell exactly how long. I had my reason, however, by turns; and in one of these intervals, I remember perfectly well, Doctor Matthews, the surgeon of our regiment, had me brought into his room, and tried to make me drink some sour punch, but I told him I could not. He asked me if I did not love it when I was well. I told him I did.

At another time I came to myself so much as to know that the body lice were eating me up, and told one of those who waited on me, to heat a tailor's goose which was in the room, and iron my blanket on both sides, which he did, and it turned it as red as blood.

Capt. Barron staid with us all winter, and the British gave him a Lieutenant's commission in the standing army, for his valour in taking Flagstaff-Hill at Newfoundland. He came to see me, and I told him I wanted to go home. He asked me if I would not have staid, if I had been well. I told him, no. He then said he would see that I was put a-board the first vessel that sailed for Boston. He asked me if I had any money. I told him I did not know what had become of my money or clothes; upon which he took from his pocket a cob dollar and gave it me, but what became of it I never knew—The captain was as good as his word, for in a few days after I was put a-board a vessel for Boston. I do not know the name of the captain, nor how long I was on the passage: but I remember they once took me up on deck, it being a very pleasant day, and combed my head, and my hair all rolled off.

While I was on board that vessel, it appears to me that I died—that I went through the excruciating pains of the separating of soul and body, as completely as ever I shall again, (and such a separation must soon take place) and that I was immediately conveyed to the gate of Heaven, and was going to pass in; but was told by one, that I could not enter then, but in process of time, if I would behave as he directed, on the set time I should have admittance. It appeared to me that my feet stood on a firm foundation, and that I stood there for the space of about a half hour. In this time there appeared to be a continual flowing up of people, as we suppose they die; and none stopped, but all passed off, one way or the other.

Just at my left hand, there appeared to be the opening of a great gulph, and the greater part of the grown people seemed to pass off there. Once in a while one passed through the gate into the Holy City. One person appeared, with whom I had been intimately acquainted, and it appeared to me that I knew him as well as ever I did: it was Doct. Matthews—(and whether I saw him or not, he died, as I afterwards learned, while I was sick on board the ship.) The one that talked with me, told me about the Revolutionary War, and showed me the British vessels in the harbour of Boston, as plainly as I saw them when they came.

And during the first year of that war, I was down there in Gen. Putnam's regiment, and I went on Roxbury hill to see the shipping in the harbour, and they looked exactly as they had been shown to me many years before.—This transition (as I firmly believe) from life to death, and from death to life, which took place nearly sixty years ago, is as fresh in my mind now as it was then: and not many days have passed from that time to this, which have not brought the interesting scenes I , then witnessed, clearly to view in my mind. But I never dared to say anything about it, for a great many years afterwards, for fear of being ridiculed. But about the last of February or first of January, 1763, peace was declared between England, France and Spain, and the people rejoiced exceedingly on account of it. I told them we should have another war soon.

They asked me why I thought so. I told them the British had settled peace with their foreign enemies, but they could not live long in peace, and they would come against us next. But I never told my own wife, nor any other person, of what happened to me on board the vessel, as above related, for nearly thirty years afterwards, when a great deal was said in the neighbourhood where I lived, about one Polly Davis, of Grantham, New Hampshire, who was taken very sick, so that no one thought she could live long, and many times the people thought she was dying. In one of these turns she had a dream or vision, by which she was assured that, on a stated Sunday, she should be healed, and go to meeting the same day.

On the Saturday night, previous to the time appointed, many people stood round her bed, expecting every moment that she would breathe her last: but when the hour she had mentioned arrived, she rose from her bed, and said she was well: and Captain Robert Scott carried her some distance to meeting, behind him on horseback, the same day she recovered. There was so much talk about it, that I ventured to tell my experience as before described and have since told it to a great many people; and, some believe it, and others do not. But to return to my narrative—When we arrived in Boston harbour, the authority of the place would not permit the sick to be brought into town, for fear of the fever; and I was carried to the castle.

A Major Gay, who was there at the time, was very kind to me, and took me into his room, and gave me some refreshment—He asked me if I had any friends that would come and take care of me, if they knew I was there. I told him that I did not doubt but that my uncle David Joy would come, if he knew it; upon which he sat down and wrote him a letter, and despatched a boat ashore, with directions to leave it at Martin's tavern, where, it fortunately happened, was a man, going directly to Rehoboth, who took the letter and carried it to my uncle that very night The second day after the letter was written, my uncle arrived with a horse and chair, and took me off by the way of Dorchester Point.

When I got into the chair, I felt nicely; and told my uncle that if the horse could stand it, I would ride home that night, a distance of forty-four miles. But my resolution soon forsook me. I became extremely weak, and my delirium returned, so that my uncle was unable to get me to a tavern. He carried me to a private house the first night, and it took him three days more to get me home, where we arrived on the ninth day of December, which was the day appointed by the civil authority for public Thanksgiving—I think I had the greatest reason to give thanks to God, of anybody in the world, for sparing my life in so many trying scenes, and safely returning me to my friends again.

I remained sick at my uncle's house about two months, and my recovery for most of that period, was considered doubtful; but in process of time it pleased God to restore me to health.

In August this year, (1762) I was twenty-one years old: Before I went on the last tour in the Spring, I agreed with my master, and got up my indentures. As he had all my wages for the former campaigns, I thought I would have them this year myself; but by reason of sickness, etc. I spent or lost them, and all my clothes, except those I had on at the hospital.

In April, 1763, I left my native home, and went into the town of Killingly, Connecticut, and agreed to work for a man, six months, at my trade. On the 12th of January, 1764, I was married; at which time I was not worth ten dollars, besides my clothes. I followed shoemaking, made a comfortable living by it, and soon was able to buy a few acres of land, upon which I erected tanworks—had a pretty good run of custom, and the inhabitants assisted all they could. Thus, for a time matters went on prosperously, and in three or four years I gained considerable property.

But there was another tanner in Killingly, named Watson, who used to have all the custom before I set up business there, and had become pretty rich. Finding his custom decrease as mine gained, he came and proposed to take me into partnership with him, so that we could carry on the business on a large scale. I closed with him, and in three years he managed to get all I had earned and left me two hundred dollars in debt.

This brings me up to our Revolutionary war. In the Spring of 1775, as there could be no accommodation of the difficulties between Great Britain and the Americans, the British troops marched out of Boston to Lexington and Concord, and killed a number of our men, which aroused every part of the country to arms! An army was immediately raised, and I was appointed a lieutenant in Capt. Fleet's company, and General Putnam's regiment. As soon as our company was full, (and it did take long to fill it) the ensign and myself marched with it to Roxbury and quartered our men in the Loring house. In a few days the captain and the other lieutenant joined us. The captain, however, was soon taken sick, and died before he had done one tour of duty.

We remained there till after the 11th of June, on which day the Bunker-Hill fight took place; but my company was not in it. This was a severe battle, especially to the British, who had 1053 killed and wounded, according to their returns, including a great proportion of officers. We had 78 killed, and 86 wounded, and among the slain was the noble Gen. Warren, whose death was a great loss to our army and country. Our regiment, immediately after this battle, was collected together on Prospect-Hill, where we built a fort. The British were in possession of Bunker-Hill, about three quarters of a mile distant, and in plain sight of our works.

This Spring Gen. Ethan Allen went and took Crown-Point from the British, together with a number of cannon, which were of great service to us, as we had but a small quantity of artillery.

When the fort was completed on Prospect-Hill, our cannon were placed within point-blank shot of the enemy, and as I was walking one day with an old experienced officer, I asked him why we did not fire upon the enemy? He said, if, by our formidable appearance, we could keep them where they were, we should do well, for we had not am-munition enough to last one day and a half. There was but little fight-ing this season, except some small skirmishes between the sentinels of the out-posts, which were soon put a stop to.

In the heat of Summer, the men were attacked with the dysentery, and considerable numbers of them died. The people flocked in from the country, to see the camps and their friends, and took the disorder; and it spread all over the New-England states: it carried off a great many more in the country than in the camp, which seemed to dis-hearten the people very much.

But in the latter part of winter General Washington marched a considerable force on to Dorchester Point, in the night, erected tem-porary batteries, and conveyed his cannon to them—and in the morn-ing, when the British came to find their fleet exposed to his fire, they sent word to him, that if he fired on their shipping, they would burn the town: but if he would let them pass out of the harbour unmo-lested, they would quit the place: and they did so.—Gen. Washington expected their next object would be New-York, and marched all his troops immediately for that city. He went by land and arrived there before the enemy did by water: but, for want of men and ammunition, he was obliged to evacuate the city to them.

About this time several regiments were raised for one year's ser-vice. Col. Durgee, who commanded one of them, pressed me hard to take a captain's commission in his regiment. But as I was poor at that time and had a wife and five small children to support, or if I went, to leave without the proper means of support, I could not comply with his wishes. I told him a soldier ought not to have anything to think of at home.

But they could not raise men enough, without making large drafts of militia. In the Fall of the year, a number of regiments were ordered to be raised for the winter. I had the appointment of a first lieutenant and was ordered to march with my company to New-York. We accordingly set out, and had proceeded one day, when I had counter orders, to go to Providence, the enemy having taken possession of Newport, I was put into Col. John Ely's regiment, which was under the command of Gen. Spencer, and remained at Providence till the expiration of the term for which we were called out, without any occurrence of importance, and then returned home.

In the year 1777, Congress, and the states individually, made an attempt to raise an army for three years, or during the war, that Gen. Washington might have an army that he could depend upon: but it was difficult to raise such a force. The government of Connecticut passed a law providing, that if any two men would procure one soldier to enlist for three years or during the war, they should be exempted from a draft during that period. One of my neighbours wished me to find a man who would enlist, and he would pay one half, and find somebody to pay the other half. I found a man as he desired: but my neighbour failed to get a partner as he proposed, and the man refused to go, unless the whole sum was paid him in advance. I was so anxious to have the man enlisted, that, notwithstanding my poverty, I paid him twenty pounds myself, although I was not exposed to a draft. This settled the difficulty; and I afterwards enlisted several others.

As there is history extant giving account of the principal events of the whole war, I will confine myself merely to an account of my domestic concerns. Nothing material with regard to them took place, until the month of March, in the year 1779, when I left Connecticut, and moved into Plainfield, New Hampshire. I lived in that town eighteen years. The inhabitants of this part of the country were not much distressed after I moved here; for Burgoyne was taken, and that pretty much stopped the enemy's progress to the northward, except a party that came and burnt Royalton, (that being a frontier town in those days,) and went off again without much opposition.

Vermont was not at that time recognised as a state. New York harassed them on one side, and New-Hampshire on the other. Finally, what was formerly called the N. Hampshire Grants; that is, three tier of towns on the east side of Connecticut River, joined with Vermont, in order to help her obtain her state privileges. They at last agreed to give N. York thirty thousand dollars to relinquish their claim, and by that means Vermont obtained of congress an admission into the union, on an equal footing with the original states.

In 1783, peace was declared between Great Britain and the United States, and the army was disbanded and returned home to their friends, without anything for their toils and sacrifices, but the consciousness of having "fought a good fight," and having won an invaluable inheritance for their posterity. The slates laid heavy taxes, in order to defray their individual expenses in carrying on the war, which were burthensome to the people. But they finally paid into the state treasuries enough to redeem the paper they had issued, to pay the soldiers their bounty, which is more than could be said of the National Government, until after the poor soldiers had disposed of their hard-earnings for a tenth or twentieth part of its nominal value.

In 1785, I took a captain's commission in the N. H. militia, signed by Meshick Ware, President; (for at that time there was no governor) and served eight years. I also served nine years as Selectman of Plainfield.

In 1797, I moved to Chelsea, Vt. and have lived here twenty-one years, last March, and helped pay the premium to New-York, in order to become a state—and for a portion of the time we have been a state much opposition has been manifested by a part of our citizens, towards the general government, and in a very bad time, too—in a time of war, when we ought to have united as a band of brothers in the common cause of our country. But we were not alone in this evil. It has pervaded most of the New England states.

I have lived to see four wars in our country, and the last was attended with difficulties harder to be surmounted than any of the other wars, by reason of the enmity towards the general government of that portion of the people, who declared there was no cause of war with England, although she had taken between nine hundred and a thousand of our vessels, impressed some thousands of our citizens, and sent the Indians to massacre our defenceless inhabitants—and notwithstanding the general government had done everything to effect an accommodation of their differences, and obtain redress for our grievances, without a resort to arms.

I desire it may never be forgotten by my posterity, for whom I have written these memoirs, that there was once a time, when party spirit raged to an extent that threatened the destruction of those liberties, which I had some small share in establishing. I hope they will never forget, that when war was declared to maintain those liberties, there were men claiming all the wealth, talents and religion of the country, who, from party, or worse motives, held back their resources from Government, and did all in their power to keep those who were disposed to lend an assisting hand, from entering into their country's service.

In the time of the Revolution we had a few such men among us, who set much by the British Government, and we drove them out of the country, or confined them at home, so that they could not meet in Convention, in the heart of the land, to plot against the government, and divide the Union. And I desire it may be remembered, that notwithstanding they boasted of their talents and religion, the Lord stood by us and put our enemies to flight in a marvellous manner, and wrought wonders for us as a nation: and we have the greatest reason to bless and praise his holy name, of any people on the earth.—Let it be remembered, as a warning to future generations, of the dangerous effects of party spirit, when carried to excess, that a governor of Vermont, at a time when the enemy threatened a powerful invasion of our frontier towns, with the avowed intention of laying them in ruins, stood on the shores of the lake, discouraging our valiant freemen from going to the assistance of their brethren, by telling them they would be killed if they went over—when he, and every other person of common sense, knew, that it would not be more than six hours before the enemy would be at Burlington, if he beat our men at Plattsburgh.

But let it also, with gratitude, be remembered, that while the chief magistrate was thus employed, the gallant Col. Fassett encouraged and prevailed on them to go forward— and they did go forward to participate in a glorious battle and victory, which preserved our towns from conflagration, and wiped the foul stain from the character of our state, which the conduct of this governor would otherwise have brought upon it.

While the enemy were thus discomfited by land, we beheld the British fleet on the lake heaving in sight of the little squadron of the invincible Macdonough, who was on his knees, praying to his God; and He answered him by fire, as in former times—and notwithstanding the enemies' superior force, they were obliged to strike—and on that ever-memorable eleventh of September, the Lord discomfited their whole force, and returned them back from whence they came: so that we may see, that the effectual, fervent prayer of a righteous man availeth much: and that the sacrifice of the wicked is an abomination to the Lord—For the great men of a great state said, that it was unbecoming a moral and religious people to pray for the success of our arms, and that we must not fight the British, because they were "the Bulwark of our religion." But I cannot but think, that they were deluded and blinded by party prejudices, and that the good hand of God was discernible at Baltimore, New-Orleans, and Plattsburgh—on Lake Erie, and Lake Champlain, and everywhere else that a traitor did not command.

Had not the Lord been on our side, and fought our battles, we must have failed to maintain our liberties against so potent a foe from abroad, aided by so many of our misguided people at home—and it becomes us as a people, (as I have before said;) to bless and praise his Holy name forever, that He caused us to overcome our powerful enemies in two wars for our independence, and that there seems now to be so happy a union taking place among ourselves—that those of our fellow-citizens who have been thus deluded and deceived, are sensible of their errors, and appear ready to unite with all real friends of their country's honour and prosperity.—And I pray God that this bond of union may continue to grow firmer and stronger, till every American citizen will be of one heart and one mind, in a determination to support our Republican form of Government to the latest posterity.

May we all remember the maxim of our illustrious Washington: "United we stand; divided we fall."—When we reflect back to our Revolutionary war, and see how much blood and treasure were spent to gain our independence, shall we, after so long an experience of the advantages arising from so good a government, be any more deceived by internal or foreign enemies? Shall we contrast the mildness of our government, and the civil and religious liberty that we enjoy under it, with the bigotry and tyranny which prevails under the monarchies of Europe, and say we are willing to exchange the former for the latter? I dare say not. Then let me conjure my posterity to stand by this government of our choice, and never be deceived by political or ecclesiastical demagogues.

Let the people keep the right and power of election always in their own hands, and at their annual freemen's meetings be sure to choose men into office, who are true friends of a Republican Government.

Let them encourage all the arts and sciences that are necessary in a Republic, and none others—and in this way they may perpetuate their liberties.—But if they are ambitious to ape the follies, extravagance, and luxury of European countries, their freedom can have but a short duration. But, above all, let us as a nation dedicate ourselves to God, and pray that he would have us in his holy keeping, and so direct the councils of our nation, as may tend to preserve its free institutions, to the latest period of time; which is the ardent prayer of

David Perry,

Chelsea, Vt. 1819.

Luke Gridley's Diary of 1757
Luke Gridley

PREFACE

The year 1757 was the nadir of the English cause during the Seven Years' War in America. Not only had it thus far distinctly the worse—having lost the control of the West at Fort Duquesne in 1755, and that of Lake Ontario at Oswego in 1756, and gained only a desert frontier on the east by depopulating one of its own provinces—but the disasters had seemingly taught the government nothing. They had not even loosed the hold of political "pulls" and jobbery which was the curse of all the administrative services. For two years a set of very unfit commanders, appointed by court or family influence, with the king's son Cumberland as military dictator, played ducks and drakes with the English chances of gaining the chief heritage of the Western Hemisphere; and they would have lost it altogether but for the provincials whom they despised, belittled, and defamed—largely for their own repute and promotions, and to the fatal misleading of English judgment as to an easy suppression of provincial revolt a few years later.

Braddock, the first, appointee of Cumberland and head of the household brigade, was by far the ablest and most courageous; but the remnant of his slaughtered regulars was saved by Washington's Virginians. A provincial governor, the energetic and sensible if tactless and over-confident Shirley, then held the field for a while, and the solitary success of nearly three years was achieved by Lyman's New-Englanders; it won a baronetcy and £5000 not for the victor, however, but for the late Admiral Warren's nephew, William Johnson, who despite the value of his Indian diplomacy, had shown neither military conduct nor courage. His jealousy of Shirley's interference began a feud which was taken up by his kinsmen, the powerful De Lanceys; and Shirley was deposed through their influence with Cumberland, probably plus the interprovincial grudge between New York and New England which wrought so much evil in the Revolution.

An English colonel, Daniel Webb, for no historically assignable reason, was then sent over as a place-warmer for two Scotchmen: James Abercrombie, another court favourite, who in turn was to be locum tenens for John Campbell, Earl of Loudoun, though all three were to remain as generals. Loudoun had also the influential earldom of Stair behind him and had managed to lose nearly all his command at Preston in 1745. Scotch noblemen were pertinacious place-jobbers and patronage hunters, but the just repute of Scotchmen as fighters seems moreover to have bred an idea that all were competent commanders. The curious feature in this case was that the chiefs did not even exhibit the personal warlikeness which distinguished so many of their underlings.

Loudoun had the hot temper and rough manners of the conventional Scot and was valorous toward civilian magistrates; but he displayed no undignified haste to engage in actual conflict and was easily persuaded of its infeasibility. Abercrombie, after his repulse at Ticonderoga in 1758, was stricken with a more cowardly panic than Braddock's mangled troops, as having infinitely less cause; and with a superior army fled from before a fort which Montcalm said could have been taken with two cannon. They were no worse than Webb, however, who was in a qualm of apprehension during his whole stay at Fort Edward; never risked his skin, and never moved without a huge escort; and after Fort William Henry and its garrison had been captured through his own fears and incapacity, thought of flying to Albany and leaving the upper settlements to the torch and scalping-knife.

These appointments again illustrate the contempt of the home government for provincial affairs, as needing little ability to manage, which alone would justify the Revolution. Respectable subordinates, or likely to be such, not one of these persons would have been dreamed of for a commander-in-chief of the smallest independent army in Europe; but almost any officer of regimental rank was good enough to plan and direct campaigns in America, with a few thousand regulars and a "mob" of provincials. Yet they would probably all have done decently well in Europe, for which they were trained; where nearly all battles were fought on open ground, with well-drilled and disciplined troops for at least a backbone, all marches were over multiplex roads thoroughly mapped out and running through settled agricultural districts, supply departments were fairly provided and officered, and practically all contingencies could be forecast if the general had a brain and experience.

But in America, where none of these things were true, they were helplessly unable to construct a new system of ideas, and except Braddock they seem to have been physically daunted. The mere fact that pretty much all battles were fought *in the woods*, as were most of the Revolutionary battles, shattered all their notions of tactics. If you could not keep your troops together, how could there be any fighting except a barbarian scramble without guidance, and how could they form and maintain columns when crawling through underbrush or making way around giant pines?

And the vast silent woods as warm with skulking savages, or suddenly breaking into blood-curdling yells and screeches, evidently appalled their nerves, as they did those of the Americans themselves wherever familiarity had not bred coolness or even over-contempt. They blenched as even Arnold could not prevent his troops from blenching when Burgoyne was marching from Skenesborough to Fort Edward, and not a hand was lifted against him in those trackless forests; as the forces of Willett and Gansevoort in Fort Stanwix were well-nigh frightened into surrender in a well-stocked fort, by half their number of Indians and a handful of white men.

Against this shifting series of second-rate military pedants was matched a Frenchman of first-rate ability and adaptability, Montcalm, succeeding another of the same stripe, Dieskau; aided by subordinates to whom the forest life and the Indians were native or entirely familiar. The American sections they led were as ill-matched in the same direction. The English provinces disliked each other only less than the French and dreaded each other more. Each was afraid of doing too much, for fear of the rest taking the advantage to do too little; and those under royal governors were glad of every occasion of public danger and demand to tie their rulers' hands, not only for the present, but as a precedent for the future. None had or would permit any standing military force; each raised what it wanted for the year, disbanded it at the close, and could not get a new one into the field till toward summer of the next.

Men, supplies, everything, were insufficient, slow, and disunited. Canada was at least a single province, with only one governor and one general to fight and paralyze each other—which truly was enough. That in spite of all this the French made but little real progress during their time of superiority and sank into irretrievable ruin as soon as the

English put stronger men in power, is the best evidence of the incurable weakness of their colonial system. It was in fact not a colonizing system at all, except in old Canada. Outside of that it lacked the one thing needful—people; and, as even there save for a slender body, was merely a set of forts with practically no settlers behind them. The command of a district hundreds of miles in extent rested on some one fort, or a few stockades; and as soon as they were reduced, the whole fabric went with them and went forever. The English control was in solid ranks of farms and villages, which could not have been expropriated wholesale even if conquered, and which could lose a hundred frontier skirmishes and regain everything by a single victory.

The operations of 1757, in which our diarist was a humble unit, need not be set forth in detail. Broadly, all forward movements and all plans for such had been suspended by the displacement of Shirley, and nothing could go on until Loudoun had decided what he wished to undertake. His plan was the old one of cutting off all French reinforcements by capturing Louisbourg and commanding the mouth of the St. Lawrence, as a preliminary to striking down what was left; but he showed his bad judgment by so stripping the centre for this purpose as to expose that to imminent destruction before the starving system could work.

This venturesomeness in plan could only have been redeemed by equal venturesomeness and energy in execution; but he showed neither. His supplies were dilatory, but so were everybody's always; and he did not reflect, like Pepperrell and his men and a thousand other minor leaders of his time, that the enemy's were sure to be so likewise. He would do nothing until he had a force to assure victory; before he received it, the French had become the stronger at Louisbourg; and when his admiral would still attack, he would bear no part in it.

Meantime Montcalm had gathered some six thousand regulars and Canadians and a couple of thousand Indians at Ticonderoga, to invest Fort William Henry and Monro's twelve hundred at the head of Lake George, the less important of the two keys of communication from Canada to Albany. Webb the while was cowering at the ultimate keypost, Fort Edward, fifteen miles off: binding Putnam with an oath not to reveal the presence of the enemy when first discovered; waiting for provincial reinforcements which could not possibly arrive in time; sending enough to Monro to be a heavy loss, but not enough to make successful resistance even probable; not daring to join him with full force lest the French should turn his rear and assail Albany, and not reflecting that if the upper fort was untenable, it was obvious common-sense to withdraw the garrison to Fort Edward, and leave the French an empty fort instead of lining it with good troops; refusing to let his provincials and incoming militia march to Monro's relief when they begged it, countermanding the permission to a small body when given; acting, in a word, like a thoroughly frightened man in presence of new conditions he could not handle—which was the truth.

Monro surrendered on promise of security; but Montcalm's In-dians had engaged with him on promise of plunder and would not have their prey escape, the fear of losing some part of their services as scouts was more insistent than humanity with some officers, and the prisoners themselves paid ransom in brandy which maddened the savage blood still more. The Indians butchered the sick and wounded at once, the Canadian officers very willing because it relieved them of a burden on their march; dug up and scalped the corpses from the smallpox hospital and were later decimated by the consequent epi-demic; dragged bodies of prisoners out of the marching column and slaughtered them, keeping some for eating at Montreal; and before they were stopped by Montcalm and some others, had probably killed five hundred sick and well. The massacre, its numbers greatly exagger-ated, is still one of the best remembered incidents in American history.

Webb's expresses and appeals had already called out great bodies of provincial militia, which came pouring in just before and just after the disaster. Connecticut alone had sent some 5000, or about one-seventh of its entire fighting population on this single call, besides the consid-erable body of its regulars already in the field, though its own borders were in no danger. As Montcalm's forces did not advance, but with-drew to Canada a week later, these were soon recalled; but meantime they were enduring great hardships from lack of food, tents, blankets, and cooking utensils, and many refused to remain without object, the New-Yorkers threatening to shoot their officers if they interfered.

At last all was settled; a small force was enrolled for winter guard and scouting: and both sides prepared for the next year's struggle, when Pitt had come into power and begun to send over very differ-ent officers. Connecticut's part in this war was one which may well be a source of pride to every citizen. She levied first and last over 27,000 troops, of whom some 14,000 were separate individuals, and 9,000 were regularly in the pay of the colony for full fighting years' services in the field, outside the militia call—even that showing her willingness to respond to the common danger and send her sons to the field. Now her population in the year 1756 was found to be 130,611. The highest proportion of males between fifteen and fifty-five known in any European country has been 280 per 1000; the lowest a little under 240.

Even the latter, taken from old settled peoples, is probably greater than that in a half-settled colony where families were very large and the number of small children very great; but in any event the number of such male adults in Connecticut was not much above 36,000, and may have been below 31,000. Taking the supposition most unfavourable for our purpose, the colony furnished, for a war which did not directly endanger herself, and simply from common loyalty, nearly two-fifths of all her fighting citizens; on the more probable supposition, nearly one-half. Even apart from the militia sent to relieve Fort William Henry, it contributed certainly one-fourth, and probably nearer one-third, of its entire adult citizenship for steady service in breaking the French power.

In 1757 the General Assembly passed an act to raise 1,400 men, in one regiment of fourteen companies, to act in conjunction with Loudoun's regulars. At its head was placed Phineas Lyman of Suffield, the eminent soldier who had won the battle of Lake George eighteen months before, had won Johnson a title and wealth, and would have seized Ticonderoga for him if allowed; had noted with unerring eye the best spot above Albany to command the road from Canada, and fortified it. Johnson, with an equally unerring eye for his own interests, suppressed Lyman's name in his dispatches and removed it from the fort.

It was then the custom, following the English fashion, for the colonel himself (English lieutenant-colonel, their colonels being titular figure-heads) to be captain of the first or "colonel's company," and Lyman so acted. The other two regimental officers were respectively captains of the next two companies: Lieutenant-Colonel Nathan Whiting of New Haven, second company, and Major Nathan Payson of Hartford, third company. Of the others in order, the captains were Israel Putnam of Pomfret, Samuel Hubbell of Fairfield, David Waterbury of Stamford, Adonijah Fitch of New London, John Slapp of Mansfield, John Jeffries of Cornwall, Eliphalet Whittlesey of Newington, Edmund Welles of Hebron, Ben Adam Gallup of Groton, Ephraim Preston of Wallingford, and Andrew Ward of Guilford.

The present diarist, Luke Gridley, was a private in "Captain Major" Payson's company. He was from Farmington, of a numerous stock which also included a missionary, and members of which were on the committee to raise subscriptions for Boston after its closure by the Port Bill. It was allied to the Boston family which produced General Richard Gridley, the great military engineer who laid out the works which reduced Louisbourg in 1745, and the defensive works at Bunker Hill and Lake George. He was in no battles; but had he been, perhaps we should have had no diary.

At all events, he marched with his company to Fort Edward, and was in camp there through the season till the troops were discharged. He gives us a set of notes upon the camp life and the outside events that came to his ears, which afford some new information, correct some old, and add to the vividness of our picture of the situation from the soldiers' point of view. As examples, we note the ever-present whip as the tool of all work for instruction and emendation. From the horrible punishment of a thousand lashes for desertion to the enemy, or five hundred for deserting from the forces of one colony into those of another (a most significant entry as a side-light on provincial separatism), or five hundred and being drummed out of camp with a rope around the neck for unspecified iniquities, we have all the way from three hundred down for arrears of a season's dereliction, for sleeping on guard (an unforgivable offense which wins the dreadful punishment of running the gauntlet also), for drunkenness (where, curiously, a "Yorker" gets three hundred to a regular's one), for selling rum without a license or to the Indians, for insubordination, for playing cards (doubtless swindling at them, as the camp was anything but puritanical), for wearing a dirty shirt on guard (quite properly, remembering what cleanliness means in a camp), for counterfeiting and passing the money, and so on; and we rejoice, with a wistful desire that our ancestors' customs were not dead, when a dirty practical joker receives fifty well-earned lashes. Riding the wooden horse with heavy weights on the feet is also not disused.

We note the constant labour of the officers to prevent or check vices, or inattention to the discipline needed for safety, for life or health: driving the worst camp-trulls out of the lines, regulating or stopping the sale of liquor, stopping the waste of stores, preventing the jaunts beyond the lines which were always liable to make one less soldier and one more scalp, punishing the shirks by making them stand guard at night, enforcing cleanliness, sobriety, obedience, and marksmanship, and respect for private property. We note that a few true-blooded New-Englanders hold Sabbath services even without a minister, in a camp where all sorts of "gaming, cursing, and swearing" are going on around them; and that the Connecticut men observe "election day" even in camp, "toping off with Bisket."

We note the never-ending scourge of small-pox which made dreadful havoc with the soldiers throughout the war, had already driven some bodies into disbanding outright, and filled the hospital which the deaths from it were constantly emptying. Rather curiously, we find pneumonia ("the Long feaver") one of the worst foes in mid-summer. We note that the allowance of rum is missed only less sorely than that of food: in those times it was thought impossible to keep a force in health and vigour except by regular if small rations of spirits.

We observe that an Indian massacre of a scouting force is prevented by the vigilance of three or four, "the rest of the gard being asleep,"— a monotonously regular tale in colonial affairs. We are reminded that the English side too had Indians serving it, the Iroquois being kept on its side through Johnson's influence; but the "Mohocks" only bring in prisoners, not scalps, and seemingly behave with decency. We see also that the descendants of the Mohegans and even the Pequots are ready to take a share in the excitement of war; indeed, the roll of Fitch's company shows a quite extraordinary percentage of evident Mohegans with craggy or grotesque names.

The negro is also well in evidence; an Afro-American could make a stirring picture of his race in the early wars. Other topics will suggest themselves, opened by the diary. The language of an untutored colonial is always of interest from its hints of contemporary phonetics, or its survivals of old names or shades of meaning or usage. The present diary is not without these. "Resigned" for surrendered, "while" for until, "peppered" for seasoned in general, instance the last-named sort; "sass" for green vegetables has no mystery for New England readers; "skeel" for cleaning off the scale or rust is an interesting dialectic survival which has missed the great general dictionaries wholly.

In pronunciations, it is interesting to observe that our Connecticut hero's name was apparently pronounced Limmon, at least by some; "Moriall" for Montreal was certainly common; "Camplain" may be a mere slip, or indicate the same attempt at pronouncing from a written word which produced "Glockster" on some tongues; "sursposed" and "Gaplop's" (Gallop's) are examples of a phonetic law more remarkably exemplified in the astounding name of "Scockerromah," applied to Lake George, and but for the inserted "c" a quite careful catching of the French pronunciation of "Sacrement"; "a Lewed" and "a Lew-ance" for allowed and allowance, and Teuchit for (probably) Toushet, illustrate the then frequent survival of the pronunciation of ow as "oo," still usual in "wound," and once universal. "Willaim" and "Jeames" accurately preserve the accepted pronunciations of our fathers later even than this. "Poywoy" for powwow and "boyl" for ball illustrate, like other colonial writings, the curious use of "y" to indicate the sound of "w," as "droy" and "soy" for draw and saw. "Er" as "ar," in "reharsth" and so on, is a matter of course.

F. M.

DIARY

March 29th *Ad* 1757
Luke Gridly his book

Aprel 8th: this day was musterd and took our oaths

Mondy the 18th Day: this day reseved wages: bounty furst month wages and biliting: 3=18=9=0 genneral Limmons Com( ) marcht ye 18th April (Lyman's personal company, the first)

★★★★★★

The bounty this year was 42 shillings, the soldier to find clothes, powder-horn, and bullet-pouch; the wages for a private, £1 12*s*. per month of 28 days; the allowance for billeting, 4*s*. per week. This would make £4 10*s*. for the first month; but the clothes were probably furnished by the colony and deducted.

★★★★★★

the 22 of Aprel we marcth. (Payson's company, the third. This first stage was from Farmington to Harwinton, through that part of Bristol afterward set off as Burlington.)

mondy 25th we marcht Licthfeel

26th to fegguts (Widow Sedgwick's) In Kornwill 36 mi (from Farmington, not Litchfield—the road from Litchfield to Cornwall was through Goshen) the next day wich was ye 27th we marcht to Landdard Robins in Carman to dine 8 miles: from thence to Landard Reeds in Solsbeary 6 miles

28th we marcht 4 mils and 6 thrugh the nine Pardenners and then 6 which was to Levenstones manners fourness *nb*: we passed by whare 3: men died: small pox a fortinnight Before haveing the wind of ye house

★★★★★★

They marched the 4 miles to the Connecticut line at the Oblong, on the west of Salisbury.

Pardenners—The Little Nine Partners, granted by New York in 1706, was the manorial estate next south of Livingstone's Manor: it was through this that the troops passed. The Great Nine Partners, south of this, had been granted in 1697.

Fourness—Furnace (Ancram). The ore beds were part of the great Middle Berkshire deposit still heavily worked in Salisbury.

★★★★★★

29 Day we marcht 20 miles and came to Clouverreck (Claverack, three miles southeast of Hudson, N.Y.): all in helth.

30th Day I went 3 miles and came to rever (the Hudson): Seeing my frinds well I pa(st) 5 miles up the river for shad

May 1th wich was the Lords Day this day we had a meating without any minister

the 2th Day our officssers devided us into fore parts in order to vittel them more regiller. ("The men complain ye most of hunger yet ever I hered in my life," says another diarist.)

The 3th wich was tusday we had orders form gennerl Limmon to be caled to geather at 7 oclock half in the morning: and 7 at night and not to be absent haveing our hats cocked up ours guns bright and our gloths cleen: and a gard to be keept: this set sum of us to washing quick:

The 4th day we trained reseveing stricker orders

The 5 d they trained But I was garding and fiching we being straitened: for Proviccon: and hungery: Johnnathan Beamman eate 3 raw fich: guts and all for 4 quarts of wine

★★★★★★

Such bestial wagers were not uncommon in this gross hard living age. A generation or two later even than this, two men ate each a raw skunk on a bet as to which should keep his meat down the longest: a noted Windham tavern-keeper named Staniford was the winner.

★★★★★★

The 6 d we trained haveing rewls so strick: that them did not sute the ofescers was train by themseuelfs

★★★★★★

This war was the first occasion when the colonial troops became a direct part of the British armies and came under their system of discipline; and in the last two years, officers like Lyman had become conversant with the official rules of drill and tried to enforce them, while the self-trained mass resented them.

★★★★★★

Sattarday the 7 day we (*i.e.*, Payson's company) was all a lowed to train afore foks But John forgoson and Shewble Reed: Gennerrall Limon reseved orders from Lord Leudon to gard the stors and get things to cook in.

The 9th (a slip for 8th) *Day was the Sabbath*: wed a meating without a minister.

★★★★★★

This was special to a few high-grade New-Englanders. A New York officer said that Sunday had been packed away with the stores in Albany and would not come up till the work was done.

★★★★★★

One man out of eevery combenny was sent up to Greean Bush for pots and kittles: Cololol l: Pheinaas Limon: C2 Whitelsy: C3P: Gallap: C4P: Putmans: 5 Captain Magor Pasons: 6 CP Slaps: 7 CP fitch 8 CP Gafas 9 CP Wells (numbering of these is not the official one, as will be noted from our list.)

★★★★★★

This individual historic name, Green Bush, is now obliterated in "Rensselaer," city, which rolls several different things into one, and the railroad and postal station of "East Albany," which represents nothing.

★★★★★★

Mondy the 9th D I was on gard we went to visiting and Captain hugabone, (Hogeboom, of Johnson's New York forces): our Landdard traind and haveing 4 men to press he gatherd 154 dollers for them to list, (*i.e.*, the men subscribed to pay bounty and hire the recruits instead of impressing them.)

the 10th day I went on to the river to fiching (canceled: I see a sturgen 6 foot long) and thare was one of Cap Gaplops negros whiped for threting of killing a man.

Wensday the 11th day we marcht 10 miles and came to Landard vanalls (elsewhere Fanall and Fondall) to dine from thens 6 which was to Canterhook (Kinderhook): we logd by ye meating: house

The 12th Day was Electshon Day (the formal celebration in Connecticut) we marcht 24 miles and came to Greenbuch: we loged Cap Dows barn:

the 13th D toping up Electshon with bisket we marcht 10 miles and came to Landard Skilars (Schuyler's): Jest a bove ye flats (Troy; but the distances in this and the next march are not intelligible even by circuitous roads. They should be about six and twelve miles instead of ten and twenty.)

the 14th D we had our Amannachtion and then we marcht 20 miles and came to Scatte Cook (Schaghticoke, east of the Hudson, a few miles southeast of Stillwater.)

the 15th D Gennaral Limon haveing his chosie to stay thaire: or come back he broute us back to the river side 2 or 3 miles that Bostton solgers might go thare:

the 16th D I went to hunting dear a monday being on gard some of ye time and one of Limons men killed one and CP Whitelses another teuchit (evidently an Indian, and apparently the same as Tousey or Toushet? or John Hatchet, found on the rolls) killed one before our offiscers had orders from Limon that no man went to hunting or passd over the river: or spoyled any boards (or houses, barns, or fences) with out his leave allso that we should be examind how maney carthirigs we had and have an a count took of how maney we had spent: and for the future every man that shot a gun without his leave was to be brough before a cort marshal and be dealt with as an abuser of the Kings stors and find for every carterrig 3 pence starting haveing but ten and one flint deliverd him

The 17th D we traind I beaing on gard: Ensine Ezekill Lewis was put under gard for not obeaying orders:

the 18 D John ashley (an incorrigible elderly "tough subject") was whiped for not obaying orders one of Limons men

the 19 Day a thursday we had an a larram 7 Ingins runing after a boye, hwo was hunting pigons to scalp him fiuerd at him and shot thrugh his shirt 5 boullet holes sume grasing his flesh bing the west side of the rever 100 rods from us sume Duch York cap penders (carpenters) his comepantions swonge thare hats a frited at lenthe one went to his releaf: thare was scouts sent out as ouick as chould be: and 2 men out of each compeney to Allbaney for more solgers: and Captain Putmans Rangers (company raised by voluntary enlistment from among the Connecticut troops, for scouting purposes, and subordinate to Major Robert Rogers): and 20 of us was sent over the river to gard (guard *against*, he means—sc. the Indians), the "cowards."3 these cowards teuset (same as "Teuchit" before mentioned) was put under gard for not obaying orders and a whiping post set up: we was all brought round in a bodey: his sentance was to be whipet 20 lachis upon his begeing faver and promising reformation his honnor (Lyman) with good advice: and strick directions to us all repreaved him

the 20th Day the solgers traind and the offiscers played boyl (ball) Cornal Limon gave us orders to march to the forts as soon a we could conveineantly his honners compeney passd over the river in order thare for

the 21 Day we was to prepare and be in a readyness to go over the river: to march: The Boston solgers Come hear

Sabath Day 22th aboute 9 o clock in the morning 7 compeneys marcht from hear and travild to the S(t)ill wartres fort 6 mils (Stillwater on the Hudson, twenty-three miles above Albany and opposite the mouth of the Hoosick): thare we refresht our selfs: and marcht 7 mils and picht our tenths which came by water

Day 23 which was monday we marcht 10 mils and picht our tents at Suratoke (Saratoga): thare we went into the river and chast ("ketcht" not chased) aboute 3000 alewifs for our super

Day 24th Tusday Leftanant wells came heare and half our compeny traind and the rest chacths ("ketcht" not chased) and salted: 3 barrills of alewifes I went to kill a dear and shot wid with my gun wet his honnor giveing no leave to skeel ("scale," or clean off rust, etc.) it out

Day 25th thare was one Dannail Boake (Bogue; a chronic offender, earning and receiving savage punishments): one of Cap Gailaps men: run the gandtelit thrugh 30 men for sleeping upon gard which cryed Lord god have mercy on me the b(l)ood flying every stroke this was a sorrowfull sight: Also one man was sintanced to ride the wooden ho(r)se for not turning out so soon as the rest to train with 4 muskits tieed to his feet: But was repreved

Day 26 aboute 9 o clock in the morning we marcht and traveld 7 miles from hear which was half a mile above fort miserry (camp nickname of Fort Miller at the rapids of the upper Hudson, on the west side; its name is still borne by a village there) and refresht our selfs: then we marcht 7 miles and in camped jest below fort Edward

******

On the west side of the Hudson near its great bend, opposite the "Great Carry" (*i. e.,* to Wood Creek, running into Lake Champlain). Originally Fort Lyman, built by Lyman in 1755, before the battle of Lake George; renamed by Johnson to curry favour with George II., after his grandson the Duke of York, brother of the later George III.

*****

Day 27th we passed over the river and piched our tents at the norwest corner of fort Edward

Day 28th sume to work highways: sume on gard sume garding teams to timber

Day 29th Sabath sume scouting others garding and regellateing there tents: the roil amarricans the Blues marcht to fort willaim henerry

******

Royal Americans, a regiment of four battalions raised in America for this war, principally among the Pennsylvania Germans, but with European officers. The famous Lieutenant-Colonel Henry Bouquet commanded one battalion.

The Blues, a New Jersey regiment raised for this war and commanded by Colonel Parker.

Fort William Henry, built by Johnson this year, and named for the Duke of Gloucester, another brother of George III. It was at the head or southern end of Lake George, close to the water and to the present wharf and railroad station at Caldwell or Lake George.

******

Day 30th we by ye post haveing heared that thare was: an army of frinch hard by william henerry thare was 70 men lent out to Rang, (Putnam's men, enlisted the day before; but they did not perhaps start for a day or two): sume one way and sume a nother: thare was 2 men convayed to the horspetall: the dockters judgeing them to have the small pox

Day 31th I was garding sume york carpenders (directing a working party in building a fence around the camp garden) Captain Putmans Rangers set out for thare scoute.

June the 1th Ad 1757 wensday was freed from duety for a coock: a party of men was sent up to the lake to gard teams.

★★★★★★

This party consisted of thirty men each from Putnam's and another company of Rangers, with their captains and two officers and forty privates of the Connecticut troops. There is a confusion of a day or two about their starting, which is curiously reflected not only in another diarist of the camp, but even in the General Orders; unless the seventy and the one hundred were different parties—but Putnam could hardly have headed both.

★★★★★★

Day 2th we being a going to worck in the highway had half a gill of rum a lewed us a day haveing the promis of a hwol gill: we marcht one mile and tayrayed that night

Day 3th we sume of us worked hard: but them which was laszy ware calld to gard us when it was night

Day 4th we hassend our bisnes: finishing before night: we returned to the fort: we heard that fore men being on gard Scattecook shot: killed 1 frinch Indian and wounded a nother: 4 or 5 run away: the rest of the gard being asleep: (usual condition except among the Rangers, and the source of many dreadful disasters.)

Day 5th which was the Sabath: our regellars had a scurmige of fireing plattoons: thare was two of mager rogers men came hear which got clear of thare captivity at Canady and sayed thare would no frinch army come hear this year they ware so stratend for provison (see the desertions to the English from hunger later on) Magor pasons arived hear.

★★★★★★

Rogers, a noted woodsman and border smuggler, was first commissioned by Johnson in the fall of 1755 to command such a company for winter scouting, and again by Shirley the next spring for permanent work; and gradually became the head of a number of semi-independent companies. He evidently had a good eye for ability, as he selected Putnam and Stark for assistants at the outset. Stark as a fellow New Hampshire woodsman he may have known, but Putnam had been only a plain Connecticut farmer.

★★★★★★

Day 6th Captain putman's Rangers with sume of our men to assist his scouting sets of for the narrows one of Captain Galops Indeains was whiped for stealing a gun 60 laches: we shot at marks (as part of the ordered practice, not at will.)

★★★★★★

Narrows; there were several familiar places in this region thus called. The one here meant was doubtless that of Wood Creek, near its mouth at Lake Champlain; a favourite place of ambush to command the boat navigation of that useful stream.

★★★★★★s

Day 7th tusday to giting pine this day one regeler died with the camp destemper thare was 6 men of the scouts came back with a drunken Indain hwo they confind:

Day 8th sum of our picked gard see whare 12 Indians had lain a boute a mile from fort Edward: we heard sume Ranngers from new york: shot 3 frinchmen: of the senterry About 2 miles Below ye narrows: allso they killed 3 more: and 4 of thare one (own) wounded:

Day 9th one man was whiped 40 laches for siting downe on gard: we had a shower of rain which made us uneasze:

Day 10th we had an a larram 15 men being sent out a boute half a mile east of fort Edward to gard aboute as many cappenders: was serrounded with 100 frinch and Ind had a shot fore of them dead (in) swamp: one Buckely and Martin hooker was two of them (these were of Whittlesey's company; the other two were Rice Edwards and William Mortawamock, probably a Mohegan of Slapp's company. The latter had his heart torn out): 5 more was mising sursposed to be taken captive: they took a horse: gennarl Limon: with 20 men by them selves went and shot upon them and firitend them so that he got 2 pikes 2 dear skins: sevearl scalping knives and packs allso thare muster role which gave an a count of thare being 100 of them and 200 more a coming and whare they was to scoute: which was reharsth (rehearsed) both to the lake and Surratoge with spead. (This skirmish is not reported by anyone else.)

Day 11th sume of the peked gard see 9 Indeains: and thare was a scoute sent after them: but cuould not find them:

Day 12th which was the Sabaths: we sume of us a lewed to seace from our labour: mary Rogers was drumed out of the camp (shortly after this there was a general medical examination of the camp women, who seem to have been of some number): and Gorge webster was put under gard for following her drum magoir.

Day 13 2 packs and read a man shot was sursposed to be taken was found dead and scalpt nearer then whare ye other was kild

Day 14 Gennarl Limon with 300 men went out scout ("Painted like a Mohog, as many other officers of the scout were," says another diarist. The scouts sometimes scalped the dead like Indians also.)

Day 15 Boston forses: 1800 of them came hear (Under Colonel James Frye. The famous Rufus Putnam was one of them.)

Day 16th thare was one andris whiped 50 lashes for sleeping on gard: Captain Putnan with his men brought into fort Edward a frinch man which told us: fore men and 5 scalps (as only four men were killed, the Indians probably practiced a mild grade of the multiplication noted later, one of the men was David Campbell of Killingly) was carryed to Ticonderoge the 12 of June: that they lost 7 of thare men the 10 of June wen these was killd and taken: allso that thare was two battalyens of regelar troops at Ticonderoge (Montcalm's grand rendez-vous there for the movement against Fort William Henry was effected in July) and a large army at Crowne Pinte

Day 17th one of the man that was taken with the small pox may 30th Died with it: he took at Allbanney thinking he had it when he was yonge (*i.e.*, exposed himself recklessly.)

Day 18th we finishing our work at the tar kill made an oven:

Day the 19th which was the Sabath gennarl Limon with his scout came in with 1 gun 2 hats and 3 packs which he took from the enemy: the Indeians killed one regellar and wounded another a mile below fort Edward: Boston forses had a sarmmon preched by thare minester with few hearers in the forenoon: In the afternoon they shot at marks: the regellars shot thare great guns at marks and made mery: &c

Day 20th thare was one Clark Robberd Knils (Robert Niles, "clark" in Gallup's company): which came home from scouting without his honnors leave: redueced to the ranks: and whiped 100

200 hampshire solgers 3 comp (From "No. 4", Charlestown, N. H., under Lieutenant-Colonel John Goffe; part of 500 raised this spring by New Hampshire, under Colonel Nathaniel Meserve, and divided by Loudoun.)

Day 21th we had an a count took of our names: haight and age werather we had been in the service before or no &c &c &c and whare we blonged &c &c &c there was 2 Indeains whipd one a 100 laches for giting drunk scouting: the other 50 for selling bark when he was bid to get it for a gard house

Day 22th one Bosston man died with camp destemper. I hear of one that died before orders to get things clean for genral webs: arivel and no man to go out of gun shot of the fort 4 regelars whipted 40 mohoacks (Johnson's influence kept the Iroquois on the English side in this war) brought in a frinch man which they took near Crown pint: they had a poywoy (*powwow*) of rejoyceing over him &c he said thare was 200 of his compantions beetween the forts (Edward and William Henry) and as many more between fort Edward and Surratoage

Day 23th Thursday we comeing jest of from dewty 100 of our men was calld away to mend highways between the forts a regler was whipd 100 lashes for hollowing and scaring the ennemy when Gennerel Limon had them partly ambusht

Day 24th three men whipt coming in from our work Gennarl web arived hear more Rodlland men Came hear

Day 25th one regellar died with the small pox.

Day 26 which was the Sabath it being ranine uncomfortable weather 80 men of us went to gard streams (a slip for " teams") to the lake and took up our logeing in the woods in mesutes (Massachusetts) rigment: one Boston man whipt 50 for pissing in a kittle of peas.

Day 27th one of our men takeen with small pox an exspress came from Lake Gorge giveing an a counte that a scout had been to Crown pint and takeing a vew of things counld see but few of the enemy thare: Leftanant John Coun (Cone, of Welles' company.) and Cap Baker was taken by Indeins from Crown pint near Scattecook:

Day 28th Came 13 frinchmen and rezined them selves up: saying they had (nothing) to eat for 7 or 8 days: allso that thare a lewance had been one pound pork 11 days. Six men taken small pox: we picth our tents the out side of the pickets so that 500 Green Regelars and 500 Roil amerrycans (both arrived this day, the "Green Regulars" were Johnson's New-Yorkers) the Blews might go with in them

Day 29th we moved our tents haveing the pleashewer of airing them and our selves: a scouting party of 200 men let out to go to the

East Beay: (Of Lake Champlain: the easternmost of the two prongs into which the long narrow southern portion divides in its extreme southern part, and into which Wood Creek empties, with Whitehall now at its mouth.)

Day 30th one regelar died:

July the 1th day was friday Captain putmans came home and told us he surround 300 frinch and Indeians 3 mile above ye south beay and fired at them 11 oclock (p.m.) and sit till 4 in the morning and one of his men was killed by our men (Elijah Sweetland of Hebron, of Welles' company.)

★★★★★★

"South beay", the western of the two prongs; he means three miles above its head or southern end. The ambush was in fact on East Bay, at a ledge half a mile above the head. The hostile party were some five hundred, mainly Indians, under the celebrated French Canadian partisan Marin; and were dreadfully cut up by Putnam's band. They murdered one of Putnam's wounded, and carried off two others.

Another party of scouts mistook Putnam's men for foes and fired into them; and Putnam told them they ought to be hanged for not killing more with so fair a shot.

★★★★★★

genral Limon with 300 men: went out scouting one compeney Rangers (Putnam's) sent home one man killd (Henry Shuntup of Welles' company; probably a Mohegan, his heart was cut out and a block of wood put in its place; this seems to have been reserved for Indian enemies) and 2 taken (Jabez Jones of Fitch's company, John Kennedy of Slapp's) 30 mohoaks came in with 2 scalps from near Crown Pinte

Day 2th six man taken with small pox: 2 men whipt for being drunk

Day 3th which was sabath it raind but no scaesation of work but a day to pay them for thare labour: 4 frinch men came hear from Crown Pint and rezined them selves up (From hunger: this occurred repeatedly.)

Day 4th galard list Ranger (*i.e.*, Charles Gaylord of Payson's company enlisted in the Rangers) 2 men died with camp destemper (this seems not to mean any one disease, but pneumonia, "Long feaver",

215

dysentery, and other non-contagious ailments) 1 Limons man the other of Boston forses: the number of men that have ye small pox (this epidemic heavily crippled the efficient force of the troops for two or three years, and drove some bodies of them home) in ye horspetell about 50 rod from the fort is 101:

Day 5th 18 men listed to fired great guns a raine day peperd with frech meat for eating. (Probably from Albany: this grateful event was an important item to all. "We took our allowance partly in fresh provision," says another.)

Day 6th out of Boston forsis one Smith died with the camp destemper the camp driners (very plain, but of course meaning "drivers") from Allbany arived hear with thares new recruts one ofesor taken with the small pox

Day 7th Johnathan Tilor John Willson: Charis Galard left our tent for Rangers thare compenney was sursposed to be verry good but thare room much better

★★★★★★

Tyler, Wilson, and Gaylord were all of Payson's company. Six companies of Rangers had been organised on the 5th: headed by Captains Putnam and Safford of Connecticut, West and Learned of Massachusetts, Wall of Rhode Island, and McGinniss of New York.

★★★★★★

Day 8th one man wipt 100 lashes

Day 9th one man whipt

Day10th which was the sabath 18 of Cap Rogers men killed and taken near Crown pint (This affair cannot be further identified. Rogers makes no allusion to it) one frinch prisner (brought in by the Indians of Stockbridge, Mass., where Jonathan Edwards then was.)

Day 11th one of genral Limons men died with the camp destemper being able to woak a bout yersterday Johnnathen Rementon of Suffeld Limons compenney:

Day 12th Dainal Boke and John Ashley whipt again (Bogue had been in the guard-house for three days, and now received fifty lashes, after his frightful experience seven weeks before. "Old Ashley" received fifteen.)

Day 13th 6 great guns was fired of 6 times a peace

Day 14th thursday one man died with the camp disstemper

Day 15th one man died the bloody flux: another ye small pox: 4 men whiped one of them 200 lashes in the morning and 200 at night thare was one man of the Bosston forses runing with one of his mates (playing ball) fell down dead emeadeately

Day 16th our tent mates had thair tents took from us and we put into other tents

Day 17th which was the sabath one drumer whipt for playing cards (probably for card-sharping, as there was great license in gaming) 200 of the Rangers let out for a 12 days scout in order to go to the vance gard which the frinch set out below the narrows (of Wood Creek as before)

Day 18th a number Bosston men went to mending high ways down to still waters

(? Day 19th) one man and one woman died

Day 20th Levi Strong and John Rogers conveyd to the horspetell tick

Day 21th one man (Dutchman named Peck) shot to death for desarting to the frinch a scoute of 40 men came in and gave an a counte that sume Indeins fired upon them and killed Leftennant Donet (of Massachusetts; probably Domett or Donnell, the Massachusetts rolls of this war are not published) and others (2 the main of them left thare packs and run home from south Bay (Another account says the lieutenant only was killed, and the rest all ran away as here told) oxford (negro from East Haddam, in Welles' company) was whipt ninety lashes for selling rume and telling fortins to the regelers (Sergeant Joseph Comstock and Drummer John Chappell of Fitch's company were punished with him for the same offense, the former being reduced to the ranks) Ceucip (probably Cujep or Chuchip, a Pequot from Groton, there were several generations of this name) Indean died with pox

Day 22th Joseph Spencer and 6 more of our compenny set out for the still waters (part of a large detachment to relieve the forces there and at Saratoga) one John Tommus a RodIlander aboute 9 oclock in the morning for passing silver mony (Spanish dollars) wich he made

217

himself was whipt 300 lashes.

Day 23th Aboute 9 oclock in the morning a considerrable number of frinch and Indeains surronded our capenders with thare covering party and they had a hot in gagement: for half an ouer aboute half a mile East of the fort 11 men was killed (and another mortally wounded, the Indians divided the eleven scalps they carried so as to claim pay for thirty-two! The assailing party was 150 Indians and a few Canadians) which was brough in and buryed 6 men was sum of them badly wound: and seaverral more missing (only one was carried prisoner by the Indians; the others scattered in the woods) Picpen (probably Pitkin; the roll of these wounded men is lost) one of these wounded men of putmans died at sun set: the regelers from Surratoage came hear 10 men carryed to the horspetill with ye small pox

Day 24th which was ye Sabbath one more of these wound men (Amos Bibben of Slapp's company) died: one Captain hardin died with ye small pox.

Day 25th Genaral web was aided up to Lake Gorge with 1000 men to wate upon his honnor

★★★★★★

Other accounts say the escort was Putnam and 200 Rangers. The diarist may have exaggerated, as he elsewhere does with the Royal Americans; but Webb's conduct makes us suspect that he took as large an escort as possible.

★★★★★★

Levi Strong one of our compeney wich belonged to Boston died with ye long (lung: pneumonia) fever: one man haveing the small pox was carryed to the horspetill: Aboute 100 regellars a rived hear from still warters Jeams Tuler (Tuller) of Simsbeary Corl Limons compeny died with the long feaver: Likewise one more of our foreces

Day 26th one man was killed by another mans gun which went of when: he was a scouring of it (in another tent) one man taken with ye small pox we hear that a scouteing party of 350 men went out from Lake Gorge to ye weast bay (of Lake George, west of the peninsula in the southern half; also called Northwest Bay, but in fact they were some miles further north, near Sabbath Day Point) and was surround with a number of frinch and Indeins which killed and took 250 of them 100 esceaped them

★★★★★★

As another diarist of the regiment says the same, Parkman's 300 is probably wrong. They were chiefly Jerseymen sent from Fort William Henry by Parker and were ambushed at the Lake George narrows by a superior body of Indians under the French Canadian Corbière. The Indians shot some, speared others in the water, and ate three on the spot; but carried most of them captive.

★★★★★★

Day 27th Johnnathen Roberds coparl and Jonnathan Word and Hezekiah Deman (Deming, these were all from Payson's company) was taken to ye horspetill: sick: one man died thare with the long feaver: one 100 and od of Cunnectecut and Bosston men set out to releave sum Reelars at half moon (peninsula at the junction of the Hudson and Mohawk, afterwards Schuyler's camp in the Revolution) 3 of (his) our compeney went thare

Day 28th one man died and one taken with the small pox: and 5 regelars whiped (One a second time, for losing his blanket and contumaciously asserting that he had received none.)

Day 29th all the capenders and battwo (*bateau*) men in ye camp set out to work at Lake Gorge: gennaral web returnd back to fort Edward (under the same escort): one regelerr died: one man taken with the small pox one Hezekiah Deman died sudenly with ye camp disstemper:

Day 30th one man died with ye long feaver

Day 31th which was ye Sabath: one man died Dockter Lord (Elisha Lord of Farmington) got in readeness to go houm

Awgust ye 1th Ad 1757 one man died and one taken with ye small pox

Day 2 Dockter Lord went houme for more things the Boston foresses and 500 Roil americans marcht up to fort willaim henorry (Only 100 in fact, with Captain Crookshank's independent company and 823 of Frye's Massachusetts regiment, all under command of Lieutenant-Colonel Young of the 60th.)

Day 3th the greate guns begun to fire at 4 a clock in the morning at Lake gorge and keep going at times and turns: thare was spies sent up thare

Day 4th these spies (James Collier, of Gallup's company, he deserted ten days later) brough in a frinch man hwo they took near Lake gorge: which was killing an ox hwo said that ye army which ware segeing Lake gorge was 11000 (He said there were 6000 regulars and 5000 Canadians, there were in fact about 8000 in all, of whom some 2000 were Indians) they had 32 cannon and 12 morter peases

Day 5th we heared fort william haner was surround with frinch and Indeains 2 Cap putmans Rangers went up and got into ye fort

Day 6th 2 men got away from thare which gave us an a counte that ye frinch was digeing trinches for thare safte (safety): But had not fired any cannon at ye fort: 3 men died with sickness

Day 7th which was ye sabath gennarl gonson (now Sir William, other accounts say he arrived the day before) ariveed hear with 1500 men: an express came from ye lake which said they were in good sperits thare haveing lost but 5 men allso that they (keap) could keap them of with thare bums sevearl days.

******

Monro is reported by Jabez Fitch, Jr., one of the "Bosston forces" here, as saying that he was "as well pleased as if he was in his own country among ye pertaters"; but that was because he expected speedy relief from Webb.

******

that they would not have gennarl web send them any healp while (until) he could cume with a party strong a nought to drive of so great an army of frinch

******

This was probably camp gossip, as Monro's existent letters to Webb contain nothing of the kind; but it would have been good sense, as any less reinforcement simply swelled the number to be sacrificed. Webb had already done exactly that, his "relief" forming part of those surrendered and partly massacred.

******

Day 8th mon the great guns keep fireing very fast at fort william henerry one Johnnathen worden of Simsbery one of our compeney died with ye bloody flux

Day 9th fort willaim henerry was resined upon these condishons our men what was left of them was to sease lifting up arms against ye frinch for 18 months they (the French) brock their artecles and